Supporting Vulnerable Children in the Early Years

of related interest

Child Protection in the Early Years
A Practical Guide
Eunice Lumsden
ISBN 978 1 78592 265 7
eISBN 978 1 78450 555 4

Supporting Toddlers' Wellbeing in Early Years Settings
Strategies and Tools for Practitioners and Teachers
Edited by Helen Sutherland and Yasmin Mukadam
ISBN 978 1 78592 262 6
eISBN 978 1 78450 552 3

Giving Children a Voice
A Step-by-Step Guide to Promoting Child-Centred Practice
Sam Frankel
ISBN 978 1 78592 278 7
eISBN 978 1 78450 578 3

**A Practical Guide to Gender Diversity
and Sexuality in Early Years**
Deborah Price
ISBN 978 1 78592 289 3
eISBN 978 1 78450 594 3

Developing Empathy in the Early Years
A Guide for Practitioners
Helen Garnett
ISBN 978 1 78592 143 8
eISBN 978 1 78450 418 2

Promoting Young Children's Emotional Health and Wellbeing
A Practical Guide for Professionals and Parents
Sonia Mainstone-Cotton
ISBN 978 1 78592 054 7
eISBN 978 1 78450 311 6

SUPPORTING VULNERABLE CHILDREN IN THE EARLY YEARS

Practical Guidance and Strategies
for Working with Children at Risk

Edited by PAT BECKLEY

Foreword by Professor Chris Atkin

Jessica Kingsley *Publishers*
London and Philadelphia

First published in 2019
by Jessica Kingsley Publishers
73 Collier Street
London N1 9BE, UK
and
400 Market Street, Suite 400
Philadelphia, PA 19106, USA

www.jkp.com

Library of Congress Cataloging in Publication Data
A CIP catalog record for this book is available from the Library of Congress

British Library Cataloguing in Publication Data
A CIP catalogue record for this book is available from the British Library

ISBN 978 1 78592 237 4
eISBN 978 1 78450 515 8

Printed and bound in Great Britain

Contents

Part 3: Supporting the Child

Part 4: A Positive Process

Foreword

Professor Chris Atkin

It can be argued that any child has the potential to be at risk. This book explores specific types of experience that make a child vulnerable, events that affect a child's life and ongoing circumstances that present risk. Contemporary research is used by Yinka Olusoga, Antony Luby and Elizabeth Farrar to provide a detailed overview of the different ways children learn. This includes the contemporary environment and indoor and outdoor approaches. The challenges and strategies used in rural school settings are discussed by Nishi Bremner and learning outdoors by Beverley Keen. Rosey Shelbourne, Gina Taylor, Sarah Howe and Helen Thornalley identify strategies to support young children and keep them safe. Vulnerable groups are considered by Julia Lindley-Baker and Pat Beckley, while Pat, Margaret Simms, Julie Percival, Anne Renwick and Emmy Sealey suggest ways to promote health and wellbeing, transition experiences and the role of the family and wider community in supporting vulnerable children. The contributors are experts in their field with backgrounds in academic research, schools and psychology. The book furthers our understanding, giving insights into children's worlds, while suggesting positive ways to support young children in society.

Professor Chris Atkin
Professor of Higher Education
School of Teacher Development
Head of the Centre for Public Policy and Professional Practice in Education
Bishop Grosseteste University
Lincoln, UK

Acknowledgements

Many colleagues helped with this project including those at Bishop Grosseteste University, Leeds Beckett University, the University of Cumbria, soundLINCS, Asra Housing Association, Christian Partners in Africa, Washingborough Primary Academy and Molescroft Primary School, who willingly shared their kindness and expertise.

Introduction

Arguably, all children have the potential to be vulnerable. Parents, carers and those in the community care for them, but some children live in challenging circumstances or are made vulnerable by difficulties or events that occur. Obtaining the numbers of those vulnerable can be very difficult, as the situation is constantly changing and young children may be classed as vulnerable for many different reasons, with some involved in more than one area of vulnerability. The challenging situations that children may be experiencing can vary from complex, life-changing cases to those requiring ongoing support to maintain appropriate learning, development and progress.

Children may be in a family group where there is an environment that includes such factors as regular substance misuse, physical abuse or neglect. They may experience economic issues, for example poverty or homelessness. A Special Education Need and/or Disability (SEND) could give rise to vulnerability, while unexpected events, such as the death of a parent, could cause a child to become vulnerable as the situation at home may become unstable and insecure. Ongoing risks, for example safety and safeguarding issues, are ever present and continual potential dangers give rise to strategies to ensure they do not arise. Children therefore live in a society that seeks to keep them safe and protected, while possibly limiting their experiences and awareness of the world around them for fear of the dangers it may pose.

This book seeks to explore issues concerning the vulnerability of children and is organised in four parts. In Part 1, The Contemporary Environment, Yinka Olusoga considers theorists and factors that influence children's views of the world and educational approaches giving them the ability to promote their agency and decision-making. In Chapter 2, Antony Luby reflects upon extensive research he has undertaken in a community of schools to share positive strategies used to support children, families and communities. Nishi Bremner then observes the challenges faced in a rural setting and presents approaches to enable partnerships to work together to enhance life chances for children.

Part 2 considers some of the groups that make up vulnerable children. This includes Julia Lindley-Baker's experiences of vulnerable children, language and poverty, as explored by Elizabeth Farrar, and children in a diverse society and looked-after children, discussed by Pat Beckley in Chapters 6 and 7, drawing on her work in inner-city schools and settings.

Ways of supporting the child are considered in Part 3, including safeguarding based on Rosey Shelbourne's extensive work in Uganda, interventions by Gina Taylor in her role as Foundation Stage Coordinator, feedback approaches used by Sarah Howe and Helen Thornalley when teaching and the outdoors by Beverley Keen, where differing teaching and learning styles and approaches can be accessed.

Part 4 includes consideration by Pat Beckley of health and wellbeing as a foundation for lifelong personal, social and emotional stability. Positive transitions are analysed by Margaret Simms who considers how these changes impact on children's lives. The section is completed with a collaboration from Julie Percival, Anne Renwick and Emmy Sealey in a discussion of the child and identity in the family and wider community. Children's vulnerability is a continuing issue for concern, with challenges for families and communities. With deeper insights into these issues, strategies can be sought to attempt to support children as they grow and give them a positive foundation for their future lives.

PART 1

The Contemporary Environment

CHAPTER 1

The Contemporary Environment

Yinka Olusoga

*Course Leader, PGCE Primary Education (3–7), leading to QTS
Leeds Beckett University*

Chapter overview

The term 'vulnerable children' is now in common use in statutory legislation, non-statutory guidance, reports and processes relating to the care and education of children. It is drawn upon by politicians, by professionals working in care, education, health and social care and by campaigners and charities who advocate for children and families. It is the focus of research by academics working in a range of disciplines. Vulnerable children have been the focus of official reports. The most recent is from the office of the Children's Commissioner for England (Children's Commissioner for England, 2017b), which sets out to count and to categorise vulnerable children in England. Debate rages regarding how best to address 'vulnerable children' in policy, practice and research.

This chapter will examine how the term 'vulnerable children' has come to be so prominent in policy and debates around practice and will consider what the term actually means. It will also explore how within 'vulnerable children' as an umbrella term, different categories of vulnerability have been identified and how these categories map onto children's real-life experiences. Alongside vulnerability, it will scrutinise how key related terms such as 'adversity' and 'risk' inform current understandings of vulnerability and how that impacts on policy and practice. This discussion will consider how critical research into children and childhood has challenged traditional concepts and practices that underpin approaches to working with, and advocating for, children.

Finally, the chapter will examine the implications for the early years sector in recognising and addressing the needs and rights of vulnerable children and their families in our practice and settings. This will include considering how research and theory can help us to critically reflect on and develop policy and practice in the current educational climate.

The journey to the contemporary context: policies and politics

In 21st-century Britain, the popular argument as far as children and childhood are concerned is that it is both the best of times and the worst of times. Childhood is physically safer than ever before. Children are less likely to die in early infancy; they are more likely than previous generations to finish their schooling and to go on to gain a university education (Bolton, 2012; NSPCC, 2014; Wolfe *et al.*, 2014). However, not all children have an equal chance at these positive experiences and outcomes. Child poverty rates, rather than decreasing as they did across most of the 20th century, since 2013 have been once again on the rise (Ivinson *et al.*, 2017a, p. 8). In their 2010 book, *The Spirit Level*, Wilkinson and Pickett highlight the growing size of the income gap between the richest 20 per cent of the population and the poorest 20 per cent, arguing that this is leading to Britain becoming an increasingly socially divided country (cited in Ivinson *et al.*, 2017b, pp. 6 and 18). Furthermore, unlike previous generations, the life expectancy of some of today's children may be lower than their parents, due to diet and lifestyle factors (Olshansky *et al.*, 2005). As a generation, children are less likely to experience free, unstructured play outside the home (Loebach and Gilliland, 2016). They are exposed to outside influences via technology and social media that, as well as bringing them opportunities to absorb and contribute to the cultural landscape, also open them up to potential harm.

Children's rights

Children's rights to protection are today enshrined in international and national law. There is also a legal recognition of their ability to exercise agency, to participate and to express their opinions. The Articles of the *United Nations Convention of the Rights of the Child* (UNCRC) (United Nations Committee on the Rights of the Child, 1989), recognise, amongst other things, the rights of children to participate in education, to have their voices heard and to have their views taken into account. They also place upon governments a duty to interpret and implement those rights within their own legal, policy and practice frameworks. As the UK is a signatory to the UNCRC, legislation in England since the Children Act of 1989 has recognised children's rights to 'provision, protection and participation' (Payler, Georgeson and Wong, 2016, p. 13). Under the Act, the right of children to protection is established in the legal duty on statutory authorities to carry out child protection enquires where there is 'reasonable cause to suspect that a child is suffering, or likely to suffer "significant harm"' (Jopling and Vincent, 2016, p. 8). Suffering or experiencing significant harm can be the result of abuse or neglect of a child, it can be the result of deliberate cruelty or it can be due to a lack of capacity for effective parenting that would meet the needs of the child. The Act also defines children as being 'in need' if they are disabled or if they are 'unlikely to achieve or maintain, or to have the opportunity of achieving or maintaining, a reasonable standard of health or development' or their 'health or development is likely to be significantly impaired, or further impaired', without the provision of services from the local authority (cited in Moss, Dillon and Statham, 2000, p. 233). The Act has been criticised for its focus on protection and provision and its relative neglect of participation. Moss *et al.* (2000, p. 242) describe the 'child in need' as its central concept, providing justification for state intervention in family life. They, and others, argue that the freedom of children to exercise their agency and to have their views not just listened to but also respected and actually impact on what happens to them is constrained within ever greater regulation and processes of surveillance.

Concepts of childhood

The dominant view of childhood is as a period of innate vulnerability, both as a chronic condition common to all children by virtue of their status as children and an acute one in some cases as a result of a range of familial and social factors. As a result, even when they are the focus of concern, children can be understood in very passive terms, as victims who need to be rescued, rather than as having an active role and voice in the unfolding of their own lives. However, since the early 1990s, this view has been challenged by academic research into the sociology of childhood. This research argues that childhood is a social construct and that children can and do exercise agency (James and Prout, 1997). They do not just exist within the confines of adult culture, but they also develop and exist within their own peer culture. In both of these cultural realms, they do not merely absorb existing cultural ideas but are actively creative and thus capable of transform those cultures (Corsaro, 2012). However, despite these insights, government policy is heavily influenced by the findings of research in psychology and neuroscience, which tends to position children as passive subjects to whom things are 'done'. This research establishes a link between negative events and conditions in childhood (particularly in early childhood) and 'physiological harm', resulting in poor outcomes in adulthood that are also costly to the economy (Daniel, 2010, p. 233). The relationship between adults and children, and between social and civic institutions and the family, is one of vigilant and accountable guardianship, poised to identify problems, actual and potential, and intervene for the good of the individual and of the state. Whilst the right of the children to be consulted on matters that involve them exists on paper, in reality that does not always equate to a right to be heard and to have a meaningful say in the decisions that impact on their lives.

The role of the state

Concern for children in vulnerable circumstances is not new. An intervening role for schools in family life, aimed at reducing the potentially negative impact of poor parenting, poverty and bad housing, was established in the discourses of the 19th century. These were the discourses that informed the framing of child labour laws that underpinned the establishment of key children's charities, such as Barnardo's, and that argued for the establishment and extension of state education. They can be detected in the pages of the 1861 Newcastle Commission, charged with investigating whether and how national provision of state-funded elementary education should be provided for the 'labouring classes'. In an echo of official reports today, the report of the Newcastle Commission identified and categorised children in relation to their exposure to poverty, parental abuse and neglect and poor parental influence. It provided a detailed and highly emotive discussion of the potential role of the state in preventing or offsetting the negative consequences of such children being 'exposed to the corruption of their vicious origin' (Newcastle Report, 1861, p. 372). These discourses are evident in the writing and work of Rachel and Margaret McMillan, who argued that nursery education was needed to advance the physical, intellectual and moral health of the poorest working-class children (Lascarides and Hinitz, 2011). Mayall (2007) argues that the introduction of the welfare state in 1945 continued and extended this pre-existing social tradition that positions the state as the protector and regulator of the lives of children. However, contemporary official priorities regarding accountability for child protection of the professionals working within services for children have hugely expanded since the turn of the millennium. Children are to be protected from actual harm and from potential future harm that is deemed 'likely' to happen. Furthermore, these expanded accountabilities for child welfare have been impacted upon by changes in government and in the national and international economic context.

The rise of the term 'vulnerable children' 1997 to 2010: the New Labour years

The New Labour Government between 1997 and 2010 placed a focus on reducing poverty rates and increasing social mobility. Emphasis was placed by New Labour on provision and services in the early years, via the expansion of universal services aimed at all children. The *Framework for the Assessment of Children in Need and their Families* was published by the government in 2000 (Department of Health (DoH), 2000). It introduced the term 'disadvantaged and vulnerable children' and described children in need as 'some of our most vulnerable children' (DoH, 2000, cited in Children's Commissioner for England, 2017a, p. 2). Under the Sure Start programme, the government demonstrated a will to broaden general access to pre-school provision and to bring together, as a means of tackling social disadvantage, the work of different family and child services. Intervention, via targeted and specialist services, aimed at children and families identified as requiring specific intervention from any of a range of child and family services, needed to happen early and to be coordinated. High-quality and accessible pre-school care and education was a key component of the 2003 Green Paper *Every Child Matters* (Chief Secretary to the Treasury, 2003), which aimed to:

- increase access to work and therefore economic productivity for parents

- give their children early exposure to early childhood care and education

- provide joined-up, multiagency services to facilitate early referral and cross-professional communication and to improve the accessibility of support for parents.

The Children Act 2004 placed on those agencies working with children and families, a 'statutory duty to safeguard and promote the welfare of children' (cited in Jopling and Vincent, 2016, p. 4). Informed by the findings of the Laming Report (Laming, 2003) into the death of Victoria Climbié, the Act also required local authorities to merge their education and social services under the newly created 'Director of Children's Services' posts. It also introduced the role of Children's Commissioner for England. The Children and Young Persons Act 2008 identified schools as a lynchpin in the exercise of this duty, with a responsibility to contribute to multiagency work with children already in the child-protection system. In addition, it emphasised schools' responsibilities to contribute to the identification, support and referral of vulnerable children not in the child-protection system. As school is a universal service, schools were seen to have a pivotal role due to their everyday contact with children and families. Thus, they should be key sites for bringing together families and agencies.

The introduction of the Early Years Foundation Stage in 2008 also reinforced the duty of the private and state early years care and education sector in this early identification and intervention work. Early years settings and schools were thus positioned as working across what Jopling and Vincent describe as 'the whole spectrum of vulnerability' (2016, p. 4). This spectrum ranges from provision of universal services to all children, via early help and targeted services for those perceived to be in suffering, or likely to suffer, harm through to statutory intervention and removal of children into local authority care. This inclusion of universal services effectively places all children somewhere on this spectrum and is underpinned by the dominant view of children as inherently vulnerable, as discussed earlier.

2010 to date: the Coalition and Conservative Governments

The Coalition Government of 2010 to 2015, and the introduction of 'austerity' measures in response to the global financial crisis, saw a move away from universal to targeted interventions and a rapid decline in funding for local services that continues today. The fragmentation of the education system, via the expansion of academies and free schools that has occurred since 2010, means that although local authorities still have responsibility for safeguarding vulnerable children, they do not have the same level of coordinated oversight of the schools in their area as used to be the case. The Pupil Premium was introduced in 2011 for specific groups of eligible children ('looked-after' children, children who have been in care, adopted children and children of serving armed forces personnel). Via Ofsted inspection, schools are held to account for their use of these targeted funds to improve educational attainment of children who qualify for the Pupil Premium (Ofsted, 2012). Across government departments, there has been a notable change in the discourse from New Labour and its talk of 'eradicating poverty'. This has been replaced by an emphasis on 'troubled families' with 'feral children' leading 'chaotic lives', as exemplified in the controversial Troubled Families Programme, also established in 2011. The economic cost to society of late intervention is also stressed i the Allen Report, *Early Intervention: The Next Steps*. Late intervention, he argues, is more expensive and less likely to work, because problems have 'become deeply entrenched' (Allen, 2011, p. 4).

The Conservative Government since 2015 has produced a continuation of this discourse and of austerity measures. Furthermore, since July 2016 the impact of the Brexit vote has seen further cuts to education budgets and children's services and huge economic uncertainty. Jopling and Vincent's (2016) analysis of policy documentation has established that the term 'vulnerable child' has become far more prevalent in policy documentation since 2010 than it ever was prior to that date. Indeed, they describe vulnerability as a key concept underpinning education policy both under the 2010 Coalition Government and under the subsequent Conservative Government. So, in summary, since 1997 schools and settings have seen a widening of the scope and responsibility of early years care and education to address the needs of disadvantaged children. However, since 2010 there has been a shrinking of the services available to children and families, but a rise in the number of children and families living in poverty.

Defining 'vulnerable' in relation to children in the early years

Defining and measuring vulnerability

Despite its growing usage in policy, vulnerability remains an under-defined and nebulous concept. In 2017 the Children's Commissioner for England set out to measure the number of vulnerable children in England. Prior to the publication in 2017 of its report, research consultants, Coram and Coram International, were commissioned to produce a technical paper, entitled *Constructing a Definition of Vulnerability* (Children's Commissioner for England, 2017a). This title is apt, as 'vulnerability' and 'vulnerable children' are indeed social constructs. Their use in language does not merely reflect reality but, via its deployment in policy, actually produces real categories, processes and events. The outcome of this work in the final, main report was a working definition of vulnerability as:

> the additional needs or barriers children face may make them likely to live healthy, happy, safe lives, or less likely to have successful transitions to adulthood. Vulnerability can take a wide range of different forms, including physical and mental health difficulties, family problems, and risks of abuse of harm. (Children's Commissioner for England, 2017b, p. 3)

After repeating the previously discussed, dominant view that in 'one sense all children are vulnerable', the report identifies 32 existing officially recognised types of vulnerability in its analysis of contemporary policy. These are then organised into four categories and estimates as to the number in each category are given (see Table 1.1).

The report acknowledges that the list is not exhaustive and that the numbers are estimates. It recognises that there is real confusion as to the extent of double counting that may be involved. Thus, it stresses that the four numbers cannot simply be added to form a grand total, as children may be experiencing more than one type and category of vulnerability. Some of the 32 types are not particularly applicable to early years. However, young children who have older siblings may find that those types of vulnerability may still be a factor for the context of their families, via their brothers and sisters.

Table 1.1 Categories of vulnerable child in England (adapted from Children's Commissioner for England, 2017b, p. 13)

Vulnerability type	Estimated number of children in England
Type 1: Children directly supported or accommodated (or previously accommodated) by the state Includes: looked-after children; care leavers; adopted children; children under a Special Guardianship Order; children with severe and/or complex mental health problems; children with an Education, Health and Care (EHC) plan for their Special Education Need and/or Disability (SEND); children who have been reported as potential victims of modern slavery.	580,000
Type 2: Children and young people whose actions put their futures at risk Includes: missing children; children who are gang members; excluded pupils, teenage mothers aged 19 and under living with their children; 16–18-year-olds not in education, employment or training (NEET).	370,000
Type 3: Children with health-related vulnerabilities Includes: children aged 17 or under who have a longstanding illness, disability or infirmity; children aged between 5 and 17 who have mental health disorders; children who have SEND but who are not on an EHC plan.	2,300,000
Type 4: Children with family-related vulnerabilities Includes: children who are homeless or in insecure or unstable housing; children in the Troubled Families Programme; children aged 5 to 17 who are unpaid carers; children under 18 who are living with adults in drug treatment or in alcohol treatment.	670,000

These issues and caveats echo the findings of Jopling and Vincent in their 2016 review for the Cambridge Primary Review Trust of key policy relating to the primary age phase. They too argue that 'vulnerability' has a range of different meanings, both in policy and in research. They identify a total 16 categories of vulnerability from their analysis of four significant policy documents and one key research publication (though no one document refers to all 16). The policy documents are:

- *Working Together to Safeguard Children* (HM Government, 2015)

- *Framework for Children's Centre Inspection* (Ofsted, 2013)

- *Families at Risk* (Social Exclusion Task Force, 2007)

- *Troubled Families* (Department for Communities and Local Government, 2015).

The research publication is *Multiple Risk Factors in Young Children's Development* (Sabates and Dex, 2012), a study examining the Millennial Cohort data that addresses the issue of very young children in families living with multiple risks and attempts to assess how this intersects with ethnicity.

Jopling and Vincent point out that the 16 vulnerabilities are described in these documents as a range of 'problems', 'disadvantages' and 'risk factors' (2016, p. 8). Some of these relate to the child themselves, some to the parents/carers and others are the result of their socioeconomic context. They identify only one vulnerability, non-attendance from school, as stemming from the child's agency, though in the context of early years non-attendance is more likely to be the decision of the parent/carer than of the child. Two vulnerabilities, Special Educational Needs (SEN) and disability, are vulnerabilities inherent in the child themselves. The remaining vulnerabilities are contextual, the result of their family circumstances that could see them, for example, witnessing domestic violence or criminality, being placed in care or having to act as a child carer. However, many of the vulnerabilities are structural, linked to poverty (poor or transient housing, unemployment, low parental education and qualification, lone and/or teenage parents) and to the reaction to poverty (poor parental mental or physical health, substance abuse).

The lived experience of vulnerability

A tendency to oversimplification of the complex, multi-layered vulnerabilities affecting children, families and communities has been highlighted in recent academic and government research. The British Educational Research Association (BERA) conducted the Poverty and Policy Advocacy Commission (Ivinson *et al.*, 2017a, 2017b) in 2016. It concluded that across the four jurisdictions of the UK (England, Wales, Scotland and Northern Ireland) child poverty is growing, and in particular the number of children in the category of 'multiple indices of deprivation' is growing. The publication of the Race Disparity Audit (Cabinet Office, 2017), also highlighted the intersectional nature of disadvantage. Its analysis of the government's own data reveals that children from some minority ethnic backgrounds are, for example, more likely than the general population to be living in poverty and to be in poor, insecure and overcrowded housing. The national evaluation of the government's Troubled Families Programme found that despite the political and media discourse their problems (and cost to the tax payer) were the result of their criminality and anti-social behaviour, in fact: '90% of adults had not committed a criminal offence and a further 93% of adults, and 88% of children, had no record of anti-social behaviour' (ECORYS UK, 2014, cited in Jopling and Vincent, 2016, p. 19).

Simpson (2013, p. 87) argues that the current government's child poverty strategy acknowledges that social justice is about access to economic, cultural and social capital. However, it takes a neoliberal approach to social justice that conceptualises the existing unequal spread of these as a behavioural rather than a structural problem. This is despite current research that shows that many children in poverty are not in workless families, but rather in underemployed families, with the rise of low wages and precarious zero-hours contracts (Ivinson, 2017b, p. 20). In government policy, poverty is treated as the result of poor individual lifestyle choices, and thus as something that can be 'educated out' of children via interventions in their care and education across pre-school and school. Rather than acknowledging the complex interplay of the impact of disadvantage on people's abilities to cope and to maximise on opportunity, society is understood here in far simpler terms as a pure meritocracy, where the outcomes of the education system are solely the result of personal effort on the part of the child, parent and teacher.

Research insights into vulnerability

However vulnerability is defined, and whatever its root causes, it is the outcome of this vulnerability that is the focus of concern. A series of key research findings in developmental psychology and neuroscience, and some influential longitudinal studies in early education that have tracked young children into adulthood, have established a link between vulnerability in childhood, negative impacts on child development and poor outcomes in adulthood. The California Adverse Childhood Experiences (ACE) study (Felitti and Anda, 2009, cited in Jopling and Vincent, 2016, p. 3) and Perry's 2002 paper 'Childhood experience and the expression of genetic potential: What childhood neglect tells us about nature and nurture' (cited in Daniel, 2010, p. 33) have been particularly influential. The striking images from Perry's article, comparing brain scans of a normally developing three-year-old and another child who has suffered severe neglect, have been reproduced extensively in research, in the media and in government reports and policy, including in the 2011 Allen Report published by the Cabinet Office (Allen, 2011). That abuse and neglect can have not just behavioural, but visible, physiological consequences has been deeply shocking and this has driven the political will to be seen to act.

Daniel argues that the concept of vulnerability is linked to the concepts of adversity and risk. All three, she argues, have 'explicit and implicit definitions' and these 'can have profound effects upon understandings about the most appropriate policy and practice response' (2010, p. 231). Adversity she defines as 'the experience of life events and circumstances which may combine to threaten or challenge healthy development' (2010, p. 232). Factors that are deemed to be adverse have come to be defined in increasingly broad terms. Thus, she argues, the duty of professionals to intervene has spread far further and 'become generalised under the umbrella of "unmet needs"' (Daniel, 2010, p. 233). Risk is defined by Daniel as 'the chance of adversity translating into actual negative outcomes for children' (2010, p. 233) and again it can be understood in limited or expanded terms. Since the 1989 Children Act, an expanded concept of risk has moved professionals from needing to make decisions based on evidence of actual harm to having to make judgements about intervention that is based on their calculations of the potential likelihood of future harm. The predictive aspect of the response to need, adversity and vulnerability is fraught with difficulty. Judgements are made against different behavioural indicators outlined in different national policies. Fear of making the wrong decision operates at the personal and institutional level. A risk-oriented mind-set will tend to focus on the deficits in a situation and to overlook the strengths. One outcome of this huge, and in some cases potentially life-and-death responsibility, has been that risk has come to be understood in purely negative terms as something to be removed entirely. Cooper *et al.* (2003, cited in Daniel, 2010, p. 235) highlight the other key tension that arises for professionals and institutions in the current child-protection approach. That is the tension between forming relationships via the building of trust and communication with families on the one hand, and the duty to diagnose and report risk factors on the other hand.

Addressing the needs of vulnerable children in the early years

Professional expectations of early years practice

The health and early years care and education sectors operate at the sharp end of policy in relation to vulnerable children, by virtue of their engagement with children from earliest infancy (and in the case of health services, prenatally), and across the formative years for key developmental milestones. Preventative measures across speech and language development, physical development, emotional attachment and socialisation that have the potential to improve children's wellbeing and attainment, and to reduce or eliminate the need for later, more expensive and less effective interventions later on, depend on early identification and intervention by professionals in these coordinated services. The expanded range of what factors count as specific vulnerabilities, coupled with a dominant discourse that views all children as inherently vulnerable, increasingly produces discourses and practices that are therapeutic and applied to growing numbers of children and their families. Increasingly, a focus has been placed on developing positive dispositions and strategies that develop personal capacity to cope and thrive in difficult circumstances. Wellbeing, social and emotional literacy, mental health and resilience are not only the focus of targeted programmes but are increasingly embedded into curriculum and practice in early years settings and schools. Targeted programmes include locally managed interventions to improve parenting skills, to reduce the social isolation of parents and to bring together and facilitate access to a range of services. An example of this would be the research-informed Families and Schools Together (FAST) programme (McDonald *et al.*, 2012). Broader curricular programmes include national policies and materials, such as the Social and Emotional Aspects of Development (SEAD), developed under New Labour (DCSF, 2008), that expanded on the personal and social education curriculum to emphasise learning as a process with strong social and emotional aspects.

This seems on the face of it a wholly positive approach. However, there has been criticism as to both the implementation and conceptual underpinning of some programmes. The interventions and programmes themselves are often based on therapeutic or counselling practices, but are delivered by other teachers, practitioners and, in some cases, other parents. They are not trained therapists or counsellors and they are not prepared or trained to cope with the issues about the lived experiences of children and families that are sometimes uncovered (Gillies, 2011). For the child and parent alike, being an object of concern can be inherently disempowering as they are processed through the system. A focus on 'resilience' can be seen as individualising and blaming the poor and the disadvantaged for failing to rise above the circumstances that others manage to adapt to and overcome. It can also be seen as effectively absolving governments from a duty to tackle structural inequalities that produce unequal distribution of advantage across class, gender, race, sexuality and (dis)ability, and the intersections between them. Instead, the new structures of the education, social care and health services hold teachers, practitioners, social workers and health professionals to account for offsetting entrenched social inequalities. This is achieved via an increasingly prescriptive regime of monitoring and inspection which, paradoxically, impacts negatively on their own mental health.

Reflecting critically to develop practice

In the context of early years practice, addressing the needs of vulnerable children involves practitioners in maintaining a focus on engagement with families, on expansion of provision, on early identification and early intervention and on multiagency working. One outcome of this has been the increase in two-year-olds now being cared for and educated in school rather than in pre-school settings. It is important not to overlook the Early Years Foundation Stage (EYFS) curriculum and, in particular, the non-statutory guidance *Development Matters* (Early Education/Department for Education, 2012). Both are informed by the findings of the Effective Provision and Pre-School Education (EPPE) study (Sylva *et al.*, 2004). Both provide the context and principles for this work to address the needs of all children. The underpinning themes of the 'unique child' and 'positive relationships' stress the need to understand the individual child in the context of their family and community context. This is supported by it being a play-based curriculum with an accompanying play-based approach to assessment that focuses on observing the child in their self-initiated play, where they are likely to be demonstrating their highest abilities. The characteristics of effective learning (CoEL) focus on identifying and developing dispositions for learning that recognise and build on children's strengths. Furthermore, the needs and the interests of the children should be key drivers of the curriculum. All of the above gives scope for practitioners to focus attention on the *participation* strand of the 1989 Children Act.

Although not directly cited in the EYFS or *Development Matters*, the Reggio Emilia Approach to early years care and education supports practitioners in developing a democratic approach to delivering a curriculum that, instead of being imposed on the child, emerges from them and their interests. It is predicated on a view of all children as capable and independent, with an innate drive to learn and an ability to generate their own meaningful ideas and projects. Thus, children are able to co-construct their own curriculum with their peers and with the adults around them. It also stresses the importance of accessing and truly hearing the voice of the child and of the family in evaluating, planning and delivering provision. This accessing of the voice of the child and the parents also lies at the heart of the Mosaic approach, developed by Clark and Moss (cited in Payler *et al.*, 2016, p. 15), that uses a multi-modal approach to capture the perspectives of children and parents. Socio-cultural approaches to researching practice advocate a respect for children's cultural worlds and the knowledge they bring with them to their early years settings. Culture here encompasses family, ethnic, gender and social class contexts and recognises that all children have their own unique 'funds of knowledge' that need to be recognised, valued and represented in the practice of early years settings (Hedges, Cullen and Jordan, 2011). All of this requires an ethical stance to working with children (Chesworth, 2016) that acknowledges the power relations between professionals, the child and the parents.

However, the current educational environment is making the above increasingly difficult. The school readiness agenda (built in to the revised EYFS of 2012) and the spectre of another attempt by government to impose baseline testing (expected to be a computer-based test, administered at the beginning of the reception year) loom over the early years. The play-based approach to learning, teaching and assessment in reception classes in particular is under threat. Pressure mounts for practice to mirror that in Key Stage 1 (Keeble, 2016), where the national curriculum is built on heavily prescribed curriculum content and an outcomes-driven, linear model of progression in learning, with no equivalent to the CoEL to focus attention on the processes of learning.

In this atmosphere of jeopardy, it is worthwhile to return to the concept of risk and to re-interrogate it. The dominant understanding of risk as something wholly negative and to be avoided, and if possible eradicated, is increasingly critiqued (as discussed by Keen later in this volume). Current accountability processes heavily dis-incentivise the taking of risk by children, but also by professionals. The language of accountability focuses on statutory compliance. However, the culture of compliance has spread and, in its wake, threatens to push out innovation, experimentation and divergent thinking. This was apparent with the Literacy and Numeracy strategies in the early 2000s. Although they were non-statutory guidance, the link between school performance outcomes and Ofsted inspection (Leithwood et al., 2004) effectively meant that schools were pressured to treat them as though they were statutory. The same internalised pressure that prevents the taking of risk is expressed in the words of a young mother (taking part in the FAST programme mentioned earlier), reflecting on the path that she has taken in life:

> I always thought I'd never be a good mum. And everyone would say 'Your children are always clean, your children are always fed. They're always happy.' I'd love to be a hero and try and save someone's life, try and save someone's house or…save someone's…just be a hero in some kind of way when I was a kid. But I never ever ended up doing that. I ended up being a hairdresser for two years, and I've been a

cleaner. And then once all me kids are in school full time I want to get back to work and be a cleaner again. I want to do something different, that I've never had the guts to ever do before. I've always took the first option, what I've always thought I could do. But now since I've had me kids and that, I think these have brought me confidence up. They always say there's always a road…something right around the corner, isn't there? Something right for you round the corner, and I think we're getting there now. (Wickham, 2005)

What she describes here is the inability to act on a dream for fear of failure. The ability to take risk, to embrace it, to experience both the euphoria of the positive outcome of having risk pay off and the sting of experiencing failure, of setting off to do something without knowing that you can actually do it, of attempting to innovate and try something new, all of this is incredibly empowering and potentially life changing. If we want this for children, if we want to inspire and empower them and their families, then we have to model it ourselves in our innovative, responsive professional practice that is shaped by the voices of children and their families.

References

Allen, G.M. (2011) *Early Intervention: The Next Steps*. London: Crown Copyright.

Bolton, P. (2012) *Education: Historical Statistics*. London: House of Commons Library. Accessed on 12/7/2018 at: http://researchbriefings.files.parliament.uk/documents/SN04252/SN04252.pdf

Cabinet Office (2017) *Race Disparity Audit Summary Findings from the Ethnicity Facts and Figures Website*. London: Crown Copyright.

Chesworth, L. (2016) 'A funds of knowledge approach to examining play interests: Listening to children's and parents' perspectives.' *International Journal of Early Years Education 24*, 3, 294–308.

Chief Secretary to the Treasury (2003) *Every Child Matters*. London: The Stationery Office Crown Copyright.

Children's Commissioner for England (2017a) *Constructing a Definition of Vulnerability – Attempts to Define and Measure*. London: The Children's Commissioner for England.

Children's Commissioner for England (2017b) *On Measuring the Number of Vulnerable Children in England*. London: The Children's Commissioner for England.

Corsaro, W. (2012) 'Interpretive reproduction in children's play.' *American Journal of Play 4*, 4, 488–504.

Daniel, B. (2010) 'Concepts of adversity, risk, vulnerability and resilience: A discussion in the context of the "child protection system".' *Social Policy and Society 9*, 2, 231–241.

DCSF (2008) *Social and Emotional Aspects of Development: Guidance for Practitioners Working in the Early Years Foundation Stage.* London: DCSF.

Department for Communities and Local Government (2015) *Financial Framework for the Expanded Troubled Families Programme.* London: Department for Communities and Local Government.

Department of Health (2000) *The Framework for the Assessment of Children in Need and their Families.* London: The Stationery Office.

Early Education/Department for Education (2012) *Development Matters in the Early Years Foundation Stage (EYFS).* London. Accessed on 11/6/2018 at: www.foundationyears.org.uk/files/2012/03/Development-Matters-FINAL-PRINT-AMENDED.pdf

ECORYS UK (2014) *National Evaluation of the Troubled Families Programme: Interim Report Family Monitoring Data.* London: DCLG.

Gillies, V. (2011) 'Social and emotional pedagogies: Critiquing the new orthodoxy of emotion in classroom behaviour management.' *British Journal of Sociology of Education 32*, 2, 185–202.

Hedges, H., Cullen, J. and Jordan, B. (2011) 'Early years curriculum: Funds of knowledge as a conceptual framework for children's interests.' *Journal of Curriculum Studies 43*, 2, 185–205.

HM Government (2015) *Working Together to Safeguard Children: A Guide to Inter-Agency Working to Safeguard and Promote the Welfare of Children.* London: The Stationery Office.

Ivinson, G., Beckett, L., Thompson, I., Wrigley, T. *et al.* (2017a) *The Research Commission on Poverty and Policy Advocacy.* London: British Educational Research Association.

Ivinson, G., Beckett, L., Thompson, I., Wrigley, T. *et al.* (2017b) *The Research Commission on Poverty and Policy Advocacy: Summary Report.* London: British Educational Research Association.

James, A. and Prout, A. (1997) *Constructing and Reconstructing Childhood: Contemporary Issues in the Sociological Study of Childhood.* London: Falmer.

Jopling, M. and Vincent, S. (2016) *Vulnerable Children: Needs and Provision in the Primary Phase* (Vol. 6). Cambridge: Cambridge Primary Review Trust.

Keeble, R. (2016) *Effective Primary Teaching Practice.* London: Teaching Schools Council.

Laming, H. (2003) *The Victoria Climbié Inquiry.* London: The Stationery Office.

Lascarides, V.C. and Hinitz, B.F. (2011) *History of Early Childhood Education.* New York, London: Routledge.

Leithwood, K., Jantzi, D., Earl, L., Watson, N., Levin, B. and Fullan, M. (2004) 'Strategic leadership for large-scale reform: The case of England's national literacy and numeracy strategy.' *School Leadership and Management 24*, 1, 57–79.

Loebach, J. and Gilliland, J. (2016) 'Neighbourhood play on the endangered list: Examining patterns in children's local activity and mobility using GPS monitoring and qualitative GIS.' *Children's Geographies 14*, 5, 573–589.

Mayall, B. (2007) *Children's Lives Outside School and Their Educational Impact (Primary Review Research Survey 8/1).* Cambridge: Cambridge Primary Review Trust.

McDonald, L., Fitzroy, S., Fuchs, I., Fooken, I. and Klasen, H. (2012) 'Strategies for high retention rates of low-income families in FAST (Families and Schools Together): An evidence-based parenting programme in the USA, UK, Holland and Germany.' *European Journal of Developmental Psychology 9*, 1, 75–88.

Moss, P., Dillon, J. and Statham, J. (2000) 'The "Child in Need" and "the Rich Child": Discourses, Constructions and Practice.' *Critical Social Policy 20*, 2, 233–254.

Newcastle Report (1861) *Royal Commission to Enquire into the State of Popular Education in England.* London: HMSO.

NSPCC (2014) *How Safe Are Our Children?* London: NSPCC. Accessed on 12/7/2018 at: www.nspcc.org.uk/globalassets/documents/research-reports/how-safe-children-2014-report.pdf

Ofsted (2012) *The Pupil Premium: How Schools Are Using the Pupil Premium Funding to Raise Achievement for Disadvantaged Pupils.* Manchester: Ofsted.

Ofsted (2013) *Framework for Children's Centre Inspection.* Manchester: Ofsted.

Olshansky, S., Passaro, D., Hershow, R., Layden, J. *et al.* (2005) 'A Potential Decline in Life Expectancy in the United States in the 21st Century. A Special Report.' *The New England Journal of Medicine.* Massachusetts: Massachusetts Medical Society.

Payler, J., Georgeson, J. and Wong, S. (2016) 'Young children shaping interprofessional practice in early years settings: Towards a conceptual framework for understanding experiences and participation.' *Learning, Culture and Social Interaction 8*, 12–24.

Sabates, R. and Dex, S. (2012) *Multiple Risk Factors in Young Children's Development.* London: Institute of Education.

Simpson, D. (2013) 'Remediating child poverty via preschool: Exploring practitioners' perspectives in England.' *International Journal of Early Years Education 21*, 1, 85–96.

Social Exclusion Task Force (2007) *Families at Risk: Background on Families with Multiple Disadvantages.* London: Cabinet Office

Sylva, K., Melhuish, E., Sammons, P., Siraj-Blatchford, I. and Taggart, B. (2004). *The Effective Provision of Pre-School Education [EPPE] Project* (Vol. 12). Nottingham: IoE/DfES.

United Nations Committee on the Rights of the Child (1989) *Convention on the Rights of the Child.* London: UNICEF.

Wickham, H. (2005) *Strengthening the Family.* Teachers TV.

Wolfe, I., Macfarlane, A., Donkin, A., Marmot, M. and Viner, R. (2014) *Why Children Die: Death in Infants, Children and Young People in the UK Part A.* London: Royal College of Paediatrics and Child Health. Accessed on 12/7/2018 at: www.ncb.org.uk/sites/default/files/uploads/documents/Policy_docs/why_children_die_full_report.pdf

CHAPTER 2

To the Stars

ADASTRA ADDRESSING POVERTY

Antony Luby

Senior Lecturer
Bishop Grosseteste University

Chapter overview

The chapter describes the journey a group of dedicated teachers, head teachers and others involved in the welfare of the children in a community made to support primary children, particularly their aspirations, outcomes and expectations of those who were living in a post-industrial area. The strategies implemented are discussed.

> *Mansfield no more*
> *Newark no more*
> *Worksop no more.*

If the Reid brothers of Proclaimers fame had been born some 300 miles south of their native Leith, then Mansfield, Newark and Worksop might have been at the heart of their plaintive cry. Rather than mourning over the devastation wreaked upon Bathgate, Linwood and Methil in the industrial heartlands of their native Scotland, their sorrow would have been poured out for the former mining towns and villages of Nottinghamshire now laid waste. I feel humbled and privileged to witness the inspiring efforts of dedicated primary school teachers who are working hard to allay the poverty wrought upon these towns and villages, and the heartfelt cry from brothers Craig and Charlie in *Letter from America* resonates clearly.

Beginnings of Adastra

But where to begin? Strangely, in a cosy pub tucked into the corner of an almost quintessential English village in Sherwood Forest. Here, I enjoyed the company of Wendy Morton, an experienced and accomplished educationist in the realm of school improvement. Wendy is a driving force in establishing the Adastra Primary Partnership that comprises six schools – one primary academy, three primary schools, one junior school and one infant school. It is expanding, and, at the time of writing, one other primary school has recently joined the partnership with another 'knocking at the door' and about to be welcomed.

All of the six founder schools share the same challenge: that of increasing progression and narrowing the attainment gap for predominantly 'white British working-class pupils in areas of deprivation'. And where are these Nottinghamshire stalwarts?

Adastra founder members

- Abbey Hill Primary and Nursery School, Kirkby in Ashfield, near Mansfield

- Forest View Junior School, Ollerton

- Hallcroft Infant School, Retford

- Jacksdale Primary and Nursery School, Jacksdale, near Mansfield

- Ramsden Primary School, Carlton in Lindrick, near Worksop

- The Sir Donald Bailey Academy, Newark.

In order to focus on what the partnership believes are significant factors affecting outcomes for their children, the schools have divided child poverty into key aspects, namely:

- material poverty

- emotional poverty

- poverty of experience

- poverty of language

- poverty of aspiration.

The Adastra Primary Partnership investigates strategies and ideas for minimising the impact of such poverty on their children. The partnership's approach is one of collaboration between equal partners working in similar contexts, but with a shared ambition to identify the best and most effective strategies to address this longstanding national and regional issue. However, let's get back to an early summer day in June 2016 and the cosy pub! For it is here that Wendy Morton outlines the backdrop to the formation of the Adastra Primary Partnership.

With her background in school improvement services, Wendy became concerned with simplistic approaches to 'closing the gap', such as free school meals (FSM). Since 2010, FSM has been used as a proxy indicator but many regard this as being too limited in both approach and understanding. In 2014 the House of Commons Select Committee produced an influential report, *Underachievement in Education by White Working Class Children*. According to Wendy, when this is cross-referenced with the Rowntree Report *Monitoring Poverty and Social Exclusion* (2014), 'it brings out the complexity'.

By the end of 2014, Wendy was thinking, 'Wouldn't it be a good idea to get a like-minded group to discuss the issue of poverty and closing the gap?' She then convened a meeting of six like-minded head teachers who she thought could collaborate with each other and, notably, whose schools were sufficiently distant to not be in competition with each other. Let me introduce these head teachers: Helen Chambers, Abbey Hill; Grant Worthington, Forest View; Jo Cook, Hallcroft; Pete Stonier, Jacksdale; Chris Wilson, Ramsden; Lee Hessey, The Sir Donald Bailey Academy.

Each head teacher read *Underachievement in Education by White Working Class Children* prior to the initial meeting which had a theme of 'No one appears to have an answer; so why don't we have a go?' Lee Hessey hosted the second session at The Sir Donald Bailey Academy and, again, there was no agenda. The group was being given sufficient 'breathing space' so that members could freely exchange knowledge and ideas. A broad agreement was emerging around a theme of 'white British working class in areas of underachievement'. However, the group needed an *identity, focus* and *commitment* from the head teachers. The *identity* issue was partly resolved through adoption of the name *Adastra* (To the Stars) that was inspired by Jacksdale school's motto 'Aim for the Stars' – but is also the name of Wendy's old home. *Commitment* was addressed through the writing up of a Memorandum of Understanding that was duly signed by all of the head teachers. Greater *focus* was achieved when, driving her car, Wendy considered that 'there is too much beating about the bush', and, in response, came up with Perspectives of Poverty and its four strands of: Material; Emotional; Language; and Experience.

Subsequently, Pete Stonier shared these four strands with all of the Jacksdale staff, and there was a great response – so much so that it encouraged the other head teachers to do likewise with their staff, and a fifth strand of 'Aspiration' was duly added. Adastra was taking its first steps and these toddler steps were recognised by a letter from Her Majesty's Inspectorate regarding Good Practice. This was an important move in building up confidence within the Adastra Primary Partnership as the head teachers came to believe, rightly, that 'they were on the right path'.

An integral feature of Adastra life is the half-termly meetings that are preceded by socialising over lunch, and this socialising is crucial to the success of these meetings. Indeed, it was through this pre-lunch socialising that I was introduced to Adastra. To begin with, I felt a little like a 'fish out of water'. A secondary school practitioner – from another country, Scotland: what did I have in common with these East Midlands head teachers? The answer? Passion. Passion for football, passion for learning, passion for theology and, of course, passion for teaching.

Discussion about the merits, demerits and seemingly endless demise of three great football clubs – Celtic, Nottingham Forest and Sunderland – revealed something of our hinterlands: we had shared common interests outside the school. Passion for learning demonstrated that we had insights to offer each other about school, pedagogy and classroom life. Passion for theology opened the way to an unexpected hour-long encounter about Catholicism, Judaism and the mysteries of life. And, yes, passion for teaching – the passion that mesmerises John Hattie in *Visible Learning for Teachers* (2012) and the bond that unites us all.

From the Adastra meetings in early 2015, it soon emerged that it would be profitable for Bishop Grosseteste University (BGU) to undertake research consultancy projects with the partnership. These projects would provide a snapshot for the schools as they engaged innovatively with addressing the five poverty strands. In the end, four of the schools undertook research consultancy (Luby, 2016a), whilst for two schools it was not relevant. Ramsden had a successful Ofsted inspection immediately prior to the scheduled research visit, and, in consultation with head teacher, Chris Wilson, it was decided to adopt a 'softly, softly' approach of gentle conversations with two groups of staff. These 'soft' conversations proved immensely helpful for developing another line of enquiry (Luby, 2016b). Also, following an extensive research and staff development project undertaken in Hallcroft by a county council speech and language therapist, head teacher, Jo Cook, consented to the production of a research commentary upon the staff's experiences. And as for the other schools?

Mansfield addressing poverty

Five miles south west of the town of Mansfield, Abbey Hill Primary and Nursery School serves an area of very high social and economic disadvantage. As indicated by school's score on the Income Deprivation Affecting Children Index, 47 per cent of pupils are living in families that are income deprived. The school receives substantial Pupil Premium funding and other indices of deprivation show that education, skills and training are significantly low in the local area. Furthermore, a significant number of families are supported by social services and the school employs a full-time Child and Family Support Worker: Sam.

Abbey Hill staff members were addressing the issue of poverty of language with particular regard to the development of handwriting skills. Their concern for this was evident from comments in the professional conversations with staff in pre-school, nursery and Years 1 and 2, for example:

- 'Been on the agenda for the last few years.'

- 'Data from boys' handwriting has been a prompt; topic has been discussed before, e.g. performance targets; school plan...'

- 'Foundation reports generally show weakness with respect to handwriting skills.'

- 'Starting from a very low base. Tracking two-year-olds from Nottinghamshire Council showed children at a significant risk of delay.'

- 'There are long-term handwriting problems.'

Further evidence of the problematic nature of handwriting is evidenced by the Ofsted (2014, p. 4) inspection report which comments that: 'The children join the Nursery with skills and knowledge that are well below those typically found. They are particularly low in speaking and listening and in reading and writing.'

Abbey Hill responded with teacher professional development through expert-led, in-service training. This led to not only a 'knowledge explosion' among the staff regarding causes of the underdevelopment in children's handwriting skills, but also changes in classroom practices, for example:

- undertaking ten-minute daily activities such as 'bean-bags'

- reducing availability of tablets as they are a 'draw' for children but they impair development of keyboarding skills

- using Storyteller with props to engage children and painting activities to help to develop gross motor skills

- encouraging use of basic mark-making, e.g. using blank paper on an easel and the children mark-make independently.

Members of staff were making professional judgements that some progress in the development of handwriting skills was being established. They cited evidences such as children:

- displaying enjoyment of writing by spending time mark-making and less time (spent by boys) on construction toys

- showing progress by not using a name card

- improving their handwriting in terms of shape and sizing.

Abbey Hill is now well placed to take forward development in children's handwriting skills. There is a depth of knowledge within the school staff as demonstrated by a training day that focused on theory, to which the staff responded with 'thought showers' comprising a welter of post-its. Indeed, there is a growing confidence and understanding within Abbey Hill, with the staff adapting the new information to their particular circumstances and implementing changes to classroom practices. Suitably impressed, I travelled a further five miles south west in the county of Nottinghamshire to the former mining village of Jacksdale.

Jacksdale Primary and Nursery School

There are 250 pupils in the school, including a number of children on roll from Amber Valley, which is in the top 10 per cent most deprived areas nationally, and 25 per cent of the children are entitled to Pupil Premium funding. Close to the Derbyshire border, the school is situated in the heart of Jacksdale village. The school was judged as 'Good' following an Ofsted inspection in February 2015.

Early in the research consultancy project, a meeting took place between the co-researcher, Elizabeth Farrar, and the head teacher, and this encapsulates the progress being made at Jacksdale with respect to addressing poverty of language. They discussed how the school had identified from the 'on entry' nursery data that children arrive with very weak communication skills. In the views of the school staff, parent–child communication is being greatly diminished as evidenced by parents actively discouraging talk through the prolonged use of dummies, and iPads, or other devices, being similarly used with the intention to keep children quiet. Recently, school staff had been teaching children traditional nursery rhymes and songs when, previously, children's knowledge of these would have been taken for granted. Worryingly, these issues are affecting whole cohorts and not just groups of children.

Members of staff at Jacksdale believe that the children are lacking in life experiences, and this promotes difficulties concerning a lack of language development. In order to address this problem, members of staff were using the National Trust's publication *50 Things to Do Before You're 11 ¾* (2016).

> This includes things like creating some wild art, making a mud pie and exploring inside a tree. These are activities which children from more affluent backgrounds might reasonably be expected to do at home with their parents, but this is not the case for the children in this community. (Luby and Farrar, 2016, p. 11)

Other initiatives to help to develop the children's language skills include the encouragement of social interaction, with the children being taught how to respond appropriately when greeted. This is reinforced through a manners award in weekly assemblies. As with other schools in the Adastra Primary Partnership, there is an overt attempt to instil the values of private, independent schools in the pupils. They wish to match the input provided by parents at other local, more affluent schools.

This is the oft-spoke Department for Education (DfE) *closing the gap* – and Jacksdale and Abbey Hill exemplify the attitude of the Adastra Primary Partnership in their efforts to 'close the gap'. It is a no-nonsense, hardworking, 'rolled-up sleeves' approach. There are no easy solutions, but it is not an impossible task – progress can be made. For instance, Jacksdale has introduced an app, *Marvellous Me*, that allows adults in the school to send good news messages directly to the phones of parents and carers. The intention is not only to encourage parents to become more interested in what their children are learning, but also to promote discussion with their children about what they have been doing at school. And so messages such as, 'Ask Freddie about his science experiment today' are being sent home. The app sends a 'Hi5' back to the school to show that parents have received the message. Jacksdale reports that this has been highly effective, and they receive thousands of Hi5s throughout the year.

Other more traditional modes of communication promoted by Jacksdale are the frequent use of drama and role play in lessons. Class assemblies and Christmas productions also give the children the opportunity to stand up in front of others to speak, and so develop their confidence. Such confidence can be a building block in developing reasoning skills that are so prized by society's elite.

Looking outward

Lessons can also be learned from elsewhere. Interesting work has been undertaken with regard to this in a deprived area on England's south coast: deploying the use of exploratory talk with pupils in Brighton in order to encourage children to 'engage critically but constructively with each other's ideas' (Mercer, 1995, p. 104). Given that the Adastra Primary Partnership is seeking and developing activities, strategies and pedagogies that address issues of poverty for disadvantaged children, then it is worthwhile to consider that:

> it seems possible that this type of pedagogical approach (exploratory talk) could be crucial in enabling these silenced, disadvantaged students to have a space for their voices to be heard and valued, an experience that could go far beyond the classroom and into the realities of the students' social world. (Haynes, 2015, p. 10)

Haynes' research has been conducted in deprived areas of the south coast and, although undertaken in secondary schools, in my professional judgement, having undertaken similar research for different purposes (Luby, 2014), the development of the dialogic skill of exploratory talk does have relevance for Adastra primary and junior schools.

Clearly, it would be difficult, because of geographical circumstances, to develop strong relationships with south-coast schools. However, relationships with schools at a regional level is not only desirable but also possible – especially given the plans from the newly instituted Chartered College of Teaching for regional hubs. These regional hubs will support members of the College to meet face to face to engage with evidence, share good practice and develop professional skills. At the time of writing, this is already happening in an embryonic fashion as the Nottinghamshire Adastra schools came together with schools from the 'Greater Lincolnshire' area at the BGU Closing the Gap conference (jointly sponsored by North Lincolnshire's Leading Learning Forward Teaching School Alliance (TSA), North East Lincolnshire's Healing Teaching School and Lincoln's Kyra TSA). These regional relationships are being further enhanced through a BGU research skills training programme, inspired by the highly successful *Closing the Gap: Test and Learn Research Project* (NCTL, 2016), at which teachers from a wide geographical area (South Yorkshire down to South Lincolnshire and west to Nottinghamshire) are supporting each other with research projects.

There is already an inbuilt expertise upon which Adastra can draw – at both local and regional levels. At the local level, there are well-established practices regarding action research at Lakeside Primary in Doncaster, and this school is situated in a similar area of high deprivation. Moreover, much can be learned from schools in different circumstances such as the leafy market town primary school of Bawtry Mayflower that, under the headship of Julie Jenkinson, has produced a cadre of teachers well versed with evidence-informed classroom practices (Crawshaw, 2017; Dunn, 2017). It is encouraging to record that, as of summer 2017, both of these schools have joined Adastra. At a regional level, Lincolnshire is blessed with one of only five national research schools: Kyra at Lincoln. And through a budding partnership, and the prodigious efforts of head teacher James Siddle, Adastra and the schools and TSAs mentioned above are participating in a prestigious research project on digital feedback funded by the Education Endowment Foundation.

But what else does the Adastra Primary Partnership have to offer the 'outside world' of education?

Newark addressing poverty

The second largest school within this partnership is The Sir Donald Bailey Academy in Newark. Their head teacher, Lee Hessey, produced a 24-page document entitled *The Speaking and Listening Functional Skills Curriculum*. This document identifies four strands to be addressed in particular:

- opportunities for children to show an awareness of their audience
- opportunities for children to speak and discuss
- opportunities for children to listen
- opportunities for children to practise non-verbal communication.

Each of these strands is supported by 10–14 exemplars; and school staff had discussed beforehand the activities and actions that required to be undertaken. The following proved to be noteworthy.

OPPORTUNITIES FOR CHILDREN TO SHOW AN AWARENESS OF THEIR AUDIENCE

- house assemblies, where older children plan and deliver an assembly linked to themes of the week
- video blog on the school website, making use of green-screen technology
- children meeting and greeting visitors and conducting school tours to potential parents
- children taking on roles in class projects such as 'project lead'
- planning opportunities to speak to different audiences; making use of the community café.

Additionally, one teacher spoke convincingly of how 'high-ability' pupils took on different roles within group work, for example as leader, illustrator, summariser or questioner. And another teacher emphasised the importance of having private conversations with reluctant pupils in areas removed from the classroom – such as the corridor – whilst preparing for an assembly. Much of this will be familiar to many schools, but it is reassuring to know that these strategies have a lasting impact.

OPPORTUNITIES FOR CHILDREN TO SPEAK AND DISCUSS

- Superstar Assemblies where children discuss and talk about their dreams

- circle time and 'show 'n' tell' sessions

- hot seating as a teaching strategy in English

- class debates using a house system and use of talk partners in lessons

- taking messages on behalf of the class teacher to other classes or departments

- children bringing in newspapers – 'What's been happening in the week?'

OPPORTUNITIES FOR CHILDREN TO LISTEN

- following instructions for 'what makes a good listener': 'Eyes looking and ears listening'

- listening to audio stories

- working in pairs and responding to a partner

- taking messages on behalf of staff and following instructions

- note taking and actively listening for key information

- having a 'look out' focus and selecting three things to spot

- visitors coming into school to speak.

A particularly good example is that of *Tinga Tinga Tales*, which are African fables from YouTube (approximately 5–10 minutes long). Children's ability to listen is 'tested' by the teacher questioning afterwards and by them acting out the stories. Again, the strategies outlined above may just offer reassurance to other schools.

OPPORTUNITIES FOR CHILDREN TO PRACTISE NON-VERBAL COMMUNICATION

- using drama and freeze frames in lessons
- children creating social stories and acting them out, paying particular attention to body language and facial expressions
- Using signs and symbols in the classroom
- training children for a range of contexts, for example, when showing visitors round school, children should be taught to use a firm handshake (and to shake the teacher's hand and make eye contact when leaving lessons)
- using appropriate bodily contact.

As part of the multi-academy Forge Trust, The Sir Donald Bailey Academy school is beginning to sponsor other schools. Initially, at least, these are likely to be in similarly disadvantaged areas. The senior leadership team (SLT) anticipates that the school systems and procedures will be rolled out across these schools very quickly. The SLT believes that they are becoming expert in poverty, and they are confident that their methods will be effective in other schools. It is noteworthy that the school was achieving 50 per cent Level 4+ at the end of Key Stage 2 but this is now over 90 per cent. And their data for the next few years suggests that they will continue to be in the top 2 per cent of schools nationally.

But the data and the teaching strategies serve a bigger purpose – that of social justice.

Worksop addressing social justice

Ten miles south of Worksop, one of the Adastra schools, Forest View Junior School, is addressing social justice within the local community. Head teacher Grant Worthington co-chairs the Sherwood Forest Education Partnership, along with Adastra convener Wendy Morton. This is an exciting development whereby local schools collaborate with Citizens Advice, a councillor, local churches, a social enterprise agency, a children's centre and retired persons, amongst others. This collaboration is founded upon the bedrock of a local community that is rightly proud of its mining heritage. This Sherwood Forest Education Partnership is developing a range of initiatives from a heritage project to a gardening programme through to reading initiatives. Each partner brings a different set of strengths to the partnership and not only are these shared, but there is also cross-pollination between the partners, for example by Citizens Advice sharing materials with local churches and schools and an educationist inviting retired family and friends onto the group to share their expertise. The partnership is in its early stages, but there is already a dynamism to the relationships that bodes well for the future.

Critics might contend that there is a degree of political activism with respect to the Sherwood Forest Education Partnership, but this is understandable and laudable. Mining communities have suffered social and economic devastation since the 1980s, and future prospects are bleak. In this era of austerity and further proposed welfare reforms, Beatty and Fothergill (2016, p. 3) have produced a hard-hitting report in which they point out that:

> The new reforms impact unevenly across the country. Older industrial areas…and a number of other towns are hit hardest… As a general rule, the more deprived the local authority the greater the financial loss… A key effect of welfare reform is to widen the gap in prosperity between the best and worst local economies across the country.

A political dimension is not something from which the schools should shy away. From an educational perspective, teachers can draw much support.

- *Common law*: In the act of teaching, teachers are no less than parents and are expected to be *in loco parentis*. Whilst in their care, teachers are expected to look after all of their children's needs.

- *Maslow's hierarchy of need*: In order to attain the ultimate level of self-actualisation, whereby children achieve their potential, their physiological needs require addressing first. Hence, the prevalence of Breakfast Clubs across many schools within the UK. And the next level is that of 'Safety', which includes security of resources, employment, family, and so on. Hence, Abbey Hill's Helen and Sam gently commanding a young pupil to come down the stairs of his home and get himself ready for school. Teachers and school staff have a legitimate interest in all areas of child development.

- *Scottish teachers' standards and social justice.* North of the border, the Scottish teachers' standards have professional values at their core, and the first of these is *social justice*. That is to say, in their professional actions, teachers are expected to 'develop and apply political literacy and political insight in relation to professional practice, educational change and policy development' (General Teaching Council Scotland, 2012, p. 10).

In my eyes, through an imaginative and determined response to the issue of poverty, the Adastra Primary Partnership is beginning to exemplify the development of political literacy and insight in schools and teachers.

Tribute

Let us finish as we started, with the voices of the Proclaimers, who claimed that they would walk 500 miles (twice!) to be with their true love.

I can't quite match walking a thousand miles, but for the last 30 months I have endured a weekly round-trip commute of 800 miles from the bonny village of Banchory in Royal Deeside to the stately cathedral city of Lincoln. The reasons for this pilgrimage are threefold. First, the School of Teacher Development at BGU has been transformed with a growing research culture that has partnership with schools at its heart. Second, developing supra-regional links with Scunthorpe's Leading Learning Forward TSA, Grimsby's Healing Teaching School, Lincoln's Kyra national research school and action research-oriented schools in South Yorkshire mean not only that the university is contributing actively to self-improving school systems, but also that it is well placed to become a regional hub for the new Chartered College of Teaching. But third, and most profound, the actions, values and beliefs of the teachers and staff involved with Adastra are inspiring and humbling.

References

Beatty, C. and Fothergill, S. (2016) *The Uneven Impact of Welfare Reform*. Sheffield: Centre for Regional Economic and Social Research, Sheffield Hallam University.

Crawshaw, J. (2017) *Engaging Boys in Writing Through Role Play: Following Their Lead*. Accessed on 6/6/2018 at www.socialpublishersfoundation.org/knowledge-base/engaging-boys-in-writing-through-role-play-following-their-lead

Dunn, C. (2017) *Engaging Children and Parents in Homework*. Accessed on 6/6/2018 at www.socialpublishersfoundation.org/knowledge-base/engaging-children-and-parents-in-homework

General Teaching Council Scotland (2012) *The Standard for Career-Long Professional Learning: Supporting the Development of Teacher Professional Learning*. Accessed on 6/6/2018 at www.gtcs.org.uk/web/FILES/the-standards/standard-for-career-long-professional-learning-1212.pdf

Hattie, J. (2012) *Visible Learning for Teachers: Maximizing Impact on Learning*. Abingdon: Routledge.

Haynes, F. (2015) 'A voice of their own: Helping silenced students to be heard through the use of exploratory talk in pairs.' *Education Today 65*, 3, 10–15. Special Issue: Re-Thinking Oracy.

House of Commons Select Committee (2014) *Underachievement in Education by White Working Class Children*. London: The Stationery Office.

Luby, A. (2014) 'First footing inter-faith dialogue.' *Educational Action Research 22*, 1, 57–71.

Luby, A. (ed.) (2016a) *Poverty and Closing the Gap: Adastra Research Consultancy Projects*. Lincoln: Bishop Grosseteste University.

Luby, A. (2016b) 'Stars and saints: Professional conversations for enhancing classroom practices.' *Education Today 66*, 3, 2–6.

Luby, A. and Farrar, E. (2016) 'Poverty of Language: Jacksdale Nursery and Primary School.' In A. Luby (ed.) *Poverty and Closing the Gap: Adastra Research Consultancy Projects*. Lincoln: Bishop Grosseteste University.

Mercer, N. (1995) *The Guided Construction of Knowledge: Talk Amongst Teachers and Learners*. Cleveden: Multilingual Matters Ltd.

National Trust (2016) *50 Things To Do Before You're 11 3/4*. Accessed on 6/6/2018 at www.50things.org.uk

NCTL (2016) *Closing the Gap: Test and Learn Research Project*. Accessed on 6/6/2018 at www.gov.uk/government/uploads/system/uploads/attachment_data/file/495580/closing_the_gap_test_and_learn_full_report.pdf

Ofsted (2014) *School Inspection Report: Abbey Hill Primary and Nursery. Unique Reference Number (URN): 136006*. Accessed on 6/6/2018 at https://reports.ofsted.gov.uk/inspection-reports/find-inspection-report/provider/ELS/136006

Rowntree Report (2014) *Monitoring Poverty and Social Exclusion*. Accessed on 6/6/2018 at www.jrf.org.uk/report/monitoring-poverty-and-social-exclusion-2014

CHAPTER 3

Inside an Early Years Rural Setting

Nishi Bremner

Deputy Head Teacher and Reception Teacher
Spilsby Primary Academy

Chapter overview

The chapter relates the initiatives implemented in an early years rural setting to enhance partnerships with parents and carers through such activities as newsletters, homework, learning journals and events, while also supporting parents, particularly those who may be in vulnerable situations themselves. Strategies to support children's wellbeing are explored.

When thinking of a rural school, most people would probably conjure the fond image of a small, old, red-brick building, set in a quaint, chocolate-box village surrounded by an inspirational landscape of open countryside. The moral heart of a community where young minds are nurtured, virtues are propagated and the most important highlight of the school year is the harvest festival. Venture inside and you are welcomed into cosy classrooms with no more than 15 model children, all sharing and communicating well together. At home time, parents might gather in the playground, perhaps chatting reassuringly to each other about how their children seem to blossom in their rustic environment, discussing the wonderful nature-based activities they had been doing over the weekend or the healthy extra-curricular activities that their children attend outside school. A perfectly pastoral educational experience.

In many aspects, this couldn't be farther from the truth.

When I first moved to Lincolnshire a few years ago, I had no preconceptions of what it would be like and was excited at the brand-new challenges awaiting me. Having successfully trained in and taught both Foundation Stage and Key Stage 1 within inner and outer London schools for many years (as well as four years of teaching in Spain), I was perfectly aware of the differing challenges that teachers face on a daily basis, whatever the type of school, wherever it may be.

What I did find, however, was that the challenges facing some rural schools are not too different to those faced by inner-city ones, the main difference being the lack of knowledge and/or professional facilities to support the families.

Allow me to set the scene. I work in a one-form entry primary school of over 210 children aged 4 to 11 in a small town in Lincolnshire. I have a reception class of up to 30 children who all start together, full-time in September. There are no children who speak English as an additional language, which, for Lincolnshire, is actually very unusual. There is an above average proportion of pupils who are eligible for free school meals and receive Pupil Premium. In fact, 38 per cent of our children receive Pupil Premium. The proportions of disabled pupils and those who have Special Educational Needs is also above average in our school.

For a true picture of the background of the children in the school, it is vital to consider the parent demographic. There is a large proportion of young parents, inexperienced parents and single, sometimes vulnerable, parents. An additional barrier faced by the teaching staff is the negative view of school that parents have, which is commonly based on their own past experiences of school when they were children themselves. Further problems also occur due to the low adult literacy levels within the community. These factors have a profound impact on the children, often resulting in very low aspirations.

On joining the school, I quickly made myself aware of the barriers that I was faced with. Given our parent demographic and their views, parental relationships were a priority. It was necessary to encourage *parental involvement* in their children's learning and to offer support to the parents in helping them *engage with their children* at home. I had to employ all the good practices that I had accumulated over the years to create effective relationships and an effective early years setting.

Parental involvement

Parents are the most prominent and important people in a child's life, especially in their formative early years. It is through their parents that they learn about the world, how to speak, how to play and how to interact with their surroundings. When a child joins a setting at that young age when they have been nurtured primarily by their parents, it can be difficult for both parent and child to have another carer be so prominent in their life. It is especially important, at this point in a child's schooling, to have a strong and positive relationship between school and home. Seeing their parents and teachers working together, with a relationship built on trust, contributes so much to the child. It impacts on the child's self-esteem, feeling of safety and security and their overall happiness and wellbeing. If this relationship is built on mutual trust and respect it will encourage the child's learning and their ability to reach their full potential. Parental engagement was clearly an issue in this particular school, or rather the lack of it, so this became a key element in the initiative that I needed to put into place to enrich the children's learning experience.

I decided to implement some initiatives straight away, even before the children started in September, so that we could explain the importance of the parents' role and equip them with all they needed to support their children. In turn, each parent could support us with information to help us engage their child.

Information sharing is the key!

Information works both ways, from practitioner to parent and parent to practitioner. There are many strands:

- practitioners collecting valuable information about the children
- practitioners collecting valuable information about the parents
- parents being informed of their children's learning
- parents being informed of their children's development and progress.

With the aforementioned parent demographic in mind, we needed to think of initiatives that were non-judgemental and easy to implement but that had maximum impact, which we could then implement to encourage the practitioner–parent partnership. A tall order indeed!

Transition meeting

We held a transition meeting before the children started school, which proved vital in explaining to the parents their own role in their child's education. We had a lot of young, inexperienced mothers and parents who needed support in parenting, so it was invaluable to have them receiving this message.

Information about the children is vital for a practitioner to make the learning more meaningful for them, so we sent out questionnaires in the July before the children started to find out their interests, abilities and any other useful information to help us support the children in their learning.

Leaflets

Leaflets were sent out to parents during the transition visits in July with tips on how to help their child at home, in reading and maths and other areas. These were kept bright, easy to read and bullet pointed so as not to overwhelm parents who may have low literacy skills and to try to engage parents who may not be likely to look at formal or 'heavy reading' letters. They included ideas for games and tips on questions they could ask their child when they were out and about.

Keeping parents informed

This was a priority, so we set up notice boards in public areas around the school to keep the parents informed about what their children were learning about on a weekly basis. These were very visual and low maintenance – simply photos and a few handwritten or typed captions to say what we'd been doing.

We added quotes from the children themselves to make it very personal to the parents of the children in our class. This highly visual and informal communication meant everyone could access it, regardless of their literacy level. Useful websites were also included in these leaflets for those who may have wanted more information.

Twitter and Facebook accounts for the school were set up and promoted to keep parents informed of events and post highlights of the school day. This has become invaluable in our communication with parents, as all of them used one or both of these social media sites – on a very regular basis!

Newsletters

These were sent out at the beginning of every term to let parents know what the children would be learning and what special events were being organised to help link to the topic. These took the shape of a topic web, again that was easily accessible to all. The parents found this extremely useful and I had several conversations with parents from all walks of life about things they had seen or talked about with their children at the weekend, which were a result of the parents knowing what the current topic was. These invaluable conversations not only engaged the parents and children, but also reinforced the bond between the parents and the practitioners in the child's eyes, as they were talking about school-based learning with their parents out of school. So simple yet so effective. Sometimes we would send out songs for the children to learn at home too for special events and this engaged parents even more. It was something they could do easily without requiring anything written and the children could teach them, making it so much fun! The added bonus was that the children got to know the songs even quicker and perform them even better. A win-win situation!

Homework

Homework is always a contentious subject, with some parents wanting more and others saying it is too much. It was becoming a task that the children would do less and less of – or even worse, the parents would complete it for their children! The purpose of homework should be to complement and reinforce the children's learning and thereby embed it. Trying to do this in a non-onerous, meaningful way is the key to homework success! Given some of the parents' attitudes towards school – formed from bad experiences from their own childhood and the adult literacy issues – it made perfect sense for it to be a more practical piece, which we hoped would be engaging for all. We needed to kill two birds with one stone: find a way of engaging parents and children with their homework, as well as learning in a fun, non-judgemental way. As our curriculum had become more topic based and cross-curricular, homework now took the shape of a topic-linked project. This was a purposeful decision, based on the needs of the children and responses from the parents regarding homework. That, at least, was the thinking behind it – engaging the parents and encouraging them to work with their child on a topic-linked piece at the beginning of the project and to talk to their children about their upcoming project so that, hopefully, they would come armed with some knowledge of the project too.

In reception, this was usually a craft-based homework, focusing on the parents working with their child on a practical piece. When the child brought it in, they were expected to talk about it in front of the class, which even the shyest children did, as they were so proud of what they and their parents had created together.

The uptake on the homework, the finished creations and subsequent feedback we received impressed us greatly and went far beyond our expectations. In fact, the parents actually became quite competitive with their creations and clearly put a lot of time and effort into them.

The icing on the cake was the look on the children's faces when we would display them in the class. The overwhelming pride in their projects and the developing sense of ownership over their classroom could clearly be seen. Priceless and powerful, moments of magic like these help to remind us why we chose a career in teaching in the first place.

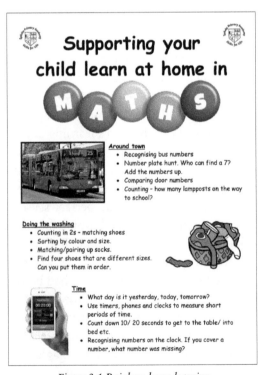

Figure 3.1 Rainbow home learning

Figure 3.2 Octopus

Figure 3.3 Under the Sea home learning

Workshops

These were set up in response to questionnaires and following conversations that I had with the parents at the school gate. Since most of the parents picked up their children from school and would be unlikely to come back in the evening for the workshops once they had returned home, we held these straight after school.

We did not call these 'meetings' but instead used the name 'workshops' and presented them in an informal way that was non-threatening and relaxed. It was a chance for the parents to ask about the theme in hand and share ideas to support their children at home and, in a small way, help the parents in their parenting roles. In the past the children were not allowed to come to these workshops, so we decided to offer a crèche facility (run by the teaching assistants, as they knew how important this was). These worked fairly well and we got a fair uptake but still had a way to go to break down the barriers and engage parents further. However, we had a few more gems up our sleeves!

Learning journals

Learning journals have been used in early years for as long as I can remember – evenings of sitting at the dining room table or the living room floor surrounded by a sea of photos and children's work; sticking these into large scrap books or folders, annotated with sticky notes and cross referenced to the early years objectives. As these were then shelved away in the class, the children only had access to them from time to time and the parents only on open afternoons or parents' evenings – perhaps three to four times a year. How could a parent really know what their child was doing at school on a *daily* basis if they didn't have daily access to their child's learning? We all know that if you asked a child, especially a child in the Foundation Stage, what they did at school, they would say one of three things: 'nothing' or 'I can't remember' or 'I played'. Although we know this may be a reactionary statement because the children may be tired or just want to come home and relax, this is not going to help any parent or carer engage with the child about what they did at school that day.

The answer was simple: to use an online journal that the parents had access to at all times and could use to see immediately what their child had been doing and learning about in school that day. The parents could see the children's learning – our annotations, photos, videos – and could like and add their own comments too.

In this way, the parent could engage, support and even choose to extend the learning at home. This would build up links between school and home, and therefore, in the eyes of the child, between practitioner and parent. In such a simple and effective way, those all-important parent–practitioner links are being reinforced again on a daily basis, adding to the security of the child as they see all the adults in their life working together in their best interest.

This has been a complete success over the last two years and parents can access them on their PCs, tablets and, most importantly for most of our parents, phones. The added facility of the parents being able to post their own observations has been invaluable for the children in building those connections between home and school, as we discuss them in class the next day. These discussions have also encouraged the other children to talk to their parents about the online journal and some children have even asked their parents to post photos of special events on their journal so they could share them with their friends.

Over the last two years in which we have been using the online journal, the uptake has steadily increased and is now at over 60 per cent, which is a great success and a figure that we expect to increase year on year. The parents from the last two cohorts have valued it so much and found it so helpful in supporting their children at home that they have asked if there will be online journals for when their children move into Key Stage 1! That speaks volumes!

Events

Events in school were next on the list of initiatives. Now that the parents were engaging with the homework projects and were informed about their child's topics and learning, we could really engage them further with fun 'Wow' events and 'Stay and Play' sessions organised and hosted by their own children. This was purposefully woven into the curriculum and became an intrinsic part of the children's learning for that topic.

The first of these we chose to implement were the Wow events, which were topic-linked. In the Early Years Foundation Stage (EYFS) our curriculum consisted of three topics per year, which would each run over two small terms. Usually there would be two mini topics within this, both being linked to the same big umbrella theme for that full term. At some point in the topic we would hold a Wow event to celebrate and share the children's learning. Parents and carers were invited to this big event, and it was a very big deal! In reception class we used this Wow event as one of the purposes to give our learning more meaning. For example, when learning about ourselves in our Rainbow World topic in the first term, we learnt about special people in our lives and all the things that made us either different, the same or special. This included what special toys we had, what we liked to do, eat and drink and other things that could be found at the end of our rainbows. For our Wow event, to knit all of our learning together and celebrate our learning, we decided to organise a Rainbow Party. We became party planners over a period of three weeks, planning what our party would look like, what food and drinks we would have, what party games we would play and what we would wear. The children made plans for the party and shopping lists to help me when I went shopping. They wrote invitations and made the decorations and, as it got closer, the children made the party food and helped to arrange it on the day.

You can imagine how immersed they were in the learning and what purpose their learning had – not to mention how many areas of the curriculum were touched on in the process and how completely focused they were to get this party organised for those special people in their lives. This, again, built on those relationships between school and home, parents and practitioners, with the children's learning being woven through it all. Needless to say, these types of events always proved to be one of the children's favourite memories when we asked them at the end of the year.

Other Wow events included performances by the children to their parents and craft-based activities with them. The type of event would depend on the theme, children's interests and how it linked into their learning.

Figures 3.5–3.10 Our Rainbow Party Wow event, organised by the reception class

Some terms we would ask the parents and carers to come into school nearer to the beginning of a topic to take part in what we in EYFS would call a 'Stay and Play' session. This would entail the parents and children working together to make topic-linked models, decorations, pictures and resources for the classroom. These activities would have been planned in advance by the children, having been asked what they feel they would need to transform the class. This would not only give the children a chance to show their parents and carers how independent they were and what they could achieve, but also give them more ownership over the class and their environment, as all their models and pictures would be displayed in the room to transform the class ready for the topic.

Figures 3.11–3.16 Our Stay and Play event linked to our Watch Me Grow topic

These events were extremely successful and engaged even those hard-to-reach parents. The attendance at these events, not only in EYFS, but across the school, has been overwhelming – usually between 90 per cent and 100 per cent!

To go from virtually no parents engaging with the school to this level of cooperation, over such a short space of time, can be considered a huge success for us in our quest to engage parents in their children's learning. The fact that this enhances the children's learning, giving it purpose and meaning along with it being so much fun, only compounds our sense of accomplishment.

Supporting parents

In a time where teachers are all too often expected to provide both education and a parent role to the children in their classes, it is imperative to give the parents the tools and techniques required to support them in parenting and supporting their own children. Through recognising what needs they have, finding the support they need and liaising with trained professionals, they can be equipped with the tools to help them to become better parents. Well, at least, that is the theory!

Support for vulnerable parents

It became clear to me at a very early stage that although I was, indeed, working in a rural school, it very much had the character and feel of an inner-city school. There is usually, however, a greater level of support offered by inner-city schools within major cities for those who need it, offering more places to receive that support and making it easier to access, even down to a geographical level (ease of commute and transport links).

I have heard the term 'green deprivation' being bandied about and this seems to fit the bill exactly – deprivation and issues similar to inner-city ones, but in rural areas and without the infrastructure to support them.

Realising that we were facing the same issues but without these support systems being as readily accessible and available, we decided to employ a full-time family welfare officer. She has proved invaluable in supporting families and their children and we cannot imagine how we could have supported these families otherwise.

To date, she has monitored and nurtured vulnerable children, supported their families, liaised with outside services, set up and attended meetings and generally provided support and advice for vulnerable parents and children in any and every way. She set up Triple P parenting courses and arranged and hosted Team Around the Child (TAC) and Child In Need (CIN) meetings. Another way to help those parents who were more reluctant to take up support was to hold these meetings on site. This way it was not threatening in the parents' eyes, as it was in a place they were comfortable with. We even decided to clear a Portakabin to host these meetings, so that they were on site but not in the school building. That way the parties involved could still feel secure in a familiar environment but not have to go through the main school building.

This has proved to work with our parents, as they are now attending their meetings and we can also monitor, very easily, those who are not, allowing us to follow up where necessary.

Wellbeing

With children and parents coming from an area of deprivation and low aspiration, we are confronted with more than just academic barriers. Another major challenge faced by our school was one of wellbeing.

The wellbeing of the children has always been the utmost priority for us, as in any school. With the needs of the children and the parents becoming more complex, we felt it necessary to put something more substantial in place.

With multiple and increasingly complicated needs now becoming more apparent in school, we soon realised that we needed to go a step further and have something more tailored to our children's emerging needs. We therefore looked for a more channelled approach. In collaboration with a children's counselling company, we have set up a counselling service for targeted children in our school. This is taking place in school time and with trained counsellors, subsidised by the counselling company and voluntary contributions from the parents of those children involved. The family welfare officer has been integral in this process and will also be further trained this year to take over the counselling sessions next year. In addition to this, the children in all classes will have a session every term linked to an aspect of wellbeing, led by the trained counsellors. These workshops will run throughout the school year to ensure that we, as a school, continue to help the children in the changing world they will inevitably face when they move on from primary school and into later life. This will enable them to recognise what 'wellbeing' actually is and how to maintain and support themselves. It will also equip the children with coping methods surrounding healthy relationships, puberty, sexual education, anxiety, emotional wellbeing, self-esteem and self-care. It is still early days, but we are hopeful that this will really benefit all the children in providing them with the best skills possible to help them to look after themselves and especially their mental health.

To complement this, in our reception class, we have introduced various new techniques to help with the children's wellbeing. These were not major overhauls of our normal practice and, in fact, we feel they are enhancing the children's experiences and helping them to be better, more independent learners.

First and foremost, we looked at our cohort and identified their specific needs. We identified a few skills that needed honing to support the children in their attitudes to learning. We then researched different techniques that we could use to support them through mindfulness approaches, which would support their wellbeing.

There were four main needs in this cohort: listening and attention; awareness of themselves; self-esteem; and, for a large group of children, calming techniques.

To enhance their listening skills, we used mindfulness techniques (supported by the Cosmic Kids website[1]) to help the children to think about *how* they listen. This was a very short (under ten minutes) calming session in which the children focused completely on listening to the sound of a bell – listening intently to hear it and then signalling when the sound had finished. It made them more aware of listening to sounds as well as being aware of the skill required to listen for sounds, whether it was listening out for sounds around them or the teacher speaking directly to them. Now, when the children lose concentration in class, they are reminded of these techniques to encourage them to focus, and it seems to be having a positive effect on a large majority of the children.

Mindfulness techniques were put in place to help the children in activities that needed more body and sense awareness. For example, prior to a tasting activity in class, we joined in with a mindfulness session and learnt not simply to gobble up the food but to use all of our senses to their fullest to enhance the experience. This included holding the food in our fingers or hand, looking at it, smelling it, licking it and holding it in our mouths and sensing how it felt. Only after these stages did the children then eat it slowly – chewing it, sensing how it felt and tasted as they chewed it and mashing it up in their mouths before finally swallowing it. During the following tasting activity we found that, once they had been reminded to follow

---

1   www.cosmickids.com

these techniques, the children made much more focused and in-depth observations on how the food tasted and were more acutely aware of their own senses that and how to use them.

Figure 3.17 Using mindfulness techniques to awaken our senses

The 'I can't monster' was another very effective technique in supporting children's self-esteem. We made up a story/scenario which introduced the 'I can't monster', who tries to tell us that we cannot do certain things. We had to pretend to be superheroes and defeat the 'I can't monster', by saying 'Yes, I can!' Then we could really try our hardest at doing something that the 'I can't monster' may think we could not do. Something so simple has become so effective by reminding the children that they can do things. They smile saying, 'Yes I can', and are now more eager to have a go at doing things more independently, from doing up their zip to writing a grapheme they have just learnt in phonics.

The imagery portrayed was very powerful in helping the children to focus themselves in all these areas and, I feel, also helped to enhance their learning experience by reducing anxiety.

Figure 3.18 Introducing the new yoga area and poster in the classroom

A large proportion of our current cohort seemed to be quite energetic and would often flit from activity to activity. Their bodies needed calming to focus their energy more constructively. A space in the classroom was created in which a poster depicting yoga poses was mounted, and we introduced this new space to the children.

They accessed this area, as any other area, independently during activities time and really enjoyed trying to learn the various poses and finding out what they were all called. We encouraged those children who had excess energy to spend some time in this area, trying out some poses with an adult.

Almost straight away, we noticed a definite improvement in the behaviour of children who found it particularly difficult to focus for any period of time and who had excess energy.

Figures 3.19–3.21 Children accessing the yoga area created in class

Just creating this small area in the classroom, including a yoga poster and focusing children on this with an adult has proved invaluable in calming and focusing the children. Some children even asked when they could do some more yoga-based activities with an adult as they, themselves, noticed that it made them feel more 'relaxed'.

This has been such a success in class that we now all have a whole-class, 15-minute yoga session linked to our topic. These sessions really do seem to focus the children, leaving them calm and relaxed.

Figures 3.22–3.23 Whole-class yoga sessions

The wellbeing of the children is paramount, but we must not forget that the wellbeing of their parents is important too. We are very aware that a child's wellbeing is closely linked to that of their parents. So, improving the wellbeing of the parents will consequently improve their child's wellbeing. Our next step, therefore, will be to provide the same wellbeing support to those parents that need it in the years to come, through counselling, which will be offered to them by our in-house trained counsellors.

Conclusion

Ask any teacher and they will tell you that working in any school offers its own unique challenges, whether it be challenging children, problematic or pushy parents or pressures from management. They are complex and interwoven challenges that need to be studied carefully to choose the most effective strategies to solve, or at the very least have a positive impact on, them. As effective early years practitioners, we all know that the most effective way to support children in their learning is to provide a curriculum tailored to their needs so that it is easily accessible, engaging and meaningful to them. We do this every day in the planning and provision we offer, from 'Funky Fingers' activities to support poor motor skills, to 'Drop Everything and Read' sessions to promote a love of reading. We also consistently build on what we know about the children's interests and strengths to make the most of the curriculum and provision we offer.

The same process is needed when identifying the challenges of the school, outside the realms of the classroom: first, identifying the barriers, thinking of ways to solve them using the strengths you have on hand and then using your invaluable knowledge of the school to create a plan to overcome them. It may not be an easy road to navigate – and the 'I can't monster' may occasionally rear its ugly head – but with the support of your setting you can defeat it and say, 'Yes I can!'

PART 2

Vulnerable Groups

CHAPTER 4

Children at Risk of Being Missed

Julia Lindley-Baker

Academic Coordinator for Special Educational Needs and Inclusion
Bishop Grosseteste University

Chapter overview

This chapter discusses the context of children at risk from global, national and classroom perspectives. Ways of supporting children, particularly in their emotional wellbeing, in the foundation years are considered. Specific case studies are presented with reflections to consider the implications of the child's situation and possible relevance to the reader.

> Jack was a quiet teenager, who might be considered sullen and withdrawn. Following an erratic pattern of school attendance and frequent rides home in police cars, Jack was placed in a non-secure residential educational setting for 90 days after being detained for joy riding. This alternative to a custodial sentence offered Jack the opportunity to develop academically and socially and stay out of prison. It also gave Jack the chance to stop glue sniffing and break away from disruptive influences at home. Jack engaged positively whilst in the centre and towards the end of his placement, a progress review, attended by professionals from social and educational backgrounds, was held. It was agreed that Jack was 'not at risk' and he subsequently returned home. Two weeks later, Jack was found dead, having fallen into a canal whilst high on glue.

Not every story is as tragic as Jack's, but neither is it an isolated one. Many young people struggle with developing identity and agency whilst balancing tensions between home and school to fulfil their potential. This chapter, with an emphasis upon development and caring in the early years, explores how children are vulnerable during childhood and adolescence. Exploring how provision and practice support children's, parents' and practitioners' emotive experiences is used to illuminate and identify ways to narrow risks of being missed.

The start of any life journey can be rich, loving and enabling, facilitated by varied opportunities in different settings to develop potential and acquire agency. A child's sense of self does not develop in isolation from other learning. Learning is intricate, is affected by prior knowledge and understanding and is shaped by interests, motivation and engagement. It is influenced by factors at home, school and community levels. It is not a one-stop destination; neither is it a single path along which children can be plotted, with defined points, hurrying them along to the next one (National Education Union, 2011). It is complex in understanding and significant in the way it is delivered. A holistic approach that encompasses different developmental domains supports this journey. Consideration of Social, Physical, Intellectual, Cultural, Emotional and Spiritual (SPICES) development is fundamental to good educational practice, and if any one domain is overlooked a child is potentially at risk. Exploration of these domains through personal stories can illuminate how care and nurturing in the early years is fundamental for lifelong growth and development.

Understanding the context

A holistic approach to development involves identification of progress and needs. An understanding of needs embraces complexities of learning environments and engagement with context-specific demands. Bronfenbrenner's Ecological Theory System offers an interpretation of how environmental interactions influence growth and development (see Beckley, 2012). As a child engages with these five different systems, from the most intimate (home) to the broadest (global), so are these systems inevitably enmeshed within each other. However, often overlooked are impacts of cultural exchange, that is relationships within and across these systems or levels of community, and their significance to learning. Rogoff (2003) identifies interrelated facets (childrearing, social relations, interdependence and autonomy, developmental transitions across the lifespan, gender roles, attachment, and learning and cognitive development) that facilitate learning, with a strong emphasis upon family and group learning. Recognising that children are social beings adds to an understanding of how learning takes place through interactions within their cultural situation. Where the learning environment is enabling, children will flourish. Equally, where children are deprived of enriching interactive experiences, their development is hampered.

Global level

In trying to reduce risk and protect vulnerable children, the significance of supporting individual children in the early years is recognised at a global level. Each individual child is valued for their contributions in transforming the world. Ensuring that all girls and boys have access to good-quality early childhood development (Sustainable Development Goals [SDGs], Target 4.2, United Nations, 2015) is identified as a global priority. Aspirations for change at a global level affirm that 'nurturing, protecting, promoting and supporting children in their early years is essential for the transformation that the world seeks to achieve' (World Health Organization (WHO), 2018, p. 7). In addition, research identifies how Early Childhood Education and Care (ECEC) supports development across all learning domains (SPICES) and provides a foundation for lifelong learning. Program for International Student Assessment (PISA) data from 35 participating countries indicates that 15-year-olds who attended ECEC settings, for one year, outperformed students who had not attended at any point in their childhood (OECD, 2017). In 2016, research promoted by the World Health Organization (WHO) and UNICEF identified the significance of Early Childhood Development (ECD), stressing that 'nurturing care' – an indivisible cluster of interventions related to health, nutrition, responsive caregiving, safety and security, and early learning – is the foundation for child development. The first thousand days (including time since conception) of nurture and support from parents and caregivers is the most crucial in determining healthy child development and instrumental with regards to lifelong and intergenerational benefits for health, productivity and social cohesion

(Lake, 2016). Nurturing care also minimises impacts of disadvantage on brain structure and function, which, in turn, improves children's health, growth and development (Singla, Kumbakumba and Aboud, 2015). Considering that:

> today's children will be responsible for the society of tomorrow, concern should be given that an estimated 250 million children (43%) younger than 5 years in low-income and middle-income countries are at risk of falling short of their potential because of adversities they face in their early, formative years. (Chan, Lake and Hansen, 2016, p. 11)

Global collaboration of non-government organisations (NGOs), through focused interventions in the early years, drives changes in national policies, striving to lessen inequities in children's learning outcomes, reduce poverty and facilitate greater social mobility.

National level

Early years education has been considered by recent UK governments as a starting point for addressing social inequalities evidenced by specific actions and policies, including free provision of early learning places for vulnerable two-year-old children. Early years settings and practitioners are crucial in providing a secure foundation for children's future attainment and life chances. Putting theory into policy and then into practice is essential given the number of external factors that might impede individual agency due to socially created vulnerabilities: gender, educational needs, neglect or abuse, ethnicity and, increasingly identified, social deprivation including poverty. Specific legislation and government-initiated reviews (Bertram and Pascal, 2014) recognise the significance of good early years provision in promoting the important foundations for continual achievement through school and reducing impacts of such external factors upon progress. Interventions with children in the 0–3 age range are key to breaking the cycle of deprivation (Cronin, Argent and Collett, 2017) and missed chances.

Classroom level

Recognising wide variations in ability presented by children when starting school and ensuring the right foundations for facilitating good development in the early years are critical. The nature of best practice is identified where teaching and play are connected (Ofsted, 2015).

MINIMISING RISK THROUGH PLAY

A play-based curriculum should be offered for children up to the age of seven and be the model for promoting seven areas of development identified in the Early Years Foundation Stage (EYFS). Play has been identified as significant for centuries: 'Plato (427–347 BC) recognised that play influenced the way children developed as adults, and proposed to regulate play for social ends' (D'Angour, 2013, p. 293); Montessori (1807–1952) advocated learning through sensory play; Dewey (1859–1952) believed that learning was active; and Steiner (1861–1925) posited that creativity and imagination are intrinsic to learning. The significance of play in psychotherapy was also researched and adapted by Anna Freud (1964, 1965), Margaret Lowenfeld (1970) and Melanie Klein (1987) (Scarlett, 2005). Theory posits and presents convincing arguments in recognition of the importance of play in developing the whole child across different learning domains. However, it can be readily assumed that a child has the necessary skills to play either independently or with others. A child might be considered to be at risk if without the skills needed for play.

REFLECTION

Steven is five and is on the autistic spectrum. He is non-verbal other than making erratic, unpredictable sounds. Upon arrival at his special school, he wanders to the corner of the room, sits down and proceeds to rock. When encouraged to engage, his rocking intensifies and he becomes agitated, biting his hands.

Jenny is four and in reception class. She has no noticeable physical differences to the other children in her class. She engages quietly with literacy and numeracy-related tasks. However, during 'free time' she does not readily join in with other children until she is encouraged, requiring regular reminders to 'play nicely'.

Consider these two situations where children are at risk of failing to develop.

- How would play help their development (SPICES)?

- What might be the difficulties in planning for play with Steven and Jenny?

PROMOTING WELLBEING

The overarching principles of the EYFS recognise the unique qualities of every child, incorporating the importance of building positive relationships that lead to resilient, capable, confident and self-assured individuals, able to progress through school and life. A majority of children achieve this experiencing good mental health. However, it is estimated that between 10 and 20 per cent of the world's children and adolescents experience at least one form of mental illness (WHO, 2014). Experiences early in life direct the nature and course of mental health and illness in subsequent years, with an estimated 50 per cent of mental illnesses in adults beginning before the age of 14 (WHO, 2014). Mental health should not be considered in isolation from physical health nor other areas of growth and development (SPICES) but recognised as a concern given that only 59 per cent of children reach a good level of development at age five where family socioeconomic status is significant (Pordes Bowers and Strelitz, 2012). Having sufficient income is important for physical and mental health, children's wellbeing and development; it enables people to afford healthy lifestyles and be in the mind-set to prioritise a healthy lifestyle (Institute of Health Equity, 2017).

The importance of positive early interpersonal environments spanning home, school and community is widely acknowledged (Beckley, 2012; Rogoff, 2003). Home is where children learn to develop an understanding of their world and part in it. With the right support they begin to develop self-confidence and coping skills. The family environment provides a child with a physical, neurocognitive and social-emotional bedrock for healthy development through childhood and into adulthood (Spence et al., 2014). Adult and child interactions within the home should provide a seamless combination of compassion, respect for feelings and boundary setting (Ginott, 1972). Positive influences of parents or carers dominate early childhood development. When home life is less affirming, teachers have a unique opportunity to counteract unhealthy influences: 'While parents possess the original key to their offspring's experience, teachers have a spare key. They too can open or close the minds and hearts of children' (Ginott, 1972, p. 301). Positive, intimate and caring relationships at home and school are fundamental to all aspects of growth, including good mental health (Bowlby, 1952). Good mental health is an individual and personal concern where school and home environment are conducive to positive wellbeing or sickness. Perceptions of a child's wellbeing are determined by observations of attitudes and actions recognising that these are bound by time, place and cultural expectations. Behaviours demonstrated at home may not be acceptable at school and vice versa. Different settings extol different expectations upon children, creating invisible norms that children are expected to learn. Determining what is important in life, understanding cultural rules for different settings and acquiring skills that enable achieving them is dependent upon an understanding of both self and others.

The capacity to understand others' and one's own behaviour in terms of mental states can be explained as 'mentalizing'. It involves a complex and demanding spectrum of capacities that are susceptible to different strengths, weakness and failings (Bateman and Fonagy, 2008). Ability to mentalize, an ongoing process, is achieved through cognitive and social discovery. Mentalizing skills are established in the early years and through strong, affirming attachment to those who care for us. These relationships help build epistemic trust, trust in the authenticity and personal relevance of interpersonally transmitted knowledge about how the social environment works and how best to navigate it (Fonagy and Allison, 2014). As children develop, they increasingly need to respond to challenges and complexities in their world, determining the 'norms'. To learn the skills for navigating their world, children need to form attachments with a close circle of people providing security and discovery. These relationships also provide the opportunity to understand who they are and the role and intentions of others. This ability to mentalize, to develop social cognition, allows adaptation and abilities to learn and cope. Attachment and mentalizing are intertwined. Without positive relationships, trust and a sense of positive self-regard are absent, and abilities to learn and engage with one's environment are reduced (Fonagy, Bateman and Campbell, 2017).

Alongside this, children are expected to learn the value of objects, cultural norms and social expectations; for example, how to respond to toys, music and daily routines. The function of these 'other' aspects can be epistemically opaque (that is, not obvious from their appearance). As children grow, they are assimilating a vast amount of cultural information that they need to process, retain and recall rapidly. The essence of epistemic trust and attachment is that children have to believe that what they are being told is important and matters.

As children grow, so does their understanding of the world. As new understandings and interpretations arise, children can be confused by contradictions in what matters to them; meanings are opaque. Children and adolescents experience temporary or permanent breakdowns in epistemic trust when earlier messages of what is important from those they trusted differs to new messages as they grow. These breakdowns can present as behavioural outbursts, personality problems and or/lack of willingness to participate in preferred patterns of social engagement. This can include being withdrawn from play, being disengaged from learning and presenting as sullen and withdrawn.

Identifying risks of being missed

Children, especially infants, the very young and children with Special Educational Needs (SEN), are not always able to verbalise how they feel. They may show emotional or psychological distress through physical pain or ill health. Some children are admitted to hospital with a mental health problem when they are presenting a physical illness with real symptoms, such as abdominal pain, headaches, tiredness and limb pain. The *Diagnostic and Statistical Manual of Mental Disorders* (DSM-5) (American Psychiatric Association, 2013), recognises seven distinct somatic symptoms and related disorders, each disorder having specific diagnostic criteria, which apply to both adults and children. All these disorders refer to an individual's subjective experience of physical symptoms. Somatic symptoms amongst children are often misunderstood and wrongly diagnosed. Risk factors that are a predictor of somatic symptoms include: changing patterns of emotions, personality types and coping styles, poor environment including trauma and stress, and parental influences, and highlight the prevalence of this phenomenon (Banks and Bevan, 2014). Subsequently, identifying mental health needs amongst children and adolescents can be difficult. Determining whether needs are long term or temporary is not easy and can be easily missed. However, it is important to recognise that some children communicate psychological distress and emotional conflict through physical symptoms.

For younger children, identification is more complex. Table 4.1 offers a range of, but not exclusive, behaviours, that, when presented in combination and over a prolonged time period, can be indicators of atypical emotional development.

Table 4.1 Indicators of atypical emotional development

Age	Possible concern if a number of the following are present
6 months	Inability to read signals and interactions
	Persistent sleep problems
	Lack of predictability in behaviour
	Failure to imitate sounds and gestures
	No affect; range of feelings/emotions are limited
	Lack of stranger anxiety (8 months)
6–12 months	No words
	Persistent sleep problems
	Withdrawn
	Excessive rocking
	Prolonged fears
	No separation distress
	Immobile, low activity
	No social engagement
	Anger and outbursts
18 months–3 years old	Eating problems
	Non-speaking
	Extreme shyness
	Lack of autonomy
	Failure in gender identification
	No enjoyment in play
	Poor problem-solving
	Total lack of self-control
	Chaotic behaviour

When concerns about these behaviours and others are present, strategies to address them should be considered.

Theory to policy: reducing risk

To minimise anxiety in childhood, structures to support development and enable trust to develop should be carefully managed. Starting nursery and changing classes have the potential to be disconcerting and anxious times for some children. To ameliorate this, children should have opportunities for 'staged transition', spending increasingly more time in the 'next' setting rather than having a single annual point of transfer for all (EYFS).When children seem to be struggling to cope with transition, consideration should be given to underlying reasons and the possible identification of a SEN. The *Special Educational Needs Code of Practice* (SENCoP) (2015) highlights the need to remove barriers to learning and for settings to put effective special education provision in place. Individualised and personalised learning through a cycle of assess, plan, do, review is stressed. Recognising that teachers, accountable for all children in their class, should set the highest aspirations for learning, development and achievement is important. No child should be missed. Managing and leading by ambitious vision is matched with identifying needs as early as possible. Where a child's needs cannot be met through this process and recourse to additional resources is necessary, then an Education, Health and Care (EHC) plan may be required. An EHC plan sets out reasonable adjustments that schools make, any therapeutic interventions needed and how combined agencies can facilitate effective delivery of the plan.

Policy to practice: at risk of being missed

Children at risk: the realities

Childhood maltreatment, including physical, sexual, emotional abuse and neglect, arguably represents the most potent predictor of poor mental health across the lifespan (Green *et al.*, 2010). Children may present outwardly visible signs of abuse and when identified interventions can be put into place. Childhood abuse can take many different forms. The cross-government definition of abuse is: 'any incident or pattern of incidents of controlling, coercive, threatening behaviour, violence or abuse between those aged 16 or over who are, or have been, intimate partners or family members regardless of gender or sexuality' (Home Office, 2013). The abuse can encompass, but is not limited to: psychological, physical, sexual, financial, emotional abuse. However, children under 16, and from early childhood who experience an indirect form of domestic abuse, are often missed. These children are hard to identify in the early years and the first signs might be noticeable differences in self-esteem and underperformance during adolescence.

The following section offers emotive cases, told from different perspectives, crossing different levels of provision. It identifies children who are at risk or who have been missed as they progressed through education. A number of these, whilst presented in plain speak, reflect that not every childhood is loving and caring. Each vignette is followed by a reflection section for you to link theory and policy, discussed previously, with practice. There are no wrong solutions, only possible ones that, as practitioners, we are constantly striving to find.

A LOOKED-AFTER CHILD MANAGER'S EXPERIENCE

Sunni is a refugee from Somalia who moved to London at 14 to live with her aunt and her aunt's partner, who started to sexually abuse her. At 15 years and 3 months she was gang raped by 12 males. A police investigation followed, and she was placed in secure accommodation outside of London for her own safety under Section 25 of the Mental Health Act. Whilst in secure care she excelled in education, gaining qualifications at Level 2 and was deemed to have A* potential. Arrangements and support were put in place for her to testify at the Old Bailey against the perpetrators through a video link. However, on turning 16, the perpetrators' lawyers said she was no longer a child at risk and had to do this in person. To her credit, she did this and the males were imprisoned. Sunni was given a new identity and relocated to supported living. She has subsequently progressed through school and now attends university.

REFLECTION

– How have interventions at different levels reduced and created risks for Sunni throughout her childhood?

A WOMEN'S REFUGE MANAGER'S EXPERIENCE

Recognition is given to protecting direct victims of emotional or physical abuse, but very little support is available for children who are witnesses of abuse, including those who spend part of their childhood in a refuge. Such children, pre-school up to 16, have experienced moving schools, having to run and being in the safe haven of a refuge only to find that the risk of violence follows them. It can be quite easy to trace partners and children given that a child of school age has to be registered with a school. Regardless of training, the school can often innocently pass on information. Sean, 13 years old, has already been to 47 different schools, fleeing with his mother to different refuges. Consequently, Sean has received very little formal education, lacks social skills and exhibits fear of adult males. His life is compromised through threat of abuse. Sean's mum is also deprived of any social relationships and friendship groups. They both lack a sense of community and have no contact with the extended family.

REFLECTIONS

—   How is Sean at risk?

—   And in relation to his holistic development (SPICES)?

—   Would you consider Sean to have additional or Special Educational Needs?

—   How might a school support both child and mother in transition?

A SCHOOL GOVERNOR'S EXPERIENCE

Thomas lives at home with his mum (Lisa) and dad (Matt). Matt refuses to let Lisa leave the home without informing him first. He expects Lisa to take full responsibility for raising Thomas and to undertake all domestic duties. Returning home from a physically demanding job each day, Matt does not talk to Thomas and discourages Lisa from doing so, Matt is the priority; he needs to be the centre of attention; Matt comes first. Lisa interacts with Thomas when Matt is not around. She takes him to school, plays with him before Matt gets home and then has 20 minutes to put him to bed. Consequently, Thomas has a confusing hot-and-cold relationship with his mum. This has started to affect his school engagement and relationships with teaching staff and peers. He varies between demanding and ignoring attention. He tears up other children's work and can be unkind in the words he uses and during play. Lisa is constantly being called into school but does not want Matt to be involved. Lisa does not want to leave Matt, and feels very secure in the relationship.

REFLECTIONS

- What might explain Matt's behaviour towards Thomas?

- Lisa says she 'knows how to manage her husband' but in managing her husband is Lisa denying what Thomas needs?

- Why have the school chosen to monitor Thomas's wellbeing, considering him to be a child at risk?

A HEAD TEACHER'S EXPERIENCE

Alison and Graham were university educated and in highly paid employment. They had a good relationship. After their first child, Sally, was born, Graham started to be physically abusive towards Alison. Alison sought advice from different services and GP intervention helped to an extent. The family became known to the police. Two years later they had a son, Mason. At this point, Graham had a mental breakdown and was sectioned and removed from the family home. He spent time in a residential setting, was administered medication and then released into the community with a restraining order that allowed family visits at designated times. However, Graham constantly breached this and a pattern of violence towards Alison started. Alison, Sally and Mason were constantly moved, to the point of being housed in accommodation with secure fittings and alarms. The alarm would be repeatedly pressed to trigger help each time Graham appeared. However, each time, before help arrived Graham would normally have physically attacked Alison in front of the children, resulting in her going to hospital. The police referred the case to public prosecution because restraints through the Mental Health Act 2005 were insufficient to keep this family safe. This referral was in process when one evening, whilst Alison was preparing the tea, Graham smashed his way in to the house with an axe. Although Alison was repeatedly stabbed, she managed to press the alarm button. When emergency services arrived, Sally and Mason were eating their tea, whilst Alison lay unresponsive on the floor.

- What might have caused Graham's violent behaviour towards Alison?

- What might explain why Sally and Mason carried on eating their tea in the midst of all the violence?

A SECONDARY SCHOOL INCLUSION MANAGER'S PERSPECTIVE

It was noticed in a secondary school, in a socioeconomic deprived area, that boys were repeatedly outperforming girls in Year 11. Observations identified that one possible explanation related to educational aspirations amongst girls being second to visions of themselves as wives and mothers. Having a baby at 13 or 14 offered some girls recognition and self-fulfilment, which seemed to increase if they had a son. If they had a daughter first, they would probably get pregnant again quite soon. In addition, particular patterns of socialisation emerged where the young mum acquiesced power to their son around the age of three to four years. The son became the 'man of the house', dominating the relationship. This form of gender compliance mirrored how these young girls viewed themselves and their own childhood. Having witnessed their mother, or through direct personal experience, these girls developed feelings of inferiority expressed through role expectations in the home. For some girls, education is perceived as an escape from existing home conditions. However, for others, moving into a new lifestyle has too many consequences and traditional female roles are considered more fulfilling than low-paid, boring work (Plummer, 2000). Low aspirations and denial of opportunity can be traced back to the relationships in the home, formed at an early age and reinforced where parents lack social capital and educational networks to support or promote progression.

- Why might this be considered a form of abuse?

- Consider where these role expectations originate and develop.

- Is intervention in secondary school too late?

A PARENT'S PERSPECTIVE

At the 36th week of pregnancy, Alex's heart stopped beating and an emergency caesarean was performed in August 2009, with Alex entering this world weighing 2lbs. Following three weeks in the neo-natal department, Alex went home with Dad and Mum, returning temporarily to hospital 12 weeks later, when problems with the left ventricle in his heart were identified. Over the following few months, Dad noticed an increasing number of restless occasions, which the GP identified as colic. However, at five months old, Alex was on the bed and his eyes started going 'skew-whiff' and twitching. Dad, who had not been convinced of the GP's diagnosis, had been Googling 'seizures' for possible alternative explanations. Clips on YouTube showed other children having exactly the same seizures as Alex. Dad took Alex back to the hospital and showed the video recordings he'd taken of Alex's fits with the possible diagnosis of West syndrome. Following many tests, West syndrome was confirmed. Early identification of West syndrome is crucial to reduce brain damage caused through seizures. For Alex, early identification and subsequent medication stopped his seizures. Alex continued to have regular monthly developmental check-ups and at two years was diagnosed with periventricular leukomalacia (PVL) linked to cognitive, sensory and physical impairment. Alex was prescribed glasses at three years of age. Alex was developing well in his early years and discharged from the neurologist, continuing with annual check-ups with his paediatrician until he was eight.

With care and support from home, Alex continued to grow, meeting expected developmental milestones, although he was noticeably smaller than most babies and toddlers. When Alex was just over two, Mum and Alex moved out. After six months they returned, and Alex's care was shared between Mum and Dad. At the end of Alex's reception year, Mum moved away, and

Dad became sole carer. Within five months of Mum leaving, Alex started having seizures again and multifocal epilepsy was diagnosed. He is currently on high dosages of steroids to manage his seizures. Alex progressed through nursery and started in reception. Previously there was little concern other than occasions where he was not paying attention during story time. Alex is comfortable at school and, whilst he has some friends, he never plays with them outside school. At eight, school reports now show that progress is slow and Alex is achieving below the expectations for his age.

REFLECTIONS

– What is the nature and what are the possible causes of Alex no longer progressing?

– What might be missed in meeting Alex's needs?

Conclusion

This chapter has explored how aspects of theory, policy and practice from global to local level can reduce possibilities of children at risk being missed. Recognition is given to the significance of supporting children in their foundation years to develop across all learning domains, particularly emotional wellbeing, to reduce risks of failing to achieve their full potential. A challenge is to facilitate opportunities and resources for young children and their families, recognising different priorities at different levels but ensuring all children, irrespective of socioeconomic background, are considered. Jack, Sunni, Sean, Thomas, Sally, Mason and Alex may be exceptional in certain settings but they are representative of the harsh realities and challenges of some childhoods. As practitioners, we are provided with the opportunity, given the key, to unlock potential through initiating or supporting trust and care within the home environment. Home and school working together is of symbiotic significance in ensuring children are not at risk. Best practice is where there is unified, seamless practice informed by theory and addressed in policy. Such practice needs to connect all social levels that impact upon a child's world. As such, recognition is given that the foundation of each child's wellbeing starts in the early years and only with considered support and care can we reduce risk and ensure that children access what they need for healthy growth, learning and development.

References

American Psychiatric Association (2013) *Diagnostic and Statistical Manual of Mental Disorders* (5th ed.) (DSM-5). Arlington, VA: American Psychiatric Publishing.

Banks, K. and Bevan, A. (2014) 'Predictors for somatic symptoms in children.' *Nursing Children and Young People, 26*, 1, 16–20.

Bateman, A. and Fonagy, P. (2008) '8-year follow-up of patients treated for borderline personality disorder: Mentalization-based treatment versus treatment as usual.' *The American Journal of Psychiatry 165*, 5, 631–638.

Beckley, P. (2012) *Learning in Early Childhood: A Whole Child Approach from Birth to 8.* London: Sage.

Bertram, T. and Pascal, C. (2014) *Early Years Literature Review.* Accessed on 7/6/2018 at www.early-education.org.uk/sites/default/files/CREC%20Early%20Years%20Lit%20Review%202014%20for%20EE.pdf

Bowlby, J. (1952) *Maternal Care and Mental Health.* Geneva: World Health Organization.

D'Angour, A. (2013) 'Plato and play taking education seriously in Ancient Greece.' *American Journal of Play 5*, 3, 293–307.

Chan, M., Lake, A. and Hansen, K. (2016) 'The early years: Silent emergency or unique opportunity?' *The Lancet 389*, 10064, 11–13.

Cronin, T.M., Argent, K. and Collett, C. (2017) *Poverty and Inclusion in Early Years Education.* New York: Routledge.

Department for Education and Department of Health (2015) Special Educational Needs and Disability Code of Practice: 0–25 years. Accessed on 5/11/2018 at https://assets.publishing.service.gov.uk/government/uploads/system/uploads/attachment_data/file/398815/SEND_Code_of_Practice_January_2015.pdf.

Fonagy, P. and Allison, E. (2014) 'The role of mentalizing and epistemic trust in the therapeutic relationship.' *Psychotherapy 51*, 3, 372–380.

Fonagy, P., Bateman, A. and Campbell, C. (2017) 'Mentalizing, attachment, and epistemic trust in group therapy.' *International Journal of Group Psychotherapy 67*, 2, 176–201.

Ginott, H.G. (1972) *Teacher and Child: A Book for Parents and Teachers.* New York: Macmillan.

Green, J.G., McLaughlin, K.A., Berglund, P.A., Gruber, M.J. *et al.* (2010) 'Childhood Adversities and Adult Psychiatric Disorders in the National Comorbidity Survey Replication.' *Arch Gen Psychiatry 67*, 2, 124–132.

Home Office (2013) *Domestic Violence and Abuse Guidance.* Accessed on 12/7/2018 at www.gov.uk/guidance/domestic-violence-and-abuse#domestic-violence-and-abuse-new-definition

Institute of Health Equity (2017) *Marmot Indicators Briefing.* Accessed on 7/6/2018 at www.instituteofhealthequity.org/resources-reports/marmot-indicators-2017-institute-of-health-equity-briefing/marmot-indicators-briefing-2017-updated.pdf

Lake, A. (2016) *Early Childhood Matters*. The Hague: Bernard van Leer Foundation. Accessed on 7/6/2018 at https://issuu.com/bernardvanleerfoundation/docs/early-childhood-matters-2016

National Education Union (2011) *Position Statement: Early Years Provision Across the UK*. Accessed on 7/6/2018 at www.atl.org.uk/policy-and-campaigns/policy-posts/early-years-provision-across-uk

OECD (2017) *Starting Strong 2017: Key OECD Indicators on Early Childhood Education and Care*. Paris: OECD Publishing. Accessed on 7/6/2018 at http://dx.doi.org/10.1787/9789264276116-en

Ofsted (2015) *Teaching and Play in the Early Years: A Balancing Act*. Manchester: Ofsted. Accessed on 7/6/2018 at www.gov.uk/government/uploads/system/uploads/attachment_data/file/444147/Teaching-and-play-in-the-early-years-a-balancing-act.pdf

Plummer, G. (2000) *Failing Working-Class Girls*. Stoke-on-Trent: Trentham.

Pordes Bowers, A. and Strelitz, J. (2012) *An Equal Start: Improving Outcomes in Children's Centre*. London: UCL Institute of Health Equity. Accessed on 7/6/2018 at www.instituteofhealthequity.org/resources-reports/an-equal-start-improving-outcomes-in-childrens-centres/an-equal-start-evidence-review.pdf

Rogoff, B. (2003) *The Cultural Nature of Human Development*. New York: Oxford University Press.

Scarlett, W.G. (2005) *Children's Play*. Thousand Oaks, CA: Sage Publications.

Singla, D.R., Kumbakumba, E. and Aboud, F.E. (2015) 'Effects of a parenting intervention to address maternal psychological wellbeing and child development and growth in rural Uganda: A community-based, cluster-randomised trial.' DOI: http://dx.doi.org/10.1016/S2214-109X(15)00099-6

Spence, S.H., Sawyer, M.G., Sheffield, J., Patton, G. *et al.* (2014) 'Does the absence of a supportive family environment influence the outcome of a universal intervention for the prevention of depression?' *International Journal of Environmental Research and Public Health,11*, 5, 5113–5132.

United Nations (2015) *Sustainable Development Goals*. Accessed on 12/7/2018 at www.un.org/sustainabledevelopment/sustainable-development-goals

World Health Organization (2014) *Child and adolescent mental health*. Accessed on 12/7/2018 at www.who.int/mental_health/maternal-child/child_adolescent/en/

World Health Organization (2018) *Nurturing Care for Early Childhood Development*. Accessed on 31/10/2018 at http://apps.who.int/iris/bitstream/handle/10665/272603/9789241514064-eng.pdf

CHAPTER 5

Poverty and Language in the Classroom

Elizabeth Farrar

Senior Lecturer, Primary
Bishop Grosseteste University

Chapter overview

Poverty tenaciously persists in the wealthiest of societies. In 2015/16 in the UK 17 per cent of children lived in households described as 'absolute low income households', with 12 per cent of these living in households of 'low income and material deprivation' as defined and reported by the Department for Work and Pensions (DWP) (2017). If these children were spread equally within our schools, that would equate to 5.1 and 3.6 children respectively in every class of 30. To consider this another way, 14.3 per cent of primary-aged children were claiming free school meals (FSM) at the time of the January 2016 census (Department for Education (DfE), 2016a), which means that in an average class of 30 children, 4.3 would be claiming FSM. When calculating income after housing costs, 27 per cent of children were living in 'absolute low income households' in 2015/16 (McGuinness, 2017). Whichever statistics we look at, we can see that in an 'average' class we would expect to find at least four or five, but possibly as many as eight, children who fall into the category of 'disadvantaged'. Obviously, no class is 'average' – there are areas of high deprivation where classes have far in excess of these numbers and, equally, schools serving areas of greater affluence with fewer FSM children. However, we can see that overall many teachers will have children in their classes who can be viewed as being affected by poverty. But do a child's home circumstances matter? What impact can they have? This chapter seeks to explore some of the potential impacts that poverty can have on children's educational attainment and how these may manifest themselves in the pupils we teach, with particular reference to language development.

What does the attainment gap currently look like?

The DfE revised results (DfE, 2017a) show that in 2016, 35 per cent of FSM children achieved the expected level in reading, writing and maths, as compared with 57 per cent of pupils not eligible for FSM. The results were generally lower for many schools in 2016 due to the introduction of the new-style Year 6 SATs, but they still clearly demonstrate an attainment gap. This gap persists throughout secondary school so by the time pupils reach the stage of GCSEs the data shows that in 2016, 43.1 per cent of disadvantaged children gained five or more A*–C grades, including maths and English, whilst 70.6 per cent of the remainder achieved this benchmark (DfE, 2017b). A 22 per cent gap at the end of primary school has therefore translated through to a 27.5 per cent difference in attainment by the end of secondary school. For all the political rhetoric around the 'closing the gap' agenda, there is little evidence of success in the statistical measures.

What initiatives have been implemented to address the attainment gap?

Over time there have been many attempts to address the connection between low educational outcomes and low socioeconomic status (SES). In the 1960s the introduction of the 'Educational Priority Areas' was intended to increase parental involvement in order to enable children to benefit more from their schooling. This deficit model implied that the children and their families were somehow culturally or linguistically deprived, placing the fault for the children's low attainment with the families, not the schools or society (Plummer, 2000; Shain, 2015). Forty years later, the Sure Start initiative was launched, again with the intention of increasing parental engagement (Melhuish and Hall, 2007). The idea of raising aspirations also took hold, with the inference being that if low SES families behaved more like higher SES families, their children's achievement would be enhanced (Gewirtz, 2001; Plummer, 2000; Power, 2008). In May 2010 the Coalition came to power, and under this government the Sure Start centre funding cuts began. In 2011 the Pupil Premium grant was introduced.

What is the focus of the Pupil Premium grant?

The focus for addressing poverty moved to the compensatory Pupil Premium grant (Burn and Childs, 2016) and the pervading notion of needing to expose disadvantaged children to the trappings of a more affluent lifestyle can clearly be seen in the choices of use of this funding (Shain, 2015). Schools often report that they are spending this money on enrichment provision, which is an obvious effort to emulate the experiences of the middle classes, whether this has been decided consciously or not. Attempts are made to raise pupils' aspirations with a wide range of heavily subsidised or fully funded activities such as music and horse-riding lessons and school trips that include visits to universities (Ofsted, 2013; Ofsted, 2014; Sutton Trust and Education Endowment Foundation, 2015). As Gewirtz (2001) observes, there are deep-seated reasons why low SES families do not behave in the same manner as the conventional middle-class family, and the initiatives introduced fail to get to the real heart of these problems. They are compensatory measures, more of a gesture than a real effort to drive through radical changes that would challenge inequality and move towards an effective solution. Cummings *et al.* (2012) suggested that attempting to raise aspirations, or even assuming they may be low in the first place, is not a useful basis for educational policy and is unlikely to produce improvement in educational attainment.

The underpinning belief seems to be maintained that academic achievement can only be secured by low SES pupils if they shun their own social background and assimilate themselves with the beliefs, language and behaviours seen in the middle classes (Gazeley and Dunne, 2005; Gewirtz, 2001; Plummer, 2000). However, the consequences of children conforming to the expectations of their social group cannot be disregarded and is considered at length by Plummer (2000), who suggests that the failure of working-class girls has gone unnoticed for a long time. Plummer makes the point that academic success serves to distance working-class children from their families and explores the 'class oppression' that a grammar school education created (2000, p. xi), as children tried to conceal their social class identity. Whilst some have hailed grammar schools as successfully increasing social mobility, the recent political debate about allowing new selective schools has reignited longstanding arguments around opportunity, accessibility and standards, demonstrating how this issue deeply divides opinion on their true contribution to reducing the social divide.

What is meant by the term 'poverty'?

Poverty itself is a problematic term. There is no commonly agreed definition of what constitutes the minimum necessities of human need (Goulden and D'Arcy, 2014). A person living in poverty does not necessarily have none of their needs met, as some things, such as attention, do not require material resources. However, other needs like social participation do require access to such resources. Poverty can be said to include those whose lack of necessities has an ongoing, persistent and wide-ranging impact on their lives, meaning that they are more likely to suffer other indicators of poverty, such as financial stress and ill health (Lansley and Mack, 2015). The key to arriving at a definition appears to be through what the members of the society in question believe to be the minimum needs, and that those seen as eligible to be judged as such have an enforced lack of these identified necessities for an unspecified length of time (Goulden and D'Arcy, 2014; Lansley and Mack, 2015; Ravallion, 1992; Veit-Wilson, 2013). 'Poverty', therefore can be seen as relative and potentially changing over time, rather than as an absolute position. This is supported by the Joseph Rowntree Foundation who publish reports based on the Minimum Income Standard (MIS). Within their reports, MIS is defined as an adequate income level below which households would struggle to manage a socially accepted living standard, based on research carried out with members of the public (Padley, Hirsch and Valadez, 2017). In 2014/15 45 per cent of children lived in families with an income below MIS and 26.6 per cent were below 75 per cent of MIS (Padley, Hirsch and Valadez, 2017). When measuring poverty in school pupils, FSM eligibility becomes the criterion used (Shain, 2015). In 2016 at the time of the Key Stage 2 tests, 16 per cent of Year 6 pupils were classed as FSM-eligible pupils (DfE, 2017a) and could therefore be considered as being the children most likely to be affected by issues of deprivation, although this may be a higher percentage if we consider the MIS data as a better indicator.

How might this affect a child's ability to learn?

Thinking about what this may mean for the children in our classrooms, Maslow's hierarchy of needs (1943) suggests that if children are not fed, warm and feeling safe as minimum requirements, they are less likely to be able to learn effectively. Perhaps one in five children live in a home that is not adequately heated, 1 in ten do not possess a warm coat and suitable footwear and 1 in 20 are underfed (Lansley and Mack, 2015), possibly resulting from the statistic that 27 per cent of children were living in 'absolute low income households' in 2015/16 (McGuinness, 2017) or that 26.6 per cent were below 75 per cent of MIS (Padley, Hirsch and Valadez, 2017) as we have already discussed. This suggests, therefore, that a potentially large proportion of pupils are not having their basic needs met as defined by Maslow, and therefore are not arriving in school predisposed to learn successfully.

What about the attainment gap?

The difficulties in addressing the attainment gap seen between the socioeconomic groups are enhanced still further by the current framework, which encourages choice and competition. Higher SES families will take whatever measures are necessary to enable their children to get the best they can out of the system, and these families have the social and economic capital to support their continued advantage. Regardless of any initiatives introduced to address the gap, this is made much more difficult if the target reached for is being moved constantly away by the competition for academic success (Ball, 2003; Gewirtz, 2001; Shain, 2015; Tomlinson, 2005).

Specific impacts of poverty

Poverty, however defined, can be seen to have a negative effect upon the likelihood of children achieving well academically. Children from low SES families often begin school already behind their peers from higher SES groups, and this is especially noticeable in the area of language and communication. The 2015/16 Early Years Foundation Stage (EYFS) data (DfE, 2016b), for example, shows that just 52 per cent of pupils who were eligible for FSM achieved a good level of development, which includes language and communication, by the end of the EYFS in comparison with 70 per cent of all other pupils.

Table 5.1 shows this broken down into the data for the three areas of language and communication.

Table 5.1 Department for Education (2016b) Early Years Foundation Stage profile results by pupil characteristics – Communication and Language Early Learning Goals

Areas of language and communication	Listening and attention	Understanding	Speaking
Percentage of FSM pupils	77	77	76
Percentage of all other pupils	88	87	87

Table 5.2 shows the data information broken down for two areas of literacy.

Table 5.2 Department for Education (2016b) Early Years Foundation Stage profile results by pupil characteristics – Literacy Early Learning Goals

Literacy	Reading	Writing
Percentage of FSM pupils	63	58
Percentage of all other pupils	79	75

The disparity is still evident in children two years older, at the end of Key Stage 1. As Table 5.3 demonstrates, the gap between the two groups in 2016 has increased by one percentage point, and the language measure is now being taken only through the medium of literacy skills. Whilst ever children are struggling with gaining proficiency in communication and language, they are unlikely to be successful in acquiring the skills to read and write effectively.

Table 5.3 Department for Education (2016c) Key Stage 1 assessments in England, 2016

KS1 assessments	Reading	Writing
Percentage of FSM pupils	60	50
Percentage of all other pupils	77	68

As discussed earlier, the gap at Key Stage 2 widens to 22 per cent and still further by GCSEs to 27.5 per cent, although these measures include a wider range of subjects, including maths. The way progress is measured, and data is collated and reported, changes not only over the different assessments carried out at various points across the education phases, but also changes over time as different governments, education secretaries and departments make adjustments, modifications and reforms to their published data reports. This makes it more difficult to extract specifics and to make precise comparisons, but the broad picture still clearly demonstrates that there is a disparity in the attainment of SES groups.

What are the effects on language development?

The acquisition of language appears to be key to children being able to access their education and the curriculum effectively so they can make the progress required of them throughout their school lives. Having the necessary language skills enables children to think and reflect on their experiences, fuelling the desire to explore further and in so doing to become self-motivated, independent learners (Tough, 1982). How children acquire language will be explored next, in order to consider whether variables within this process may be having some effect on the differences seen between the competencies of the low and high SES groups. As children's knowledge of language can be seen to be a crucial factor in their chances of making good academic progress, the possible connections between low SES and weaker linguistic skills will be investigated with a view to considering whether and how these effects may be possible to mitigate to some degree within the school system.

Language acquisition theories

In general, most children appear to acquire language almost effortlessly and usually arrive in school able to construct grammatically correct, complex sentences. Language learning is thought to begin even before birth (DeCasper and Spence, 1986), continuing to develop so that the average six-year-old has a vocabulary of around 10,000–14,000 words, according to Saxton (2010). Nation and Waring (1997) suggest this figure is 4000–5000, but they qualify this as being word families, which may explain the apparently large discrepancy. However, regardless of how many words are acquired, there is no single definitive explanatory theory of precisely how language is acquired. There are a number of approaches that attempt to illuminate the process of language learning, exploring the independent variables that may be involved and considering how these could be defined. For example, behaviourists approach language development as a type of behaviour and were among the first to produce a theoretical framework for the process of language learning. Adults were seen as reinforcing a child's linguistic output, selectively encouraging the use of language progressively close to the required adult speech. According to their learning theory, the child was a passive recipient rather than playing an active role in the process (Garton and Pratt, 1998; Skinner, 1957).

Contrastingly, Chomsky's nativist approach recognised children as being born with an innate ability to learn language, the so-called Language Acquisition Device (LAD). This was claimed to be equipped to receive an input of language data that it would process and produce comprehensible language output (Chomsky, 1968). Chomsky's theory stands opposite the behaviourists' position and totally depends on the belief that children are innately inclined to learn language. Critics have contended that any consideration of environmental influences on language development is lacking from this approach (Garton and Pratt, 1998), such as the child's hearing capacity or their attention span, for example. Both nativist and learning theories have their limitations, as they view language development as a predetermined sequence of events that happen in isolation.

More recent approaches to language acquisition have appeared in the form of learnability theory and parameter setting, both of which stem from Chomsky's work. These approaches allow for greater flexibility in the acquisition of grammatical rules. Parameter setting suggests that the child possesses some innateness, but that this changes through input from the linguistic community where the child resides (Atkinson, 1986; Chomsky, 1981; Meisel, 1995; Wexler and Culicover, 1980).

How might theories explain the variations in language acquisition of SES groups?

Given that there are differences seen in children from different SES groups, it may be that exploring theories of child development could potentially illuminate the possible reasons for these variations.

Theories tend to consider how language, thought and social interaction interrelate and, dependent upon the focus of the theory, these features are then defined and connected in different ways. Hickman (1986) notes that whilst Vygotsky attaches much importance to social interaction, Piaget places it in a comparatively subordinate role, and that this partly arises both from their definition of language and their understanding of its development. Piaget believed that language was neither necessary nor adequate to drive cognitive development prior to the point of higher levels of reasoning. Hickman (1986) deems that for Piaget, cognitive development is independent of language acquisition. However, contrastingly, Vygotsky held that language development powers cognitive development, with constant interaction between the two. He believed that social interaction was the primary element in cognitive development, whilst Piaget thought that children produce a mental model of their world, which they then reconstruct and assimilate depending upon the experiences they have (Saxton, 2010).

How do adults contribute to language learning?

A great deal of research since the 1970s has focused on the direct impact that adult speech has on the rate and sequence of language development in young children, as noted by Garton and Pratt (1998). What social interaction consists of for young children and the relationship of adults' speech in their language development was often centred around mothers' linguistic input, which led to early researchers using the term 'motherese' to describe particular characteristics of speech being aimed at a young child (Cross, 1975; Snow, 1972). Snow (1986) later adopted the term Child Directed Speech (CDS), as 'motherese' implied that only mothers were found to use the features that characterised child-directed adult speech. This new term also put the child at the centre of the learning process, rather than the emphasis being placed on any adult input. Snow also observed conversations between adults and children in a range of cultures, with some being seen to utilise highly explicit teaching of correct speech, and not adapting or simplifying the language used toward the child.

What can be concluded is that a successful language teaching environment can be regarded as any that offers sufficient numbers of utterances within a context that can be recognised by the child. Language is reliably acquired in a wide variety of social settings, demonstrating that there are a variety of learning systems and which ones are employed depends on the prevalence of enabling conditions. Further studies, carried out since Snow, confirm the findings that the use of CDS is common across many cultures and languages, and, equally, there are those where CDS is not used. Indeed, Rowland (2014) poses the question of whether CDS does facilitate the acquisition of language. Hart and Risley (1995), Hoff-Ginsberg (1998) and Huttenlocher *et al.* (1991) support the notion that those children who have exposure to more words, in both amount and variety, are the children who acquire language most rapidly, and that this happens regardless of whether CDS is used.

Does context matter?

It can be seen that although we have a good understanding of some processes, our knowledge regarding the effects of context is still patchy. We do not know to what extent the properties of children's speech reflect their linguistic understanding opposed to the context in which they are producing their speech. That family economic status is a strong predicator of language ability adds credence to the view that aspects of language development do depend on the properties of language experience, as it is these experiences that have been found to differ between the SES groups (Hart and Risley, 2011; Hoff, 2003; Hoff, 2010).

What differences have been seen in language acquisition of the different SES groups?

Snow describes language as 'a highly complex skill…acquired with a very low failure rate' (1986, p. 87). Exactly what 'failure' might look like is unclear, but there is a widely held view that some children do not acquire sufficient language to enable academic success in comparison with their peers. Bernstein (1975) suggested that the quantity and quality of linguistic exchange a child is exposed to at home is a strong indicator of their likely academic attainment. This is supported by Hart and Risley's US longitudinal study (1995) involving 42 families from a range of socioeconomic backgrounds (Hart and Risley, 2011). The study set out to determine if and how the language exchanges in the families impacted on the children's language and vocabulary acquisition. Over a four-year period, high SES families uttered over 30 million more words than those deemed the lowest status. It was also observed that children from the low SES families were exposed to a greater proportion of negative utterances than the children from other groups. When the children reached nine years of age, follow-up studies, using various language development, vocabulary and reading comprehension measures, revealed a high correlation between the children exposed to more words and rate of academic progress.

Does the use of language children hear, rather than the quantity, have any effect?

Mercer and Littleton (2007) suggested that the SES group gap that is evident as in Hart and Risley's findings relates to opportunities to develop language as a tool for learning and is nothing to do with the differences that reflect social origins. They believe that a lack of experience in ways of using language to develop problem-solving capacity is what impacts negatively on academic attainment, recommending that schools should explicitly teach the type of language required to facilitate reasoning and working collaboratively, which would support learning and help to develop positive intellectual habits (Mercer and Littleton, 2007). Tough (1982) also argues that the real problem with children from families in poverty is not that they lack language, but rather that the way in which they use it does not support their learning.

Disparities in the rate and sequence of language development are known to occur, but then studying a sample of children will enable many differences to be identified between them, in any number of categories we choose to construct (Wells, 1986). The speed as well as the course of development can be examined in relation to possible reasons for variations and also to the results of these – for instance the effect on school attainment. Wells (1986) proposed a framework that would enable findings to be considered and within this states that social background is not seen to have a direct influence on children's linguistic behaviour. Rowland (2014) disagrees, citing many studies that have found children from high SES families acquire more language earlier than children from low SES families. The reason suggested is the language-rich environment that appears to characterise high SES groups, but why they have this environment is not apparent. Rowland offers two possibilities. One may be the differing language skillsets of the parents. Research has found a correlation between parents' level of education and language use, including the understanding of complex sentence constructions (Bradley and Corwyn, 2002; Street and Dabrowska, 2010). Another possibility suggested is that SES groups have contrasting views about child language development, and this then has an effect on how they communicate with their children. Other studies have reported findings supporting this hypothesis (Huttenlocher *et al.*, 2002; Pye, 1991; Rowe, 2008).

Does reading affect language development?

Another aspect to be considered is the impact of reading on children's linguistic capabilities. It has been found that children with parents who read more to them are exposed to a wider range of vocabulary than children with parents who tend to read less (Bus, van IJzendoorn and Pellegrini, 1995; Rowe, Raudenbush and Goldin-Meadow, 2012). It is easy to see that the accelerated vocabulary growth produced by reading to children early in life has the potential to rapidly increase the size of a child's vocabulary and, as a result, to improve school readiness (Rowe, Raudenbush and Goldin-Meadow, 2012). This is another aspect that contributes towards the more developed linguistic capabilities seen in children from higher SES families, as this activity has been found to be more habitual for those groups than for children from lower SES households. There has also been found to be more instances of adult readers, particularly males, who act as role models to young children in higher SES households.

Do children who are initially behind catch up?

Marchman and Fernald (2008) looked at longer term effects, discovering that children in their research sample who showed faster processing speeds at 25 months were still outpacing their peers in language, cognition and working memory tests at eight years old. Correspondingly, those with the slowest speeds at 25 months of age were those at risk of weaker school performance, scoring below all other groups when they were eight years old. This was a small-scale study, but it does seem that there is some evidence that suggests those children with faster language processing speeds are placed at an advantage for a range of intellectual aptitudes, which in turn gives them long-term educational benefits. These findings support those proposed by Hindman, Erhart and Wasik (2012) regarding the so-called 'Matthew Effect', which will be discussed later in the chapter.

Could schools be contributing to the variation between SES groups' academic attainment?

Over the last 50 years or more there have been numerous policies and initiatives introduced by successive governments, but evidence suggests these have done little to narrow the socioeconomic gap. Gove's attitude to the situation was made clear when he labelled the achievement gap as a 'tragedy' caused by 'accidents of birth' (DfE, 2010, pp. 6–7), whilst placing full accountability for closing the gap with the school system. In their 2012 report, Cummings *et al.* suggest there is evidence that teachers and other education professionals misjudge the aspirations of disadvantaged pupils and the value their families place on education. Teachers could be operating from a deficit model, with significant differences between their values, attitudes and beliefs and their pupils' (Plummer, 2000; Thompson, McNicholl and Menter 2016). The Teachers' Standards however, do not specify any requirement to engage with poverty or social disadvantage (DfE, 2011). Whilst the Standards are written to apply to all teachers and not all will work in areas of high disadvantage, society in general is unequal and, as we have seen, 17 per cent of children lived in families of 'absolute low income' levels in 2015/16 (DWP, 2017). It seems reasonable to suggest that many teachers will, at some stage in their career, be responsible for the learning and progress of a child in poverty.

How might teachers' assessments of children be affected by linguistic ability?

More able pupils are often identified as such through their oral communication skills. These can often be children who enter school able to learn quickly, with a rich vocabulary and a well-developed understanding of social conventions. Attributes related to oral ability are often ascribed to intelligence, but we need to question whether those children are actually gifted and talented or whether they are just comparatively advanced due to the support at home that has coached them in their development of these skills (Hart and Risley, 2011; Rask and Paliokosta, 2012). Higher SES families may have a tacit understanding of the requirements for success in school, and so be better placed to prepare their children appropriately.

Are school staff always aware of their own views about poverty?

Jones (2016) carried out a study giving trainee teachers the opportunity to discuss their views around the issues of poverty. Through this research it became apparent that without the opportunity provided by such conversations, the trainees may not have necessarily even been aware that others did not have the same opinions, values and beliefs as themselves. It is important that systems are in place to enable teachers to become aware of the harm that can be done by prejudice, labelling and low expectations that arise from deficit views of disadvantage (Gorski, 2012; Thompson et al., 2016).

Gorman's research (2005) was within a different profession, but is equally valid amongst teachers as lawyers, as he suggests that we are much more likely to notice things that confirm a stereotype we subscribe to than something that opposes our view. We also have strong tendencies to attach more negative qualities to a group we do not belong to, and we draw on what we know from stereotypes to furnish us with information about groups that we are not part of (Gorski, 2012). Therefore, because of these predispositions, if a teacher has not been able to properly explore their own value system and the stereotypical ideas they may hold, to challenge their cultural and social assumptions about the impact of poverty or to question the deficit model they may accredit to disadvantaged pupils, then the prospect of low expectations and less effective teaching of these children appears to be a real risk (Gorski, 2012; Plummer, 2000; Thompson et al., 2016). Providing opportunities for teachers and other adults in school to discuss issues of poverty and to investigate and share their own opinions is suggested to be a vital step in helping to both address the deficit model and avoid potential mismatches between the understandings of staff and the needs of the children.

How else can schools help?

Teachers need to be aware of the effects of poverty on their pupils, but also the part that they themselves can play in redressing the balance. Hindman *et al.* (2012) discuss the so-called 'Matthew Effect', which results in the children who start school with the strongest skills being the ones who show the fastest progress, which exacerbates the problem of the initial attainment gap. They believe that teachers who systematically expose children to high-quality teaching within a language-rich environment facilitate their swift acquisition of new vocabulary, thus enabling those who are initially less adept linguistically to catch up with their more proficient peers. This view is supported by the findings of Huttenlocher *et al.* (2002), who found that children with teachers who produce many complex utterances containing more than one clause are often more adept at both understanding and producing complex sentences themselves. They discovered that the rate at which children developed grammar was strongly related to the proportion of complex sentences used by their teacher, and that this was demonstrated irrespective of the child's linguistic starting point. These findings make it very clear that habitually simplifying language for children is actually unhelpful with regard to their language development. Ensuring in school that all adults' speech is rich, complex and varied will contribute positively in developing the communication skills of all pupils.

Conclusion

It is certainly the case that there is an attainment gap linked to the SES of pupils, which may well worsen with the continuance of austerity measures and public-sector cuts affecting the disadvantaged most acutely. Children's language development is negatively affected by living in poverty, and these effects go beyond grammar and vocabulary, appearing to make a difference in cognitive ability, which has ramifications for general academic success. Having a consistently strong focus on stretching children's linguistic skills through the use and promotion of a wide vocabulary couched in grammatically complex communication both between and around children by all school staff appears likely to have a positive effect. Teachers and other adults in school also need a raised awareness of issues of social justice, otherwise a deficit view of families in poverty can result, which may in turn lead to lowered expectations as well as a lack of understanding about overcoming the consequences of disadvantage.

References

Atkinson, M. (1986) 'Learnability.' In P. Fletcher and M. Garman (eds) *Language Acquisition* (2nd ed.). Cambridge: Cambridge University Press.

Ball, S.J. (2003) *Class Strategies and the Education Market: The Middle Classes and Social Advantage.* London: RoutledgeFalmer.

Bernstein, B. (1975) *Class, Codes and Action. Volume III: Towards a Theory of Educational Transmissions.* London: Routledge and Kegan Paul.

Bradley, R.H. and Corwyn, R.F. (2002) 'Socioeconomic status and child development.' *Annual Review of Psychology 53*, 1, 371–399.

Burn, K. and Childs, A. (2016) 'Responding to poverty through education and teacher education initiatives: A critical evaluation of key trends in government policy in England 1997–2015.' *Journal of Education for Teaching 42*, 4, 387–403.

Bus, A.G., van IJzendoorn, M.H. and Pellegrini, A.D. (1995) 'Joint Book Reading Makes for Success in Learning to Read: A Meta-Analysis on Intergenerational Transmission of Literacy.' *American Educational Research Association 65*, 1, 1–21.

Chomsky, N. (1968) *Language and Mind.* New York: Harcourt Brace Jovanovich.

Chomsky, N. (1981) *Lectures on Government and Binding.* Dordrecht: Foris.

Cross, T. (1975) 'Some relationships between "motherese" and linguistic level in accelerated children.' *Papers and Reports on Child Language Development 10*.

Cummings, C., Laing, K., Law, J., McLaughlin, J. *et al.* (2012) *Can Changing Aspirations and Attitudes Impact on Educational Attainment? A Review of Interventions.* Accessed on 7/6/2018 at www.jrf.org.uk/sites/default/files/jrf/migrated/files/education-attainment-interventions-full.pdf

DeCasper, A.J. and Spence, M.J. (1986) 'Prenatal maternal speech influences newborns' perceptions of speech sounds.' *Infant Behaviour and Development 9*, 133–150.

Department for Education (2010) *The Importance of Teaching. The Schools White Paper 2010.* Accessed on 7/6/2018 at http://webarchive.nationalarchives. gov.uk/20130401151715/https://www.education.gov.uk/publications/eOrderingDownload/CM-7980.pdf

Department for Education (2011) *Teachers' Standards: Guidance for school leaders, school staff and governing bodies.* Accessed on 7/6/2018 at www.gov.uk/government/publications/teachers-standards

Department for Education (2016a) *Schools, Pupils and Their Characteristics: January 2016.* Accessed on 7/6/2018 at www.gov.uk/government/statistics/schools-pupils-and-their-characteristics-january-2016

Department for Education (2016b) *Early Years Foundation Stage Results: 2015 to 2016.* Accessed on 7/6/2018 at www.gov.uk/government/statistics/early-years-foundation-stage-profile-results-2015-to-2016

Department for Education (2016c) *Phonics Screening Check and Key Stage 1 Assessments in England, 2016.* Accessed on 7/6/2018 at www.gov.uk/government/uploads/system/uploads/attachment_data/file/577806/SFR42_Phonics_KS1_2016.pdf

Department for Education (2017a) *National Curriculum Assessments at Key Stage 2 in England, 2016 (revised)*. Accessed on 7/6/2018 at www.gov.uk/government/uploads/system/uploads/attachment_data/file/577296/SFR62_2016_text.pdf

Department for Education (2017b) *Revised GCSE and Equivalent Results in England, 2015 to 2016*. Accessed on 7/6/2018 at www.gov.uk/government/uploads/system/uploads/attachment_data/file/584473/SFR03_2017.pdf

Department for Work and Pensions (2017) *Households Below Average Income: An Analysis of the Income Distribution 1994/95 to 2015/16*. Accessed on 7/6/2018 at www.gov.uk/government/uploads/system/uploads/attachment_data/file/600091/households-below-average-income-1994-1995-2015-2016.pdf

Garton, A. and Pratt, C. (1998) *Learning to Be Literate: The Development of Spoken and Written Language* (2nd ed.). Oxford: Blackwell Publishers Ltd.

Gazeley, L. and Dunne, M. (2005) *Addressing Working Class Underachievement*. Accessed on 7/6/2018 at www.sussex.ac.uk/webteam/gateway/file.php?name=addressing-working-class-underachievement.pdf&site=319

Gewirtz, S. (2001) 'Cloning the Blairs: New Labour's programme for the re-socialization of working class parents.' *Journal of Education Policy 16*, 4, 365–378.

Gorman, E.H. (2005) 'Gender stereotypes, same-gender preferences, and organizational variation in the hiring of women: Evidence from law firms.' *American Sociological Review 70*, 4, 702–728.

Gorski, P.C. (2012) 'Perceiving the problem of poverty and schooling: Deconstructing the class stereotypes that mis-shape education practice and policy.' *Equity and Excellence in Education 45*, 2, 302–319.

Goulden, C. and D'Arcy, C. (2014) *A Definition of Poverty*. York: Joseph Rowntree Foundation. Accessed on 7/6/2018 at www.jrf.org.uk/report/definition-poverty

Hart, B. and Risley, T.R. (1955) *Meaningful Differences in the Everyday Experience of Young American Children*. Baltimore, MD: P.H. Brookes.

Hickman, M. (1986) 'Psychosocial Aspects of Language Development.' In P. Fletcher and M. Garman (eds) *Language Acquisition* (2nd ed.). Cambridge: Cambridge University Press.

Hindman, A.H., Erhart, A.C. and Wasik, B.A. (2012) 'Reducing the Matthew Effect: Lessons from the ExCELL Head Start Intervention.' *Early Education and Development 23*, 781–806.

Hoff, E. (2003) 'The specificity of environmental influence: Socioeconomic status affects early vocabulary development via maternal speech.' *Child Development 74*, 5, 1368–1378.

Hoff, E. (2010) 'Context effects on young children's language use: The influence of conversational setting and partner.' *First Language 30*, 3–4, 461–472.

Hoff-Ginsberg, E. (1998) 'The relation of birth order and socioeconomic status to children's language experience and language development.' *Applied Psycholinguistics 19*, 4, 603–629.

Huttenlocher, J., Haight, W., Bryk, A., Seltzer, M. and Lyons, T. (1991) 'Early vocabulary growth: Relation to language input and gender.' *Developmental Psychology 27*, 2, 236–248.

Huttenlocher, J., Vasilyeva, M., Cymerman, E. and Levine, S. (2002) 'Language input at home and at school: Relation to child syntax.' *Cognitive Psychology 45*, 3, 337–374.

Jones, H. (2016) 'Discussing poverty with student teachers: The realities of dialogue.' *Journal of Education for Teaching 42*, 4, 468–482.

Lansley, S. and Mack, J. (2015) *Breadline Britain: The Rise of Mass Poverty.* London: Oneworld Publications.

Marchman, V.A. and Fernald, A. (2008) 'Speed of word recognition and vocabulary knowledge in infancy predict cognitive outcomes in later childhood.' *Development Science 11*, 3, F9–F16.

Maslow, A.H. (1943) 'A theory of human motivation.' *Psychological Review 50*, 4, 370–396.

McGuinness, F. (2017) *Poverty in the UK: Statistics. Briefing Paper Number 7096.* Accessed on 7/6/2018 at http://researchbriefings.files.parliament.uk/documents/SN07096/SN07096.pdf

Melhuish, E. and Hall, D. (2007) 'The Policy Background to Sure Start.' In J. Belsky, J. Barnes, and E. Melhuish (eds) *The National Evaluation of Sure Start: Does Area-Based Early Intervention Work?* Bristol: The Policy Press.

Meisel, J.M. (1995) 'Parameters in Acquisition.' In P. Fletcher and B. McWhinney (eds) *The Handbook of Child Language.* Oxford: Blackwell.

Mercer, N. and Littleton, K. (2007) *Dialogue and the Development of Children's Thinking: A Sociocultural Approach.* London: Routledge.

Nation, P. and Waring, R. (1997) 'Vocabulary Size, Text Coverage and Word Lists.' In N. Schmitt and M. McCarthy (eds) *Vocabulary: Description, Acquisition and Pedagogy.* Cambridge: Cambridge University Press.

Ofsted (2013) *The Pupil Premium: How Schools are Spending the Funding Successfully to Maximise Achievement.* Accessed on 7/6/2018 at www.gov.uk/government/uploads/system/uploads/attachment_data/file/413197/The_Pupil_Premium_-_How_schools_are_spending_the_funding.pdf

Ofsted (2014) *Pupil Premium: Update on Schools' Progress.* Accessed on 7/6/2018 at www.gov.uk/government/publications/the-pupil-premium-an-update

Padley, M., Hirsch, D. and Valadez, L. (2017) *Households Below a Minimum Income Standard: 2008/09 to 2014/15.* Accessed on 7/6/2018 at www.jrf.org.uk/report/households-below-minimum-income-standard-200809-201415

Plummer, G. (2000) *Failing Working-Class Girls.* Stoke-on-Trent: Trentham.

Power, S. (2008) 'How should we respond to the continuing failure of compensatory education?' *Orbis Scholae 2*, 2, 19–37.

Pye, C. (1991) 'The Acquisition of K'iche' (Maya).' In D. Slobin (ed.) *The Cross Linguistic Study of Language Acquisition* (Vol. 3). Hillsdale, NJ: Lawrence Erlbaum Associates.

Rask, H. and Paliokosta, P. (2012) 'Fostering Speaking and Listening in Early Years and Foundation Stage Settings.' In D. Jones and P. Hodson (eds) *Unlocking Speaking and Listening* (2nd ed.). Abingdon: David Fulton Publishers.

Ravallion, M. (1992) *Poverty Comparison: A Guide to Concepts and Methods.* Washington, DC: The World Bank.

Rowe, M.L. (2008) 'Child-directed speech: Relation to socioeconomic status, knowledge of child development, and child vocabulary skill.' *Journal of Child Language 35*, 1, 95–120.

Rowe, M., Raudenbush, S. and Goldin-Meadow, S. (2012) 'The pace of vocabulary growth helps predict later vocabulary skill.' *Child Development 83*, 2, 508–525.

Rowland, C. (2014) *Understanding Child Language Acquisition.* London: Routledge.

Saxton, M. (2010) *Child Language Acquisition and Development.* London: Sage.

Shain, F. (2015) 'Succeeding against the odds: Can schools "compensate for society"?' *Education 3-13 44*, 1, 8–18.

Skinner, B.F. (1957) *Verbal Behaviour.* New York: Appleton-Century-Crofts.

Snow, C. (1972) 'Mothers' speech to children learning language.' *Child Development 43*, 549–565.

Snow, C. (1986) 'Conversations with Children.' In P. Fletcher and M. Garman (eds) *Language Acquisition* (2nd ed.). Cambridge: Cambridge University Press.

Street, J.A. and Dabrowska, E. (2010) 'More individual differences in language attainment: How much do adult native speakers of English know about passives and quantifiers?' *Lingua 120*, 8, 2080–2094.

Sutton Trust and Education Endowment Foundation (2015) *The Pupil Premium: Next Steps.* Accessed on 7/6/2018 at www.suttontrust.com/wp-content/uploads/2015/06/Pupil-Premium-Summit-Report-FINAL-EDIT.pdf

Thompson, I., McNicholl, J. and Menter, I. (2016) 'Student teachers' perceptions of poverty and educational achievement.' *Oxford Review of Education 42*, 2, 214–229.

Tomlinson, S. (2005) *Education in a Post-Welfare Society.* Buckingham: Open University Press.

Tough, J. (1982) 'Language, Poverty and Disadvantage in School.' In L. Feagans and D. Farran (eds) *The Language of Children Reared in Poverty.* London: Academic Press.

Veit-Wilson, J. (2013) *Measuring Child Poverty: A Response to the Consultation.* Accessed on 7/6/2018 at https://northeastchildpoverty.wordpress.com/2013/02/12/measuring-child-poverty-a-response-to-the-consultation/

Wells, G. (1986) 'Variation in Child Language.' In P. Fletcher and M. Garman (eds) *Language Acquisition* (2nd ed.). Cambridge: Cambridge University Press.

Wexler, K. and Culicover, P.W. (1980) *Formal Principles of Language Acquisition.* Cambridge, MA: MIT Press.

CHAPTER 6

Children in a Diverse Society

Pat Beckley

Senior Lecturer for Research
Bishop Grosseteste University

Chapter overview

The chapter celebrates the diversity of our society and considers factors that have influenced this. It explores how early experiences, routines and planning in settings and schools can embrace this diversity and discusses how young children new to this country can be supported. Challenges of transitions for children and their families will also be considered.

We are fortunate to live in a diverse society with the ability to celebrate everyone's unique talents. Why is such a discussion concerning living in a diverse society needed? The UK, for example, consists of people with multiple backgrounds from waves of immigrations throughout the centuries. Yet extremist organisations exist and those recently moving countries through employment, war or other reasons who should have the opportunity to be valued members of a changing society are not always able to access this inclusion. Adams, Bell and Griffin (2007, p. 151) state:

> Globalization increases the vulnerability of populations...who exist on the bottom of the global economy. Forced by harsh economic conditions at home, in large part spurred by globalization as well as famine and war, many thousands of people must move simply to survive.

Others may have moved to be with family members or invited through their employment networks. The 'shrinking world' enables individuals to gain awareness of other countries, through international educational agendas, human rights issues and technological advances. Issues, for example environmental concerns such as global warming, are increasingly seen as affecting the planet on a global scale.

Social knowledge, understanding and appreciation of different cultures and traditions can be fostered in the early years to promote harmony in this constantly changing environment. This needs the understanding of all communities, not only the dominant culture within a society. What constitutes an ethnic minority? The online Oxford English Dictionary definition states, 'A group within a community which has different national or cultural traditions from the main population', and notes, 'a group of people of a particular race or nationality living in a country or area where most people are from a different race or nationality'. The very notion of ethnic minority causes difficulties as it fosters perceptions of stereotypical ideas. Beaver *et al.* (2002, p. 18) state, 'stereotyping contributes to the development of negative attitudes. It involves making assumptions about people… Stereotypes are harmful because they perpetuate negative, unthinking attitudes: they are limiting because they influence expectations.' They highlight the negative effect of racism, which 'describes when people of one race or culture believe they are superior to another' (Beaver *et al.*, 2002, p. 18). This can be identified in organisational routines, for example when food does not meet dietary needs of a religious group. The notion of a 'group' can be problematic, as individuals make up society. This embraces their new environment while wishing to celebrate and maintain links with other cultures within their families and communities. Therefore, a personalised approach to each child is essential to gain understanding of each child's needs and expectations. This can be achieved through effective partnerships with parents and carers, as well as with ongoing discussions with the child themselves.

REFLECTIONS

- Think about the diverse backgrounds of the babies and young children you are involved with.

- Consider how you meet their diverse, specific needs. What strategies are in place to ensure individuals are not excluded in your practice?

Links with children in other countries promote understanding of diversity and help relationships between peers to enhance awareness and reciprocal appreciation.

CASE STUDY

An English, early years setting linked with one in Germany. The similar aged children kept a diary, through their adult facilitators, of the routines of their days. The children in both countries were fascinated by the differences in their daily patterns, particularly sleep times after lunch. This developed to further links and drawings of their 'view from my window', leading to discussions, activities and insights from their paintings of their homes outside the setting, to Norwegian mountains and the Mediterranean from Malta.

According to Cole, 'education should be about empowerment, where visions of an alternative way of running the planet become part of the mainstream curriculum' (cited in Hill and Robertson, 2012, p. 33). He suggests 'equality and equal opportunity issues have both an institutional and legislative dimension and an individual dimension'. What better way to encourage the outlook of equality and an individual's unique value than at the earliest beginnings in a child's life. Views of equality, it can be argued, develop through social constructions and it can be observed when noting children at play that they view others from a personal perspective and have an understanding of parental or community views that may not be their own.

CASE STUDY

Sarah played happily in the sand tray, sieving and marking tracks. Another girl joined her. The two girls had different ethnic backgrounds and had been told by their parents not to play with each other. The girls clearly liked each other and started to play together in the sand. This led to excited talk and the beginnings of a shared understanding and lifelong friendship. The adult spoke to the parents at the end of the session and mentioned that the children had told her of their views and what had happened. It began some understanding of each other and shared interests of their children. The young girls had changed their parents' views.

REFLECTIONS

- How do you promote understanding of diversity in your setting?

- Have there been any challenges to this work?

- How did you resolve it?

- What positive outcomes have you observed through your strategies to encourage an understanding of diversity?

Kum suggests, 'The specific educational needs for children from refugee communities is distinctive, especially as the children may have experienced considerable trauma through rapid relocation, often under physical threats, to a very new society where their own language is not understood.' With reference to schools he continues, 'When dominant ethnicity in most British schools is white, it is difficult for cultural differences to be recognised, represented and respected in schools' (cited in Hill and Robertson, 2012, p. 66).

Children entering early years provision in a different country, either in a child group setting or one with different expectations from those they are familiar with, may exacerbate anxieties when faced with new requirements of behaviour and practice. International early years provision varies considerably. In a Norwegian setting, a parental complaint was observed that a four-year-old child had not got her outdoor suit dirty. 'Hasn't she been doing anything today? Her outdoor suit is still clean! She hasn't learnt anything!' explained her parent. However, a later observation noted a Chinese girl attending the setting on her first morning had not brought an outdoor coat, simply a pencil and a paper pad to begin writing indoors. The parental expectation was that she would be writing and working on formal tasks given indoors.

The importance of gaining awareness of other cultural mores is relevant. For example, it may not be acceptable for a strict Muslim woman to be in the presence of a man other than her husband unless the husband is also present. This could have implications for meetings arranged to ensure all participants are comfortable with the arrangements.

Children may enter a setting displaying extreme anxiety, for example if they have only very recently arrived in the country and have had to adjust to the surroundings such as climate or pace of life. This could be heightened, particularly if a parent is also anxious and has pressing needs to manage, for example, financial or housing requirements. Parents in this situation may be unable to give the time they would like to the child to reassure them, as they are exceptionally busy with urgent issues to address. Throughout the happenings and transitions for the child, it is crucial for the key person, designated to support the holistic development of the child, to listen to the child's views and perspectives of what is happening to them. Parents may be very busy organising daily life, while the key person could be a source of time for talking to the child and gaining knowledge of the child's concerns and feelings about what has and is happening.

Visual clues will help a new child, and the support of a peer 'buddy' seems to give a young child an understanding that they are safe and secure in the provision and are welcome. The new child may observe silently for a few days, absorbing their surroundings and gaining a knowledge of how things work, routines and how children play together. English may be their second language, so it may be possible to access the help of someone who can support bilingually. Wider discussion concerning immigration, for example when incorporated into deliberations about legislation such as Brexit, impact negatively on confidence through feelings of security and awareness of what the future might bring.

A diverse learning environment

A welcoming environment is the foundation to begin the partnership, through communication with parents/carers and children and the surroundings created. This can reflect the diverse nature of the setting and how this diversity is valued. Resources, such as bilingual books or artefacts in the role-play area, demonstrate some understanding and shared thinking, which can form the beginnings of open dialogue to gain further knowledge of the child. This dialogue can inform any specific requirements needed in the setting or aspects to consider for inclusion. Opportunities to encourage bilingualism can promote learning from all involved. Shared communication and collaborative talk promotes positive meaning-making and understanding, supporting the development of activities achieved together. Sage argues, 'Differences in language reveal a variety of beliefs, rules and general ways of living so that those who deviate from what is the majority norm are often rejected' (2010, p. 155). She continues, 'The "contact hypothesis" suggests that close and frequent interaction between people is all that is needed for positive attitudes to develop between them,' with education a component of this outcome. Non-verbal communication is important and can identify a range of emotions and feelings such as friendliness, interest, understanding, empathy or care, through gestures, voice tone or facial expression. For young children, most may be learning the social mores relevant to support positive interactions, for example to say please and thank you.

REFLECTIONS

- What discussion times for sustained shared thinking do you introduce?

- How are the children encouraged to talk during their independent activities and play? Have you observed different levels of talk? Are children from different cultural backgrounds able to access higher levels of complex discussions?

- Are talk times planned into daily routines?

- Which discussion times between children or children and adults have been most successful?

Positive strategies can be implemented to ensure all children are able to access the provision provided. When appropriate interventions are used to support a child, for example when a child may not be used to certain procedures – such as using tools when making things – and is anxious about participating in them, it can broaden their experiences and enjoyment of learning. With this understanding comes tolerance and mutual respect – as well as having much fun by interacting and learning about others, as those involved with young children will know. Culture is complex and ever-changing, continually redefining society.

Early years experiences form a crucial basis of babies' and young children's understanding of the world. The age phase forms the beginnings of their educational journey. Lynch (1992, p. 21) states:

Education has a unique, fundamental, powerful and heretical role to play in the process of defining a new paradigm for economic, social and cultural nation-building and the internationalization of citizenship, which at the same time can encourage a plurality of communities and greater attentiveness to the environment.

Learning about cultural differences, including through interactions with individuals and communities around the child or care and education provision, can only serve to increase understanding of the nature of the multicultural society and the global world we live in. Those who have knowledge of other cultures through experiences while living there can be a useful resource to promote a wider perspective of the world. Discussions about diversity can promote a celebration of the cultural backgrounds each individual has. In this way, the participation in international dialogue will equip our young children for global awareness and citizenship.

References

Adams, M., Bell, L.A. and Griffin, P. (2007) *Teaching for Diversity and Social Justice.* Abingdon: Routledge.

Beaver, M., Brewster, J., Jones, P., Keene, A., Neaum, S. and Tallack, J. (2002) *Babies and Young Children: Early Years Care and Education.* Cheltenham: Nelson Thornes Ltd.

Hill, D. and Robertson, L.H. (eds) (2012) *Equality in the Primary School: Promoting Good Practice Across the Curriculum.* London: Continuum International Publishing Group.

Lynch, J. (1992) *Education for Citizenship in a Multi-Cultural Society.* London: Cassell.

Sage, R. (2010) *Meeting the Needs of Students with Diverse Backgrounds.* London: Continuum International Publishing Group.

CHAPTER 7

Looked-After Children or Those in Care

Pat Beckley

Senior Lecturer for Research
Bishop Grosseteste University

Chapter overview

This chapter gives an overview of the diverse meanings of 'children in care' or 'looked-after children'. It explores reasons why children may have found themselves in that situation and what impact it may have on their development. It considers how those working in early years schools and settings can support children to enable them to enjoy life to the full and progress.

Children may be taken into care by accessing children's homes, foster carers, adoption services or other family members, through a whole range of events and happenings. It could be through parental ill health, difficulties associated with parenting or a choice to place a child with another form of caring for their upbringing. Vulnerable groups in this category (cited in Longfield, 2017, p. 8) could include:

- Children Looked After (CLA) (including those in adoption)

- children who are subject to a Child Protection Plan (CPP)

- children in children's homes

- Children In Need (CIN)

- children who are subject to a Special Guardianship Order (SGO)

- adopted children

- children with special needs and disabilities

- children who have physical health issues

- children in workless families

- children in low-income families

- children who are homeless or who are in insecure/unstable housing

- children who do not meet the threshold for social worker intervention

- children in non-intact families

- children in troubled families

- children whose parents use substances problematically

- children whose parents may have limited parenting capacity

- children in need who have experienced childhood trauma or abuse

- children who have been victims of modern slavery and missing children.

Young children may be placed with a carer while accessing early years provision nearby. The setting may be notified of a referral via social services, who may provide contact with foster carers or relevant family members supporting the child to help the provider liaise with the carer for the enhanced assurance of the child's transition to a new situation. Multiagency working supports the smooth transition of the child from one home and setting background to another.

Understandably, this may be traumatic for some children, as well as being a positive experience for others. Some children may appear to regress as they struggle to come to terms with their experiences.

CASE STUDY

Kyle entered a reception class and had great difficulty following the norms and routines of the classroom. His screams when realising he needed to attend assembly could be heard throughout the school. He struggled to concentrate in formal work and frequently shouted and hit other children. It was decided that he would be allowed to spend a period in a less formal routine in the nursery. He watched the others play and sought the company of adults. He gradually learned how to play with others and that it was not aggressive or frightening. He began to enjoy stories and music times and demonstrated his creatively in art, plus his sense of humour during his play. He joined assemblies in the hall, surrounded by his friends, being ready and confident to gain new experiences. Later, he happily re-joined his year group when he felt secure and safe.

REFLECTIONS

- Have you supported a child in an early years setting who was afraid and hesitant?

- What strategies did you use to help them?

- What effect did this have on the child and the children and adults around them?

From their earliest moments, children appear to be attempting to make sense of their world – trying to focus on images around them. As parents/carers may know of small babies, it can sometimes be disconcerting when a tiny infant's gaze is transfixed on the adult's face. According to Bronfenbrenner (1979), children learn who they are from their surroundings and those who are in it. Initially this would be the adults around the child, then developing outwards through greater understanding of a widening world. Thus, the individual child would initially have contact with others through a microsystem consisting of family, siblings and peers. This develops to an exosystem comprising the extended family, the parents' workplaces, neighbours, social services, health services, family friends, mass media and local community. The widening awareness of a macrosystem includes laws, government, culture, economic systems, social conditions and belief systems and customs.

In this way, if the adults around the child have negative life experiences, this may influence the child's outlook on the world and those they meet from the beginning of their life.

The Barnardo's website (2014) states:

Children are taken into care for a number of reasons; they may have been abused or neglected, or they may have families who are struggling to cope in difficult circumstances. Whatever the reason, these children are highly vulnerable. Their problems are made worse by the number of moves that many of them are forced to make during their time in care, which can seriously disrupt their education. Not surprisingly, many of them do less well at school than their peers. This has a lasting effect on their adult lives; care leavers are more likely than children who have not been in care to be unemployed, get in trouble with the law and they often have trouble forming stable relationships.

Stein (2005) furthers these perspectives, suggesting, 'Many care leavers, as a consequence of their pre-care and care experiences, are unable to take advantage of educational opportunities. Instead, there is the expectation of instant adulthood on leaving care' (p. 25). This could lead to challenges in later life. Difficulties following care could include coming to terms with a lack of stability in their upbringing and poor family background, a lack of a parental role model, self-esteem issues and resilience, a lack of emotional support, a possible mistrust of organisations or inputs, poverty, challenging levels of educational attainment and inexperience of running a home such as budgeting, housing difficulties and isolation.

Stein (2005) organises those who have experienced care systems as victims, survivors or successors. Those in the victim category may find their experiences so difficult to manage, live with and come to terms with that they are unable to break free of their experiences, constantly reliving their negative pathways and finding new unhappy challenges. Survivors manage their situations and are able to keep going on a steady path…just. Those in the successors category, however, have been able to come to terms with their experiences and move forward from them, embracing all that life has to offer, with perhaps enhanced resilience shown, which developed as they met challenges in their earlier lives. The low numbers of those in care can mean they are missed within systems, through frequent changes in living locations. Adults working with them may feel they just get to know them when they move again. As Jackson (cited in Cox, 2000, p. 66) noted, 'There is still a strong tendency to attribute low attainment in characteristics of the children themselves', while it could simply be a result of the continued adjustments and transitions made. It does not have to be a deficit model if early support can help young children develop happily.

Support for early years children and how practitioners can facilitate appropriate strategies and environment

Family make up varies widely, for example: a nuclear one, consisting of a mother and/or father and child or children; an extended family make up, with close familiar ties, including people such as aunties, uncles or those once or twice removed, for example a distant cousin; or any set of relationships that make up a family unit, such as single parents or same-sex parents. It could also include those who do not have close family members or who have family members who are abusive towards them. The learning environment can reflect the diverse backgrounds of children in contemporary society, rather than simply mirror that of the adult working with the child. It was highlighted in Chapter 4 that the close adults around the child in Bronfenbrenner's Ecological Theory hold great significance for the child's development, therefore the child's existing structures can be built upon. Multi-agency team meetings will occur for children in care, and guidelines for an individual child's needs can be developed from knowledge of the child's circumstances and needs. 'Looked-after' children may be the subject of a care order or be 'accommodated' to support parents or a parent during difficult times. In a care order, parental responsibility is shared. A social worker will have involvement in the development of the child as an information link between the setting and ongoing liaison with parents or carers. Links can be made if the child is in a children's home. Foster carers may care for children on a short- or long-term basis. It is highly beneficial to maintain communication with the key foster person to enable a shared rapport and understanding between the roles at the foster home and in the setting. In this way, matters that have to be attended to urgently can be addressed immediately, for example an overnight referral.

According to Brodie, 'Research into the educational attainment of children "looked after" has shown that a disproportionate number fail to achieve the standards of their peers' (cited in Rix et al. 2010, p. 35). Jackson (2000, p. 66) highlights that in relation to the figures she had, four out of ten children in care are nine years old or younger.

> Nearly half the children in care are looked after for less than eight weeks and two out of three return home in less than six months. But those who remain for more than six months are likely to stay for long periods, and may spend the rest of their childhood in public care. (Jackson, 2000, p. 67)

A challenging start in life can have a significant influence on a child's sense of self-worth and confidence. This can be alleviated by a safe, secure and understanding environment, including an awareness of a child's anxiety if a routine occurrence triggers unhappy memories and events. The importance of teamwork around the child to ensure all adults are aware of challenges the child has experienced and strategies to influence positive outcomes can be crucial to support the child's development.

It is useful to observe a child initially to identify strategies that are relevant, for example encouraging in play, helping the child learn about setting routines or supporting areas of learning such as when having difficulties or specific talents. This can be incorporated into information gained at entry to become aware of the holistic, specific nature of requirements. These can be used to inform a child's next steps either for the key person or with a multiagency team. Initially, individual children may need frequent reassurance that the environment they have accessed is safe, and it may take a while for them to trust the adults working with them.

Conclusion

Children's earliest experiences impact on their understandings of the world around them. They will internalise experiences and develop their self-identity through their own and others' perceptions of them. Through support of 'looked-after' individuals by an interest in their holistic development, secure liaison with other agencies and those involved with the child – either as parents, carers or social workers – key persons and others supporting the child can provide opportunities for the child to develop happily. This crucial time can impact successfully on the child for the rest of their life.

References

Barnardo's (2014) *Five to Thrive: The Things You Do Every Day that Help Your Child's Growing Brain.* Dursley: Kate Cairns Associates.

Bronfenbrenner, U. (1979) *The Ecology of Human Development.* London: Harvard University Press.

Cox, T. (ed.) (2000) *Combating Educational Disadvantage: Meeting the Needs of Vulnerable Children.* London: Falmer Press.

Jackson, S. (ed.) (2001) *Nobody Ever Told Us School Mattered: Raising the Educational Attainments of Children in Public Care.* London: British Agencies for Adoption and Fostering.

Longfield, A. (2017) *On Measuring the Number of Vulnerable Children in England.* London: Children's Commissioner for England.

Rix, J., Nind, M., Sheehy, K., Simmons, K., Parry, J. and Kumrai, R. (2010) *Equality, Participation and Inclusion: Diverse Contexts.* Abingdon: Routledge.

Stein, M. (2005) *Resilience and Young People Leaving Care: Overcoming the Odds.* York: Joseph Rowntree Foundation.

Bibliography

Belsky, J. (1984) 'The determinants of parenting: A process model.' *Society for Research in Child Development 55,* 1, 83–96.

Deutscher, B., Fewell, R. and Gross, M. (2006) 'Enhancing the interactions of teenage mothers and their at-risk children: Effectiveness of a maternal-focused intervention.' *Topics in Early Childhood Special Education 26,* 4, 194–205.

Leishman, J.L. and Moir, J. (2007) *Pre-Teen and Teenage Pregnancy: A Twenty-First Century Reality.* Keswick: M and K Publishing.

Lounds, J., Borkowski, J. and Whitman, T. (2006) 'The potential for child neglect: The case of adolescent mothers and their children.' *Child Maltreatment 11,* 3, 281–294.

Preston, G. (ed.) (2005) *At Greatest Risk: The Children Most Likely to Be Poor.* London: Child Poverty Action Group.

| PART 3 |

Supporting the Child

| CHAPTER 8 |

Safeguarding

A JOURNEY OF TRANSFORMATION

Rosey Shelbourne

CPA Director
Christian Partners in Africa

Chapter overview

This chapter describes how a group of teachers in a rural Ugandan primary school devised ways to safeguard children that would challenge and change entrenched views in their school and local community. Through a series of interactive workshops they were able to develop their own safeguarding policies and procedures which became central to the ethos of the school. A tool kit was devised that comprised guidelines, games and activities to emphasise key aspects of the policies. In this chapter, a child is defined as being under the age of 18.

There is a tradition in Uganda that when you leave a place, maybe to walk home, your friends will go with you some of the way. 'Let me give you a push,' they will say, so that you share some of the journey together. This is very much how we see our partnership with St Paul's Community Primary School in Uganda.

On a trip to Uganda in 2001 I came face to face with child abuse and its fallout in many forms; this is an account of what came next. Although the school is based in Uganda, the principles apply to all cultures, including our own.

Our story involves both challenging a worldview held by many in Uganda and supporting a group of willing, passionate teachers in a rural primary school as they attempt to change entrenched attitudes in their school and community, demonstrating and modelling new and better ways of working.

In 1995 my husband Chris and I founded a Lincoln-based charity called Christian Partners in Africa (CPA). Feeling compelled to help the poor in Africa, and with very little experience, we went on our first trip in 1994. So much has happened since then and we have been privileged to meet, support and work alongside many people who have found themselves in desperate circumstances. Several of our projects are based around children and education, and 'safeguarding' has become a central and vital component of the work we do – to ensure that children feel valued, respected and safe and that the adults who care for, or teach, them feel equipped to cope and are able to provide the support that children may need.

Over the first few years it seemed relatively easy to see a measure of positive change with individuals and groups. As we got more familiar with Ugandan culture, building relationships and friendships, we gained a deeper understanding of their belief system and we realised that underneath the surface there was a lot more going on: in its most extreme form, witchcraft and child sacrifice.

In a 2005 study, *Raising Voices*, a Kampala-based organisation that works to prevent violence against women and children, shockingly reported that 98.3 per cent of children in Uganda had experienced some form of violence and 76 per cent had experienced sexual violence. Abuse, in its many forms, was being cleverly disguised as 'the norm' in a no-shame culture.

Starting places

The challenge was how to start. I didn't have any training or experience in safeguarding and had grown up in a safe and flourishing environment. Yet I felt compelled to do something to reach out to these children and to try to stimulate a change of attitude that would create a better world for the children in Uganda – on our projects and within the communities in which they lived, anyway. Our story proves that anyone who feels passionate about something is capable of inspiring change.

On my return to the UK I met with a small group of friends to see if it was possible to create some workshops that would challenge norms in Uganda and that could unlock preconceived patterns of thinking and empower adults to keep children safe – all in a way that would sit well in the Ugandan culture, be culturally appropriate and become owned by the local people. We decided to try but realised that it would require a revolutionary change of worldview in the way children were seen, nurtured and accepted in Ugandan society.

What follows is an overview of our initial research, and what I wish I had known when we first began! Our starting places were to be: universal child rights, the *Keeping Children Safe* tool kit, faith-based approaches and any on-the-ground provision that was available in Uganda.

Universal child rights

Finding a point of reference in a cross-cultural situation is never easy, but it is crucial in the process of finding common ground, building trust and laying a solid foundation on which to build. The *United Nations Convention on the Rights of the Child* (UNCRC) is the most widely ratified human-rights treaty in the world. Signed up to by 196 nations, its protocols are bound by international law. It recognises that every child has rights, whatever their ethnicity, gender, religion, language or abilities, and it advises adults and governments on how to work together to achieve its ends. It deals with all aspects of a child's life, including the civil, political, economic, social, health and cultural rights that all children should be entitled to everywhere.

Its principles cover areas such as: the best interests of the child; the right to life, survival and development; the right to be heard; protocols for children in armed conflict and the sale of children, child prostitution and child pornography. Each 'right' is equal, so, for instance, the right to play is equally important as the right to be protected from violence.

It was signed by the UK in 1990, becoming law in 1992. Interestingly enough, Uganda signed up in 1990 and went on to produce the Children's Statute in 1996, covering children's basic needs such as food, shelter, housing, clothing, education and health.

This made it a credible starting point for us. As we began to unpack the UNCRC and compare it with Uganda's Children's Statute, a pattern began to emerge. We found that not only did the 'rights' sit well in any culture, but they also opened up many useful cross-cultural and diverse discussions.

The tool kit

When starting from scratch, a tool kit, or similar, is always useful to help organise and formalise your thoughts and make sure that you don't miss anything out.

Keeping Children Safe: A Toolkit for Child Protection (Save the Children UK, 2006) is a very comprehensive and user-friendly guide. It was produced by the Keeping Children Safe Coalition and includes input from UK and overseas charities, such as NSPCC, Oxfam, Save the Children, World Vision and more.

The Keeping Children Safe Coalition's multicultural approach is particularly useful in helping organisations at home and abroad to develop their own child protection policy and procedures. The tool kit then equips them to implement and monitor the organisations. It covers areas such as: understanding, recognising and responding to child abuse; making your organisation safe for children; meeting the standards in different locations; communication, education and training. The self-audit tool is particularly helpful, both as a starting point for any organisation but also to use as an annual check-up. We found this to be a helpful and positive process. It is also simple enough to be an effective and empowering tool on the ground in Africa.

Using a faith-based approach

There are many different traditions and customs involved in bringing up children around the world. Many are based on culture and religion, and most contribute to helping children to understand their history and give a sense of wellbeing, thus playing a significant part in safeguarding children.

Religious groups often have a strong common ethos to 'do good', and this provides a good support group for change. Religious texts can be familiar, relevant and supportive; they can be used as a framework to challenge traditional and cultural practices that are harmful to children and can be a good starting point for discussion. Enlightened leaders can be influential, reaching places and people that would normally be difficult to access, such as church congregations in rural areas, parents who would never attend training or those who can't read.

Occasionally, unacceptable and abusive practices hide under the banner of culture or faith, and in these cases it is important not to judge without first understanding and to find a way of working with a community to help them recognise the impact on children and how to change things for the better.

On the ground

At that time, a local organisation called Raising Voices was developing the *Good School Toolkit* (2005a), with the core aim of preventing violence against children in schools. Although the school team that I was to work with wrote and developed its own policies, including those on safeguarding, *Raising Voices* proved to be a great inspiration to us.

Beginnings

So we began, fuelled by a passion to at least do something. In 2001 we had been invited to partner with St Paul's Community Primary School in Rukungiri, Uganda.

The school was established by a group of friends, who, inspired by their Christian faith and moved by the level of poverty among their neighbours, wanted to provide a source of hope in the form of education for the orphans in their community. Initially, we were invited to fund 20 free scholarships for local orphan children, allowing them to attend school with no cost to their families or guardians. Today the school has over 700 pupils with 150 children on the scholarship scheme.

Figure 8.1 Justus (Head Teacher) and Moses (Project Director)

In the early days, the school was small and rural and the facilities basic: teaching took place in four classrooms and there was a tin shack for the nursery children. There was no electricity and there were few resources, but the teachers were committed and the founders driven by faith and vision. Over the years, we worked with the school on many initiatives, but safeguarding was to be one of the most transformative.

Figure 8.2 The school in its early days

We made a decision to keep all training interactive and in workshop style, as 'ownership' was key, rather than coming from the perspective of, 'We know better than you – this is what you should be doing' (interestingly enough, in the UK we are not as advanced as we like to think we are in preventing abuse).

We also knew from Raising Voices' research (2005b) that if a shocking 98.3 per cent of children in Uganda were being abused in some way, then most of the adults with whom we would work would also have experienced child abuse. This was to be an important consideration, and consequently we began each session by creating a 'safe space'. We didn't know what effect talking about safeguarding would have, or what it may trigger from the past. We found it useful to begin with something like:

> Everyone needs a safe place where we can share our thoughts without fear of being judged or criticised. Our safe place must be a place of confidentiality, and team members' views and opinions should not be discussed outside of the safe place. The safe place can be an opportunity to voice our own views and a place where problems can be addressed in an environment that endeavours to be honest, open and non-threatening.

Myths and facts

We started with a 'Myths and Facts' game, where statements were read out and individuals had to move to the end of the room representing the appropriate answer, fact or myth. It worked well, creating a lot of discussion and laughter and breaking the ice. It also highlighted cultural differences and beliefs, which was as useful for us as it was for our trainees, helping us to gel more easily. The activity also highlighted that the Ugandan team were not used to active learning in this way. Most had come through an education system where 'chalk and talk' was the norm, and learning was a matter of memorising (often by rote) and then reproducing when required. Funnily enough, when our trainees got used to this new way of working, it actually freed them up to begin to think for themselves.

Some of the statements in the game like, 'People employed to work with children are less likely to abuse them,' 'Children are usually abused by strangers,' 'Children are always safe in groups,' and 'Children often lie about being abused,' stimulated lots of interesting debate as we strived to understand each other's preconceived ideas.

Definitions of abuse

Initially, it was important to look at some definitions of what 'constitutes' child abuse, not only for cross-cultural clarity but also for clarity between the sexes. The World Health Organization (WHO) defines child abuse or maltreatment as constituting:

> all forms of physical and/or emotional ill treatment, sexual abuse, neglect, or negligent treatment or commercial or other exploitation resulting in actual or potential harm to the child's health, survival, development or dignity in the context of a relationship of responsibility, trust or power. (WHO, 1999, p.16)

This was a lot to comprehend, so we divided it into three sections: types of abuse and their definitions; what actually constitutes abuse; and memorising the definitions.

We made up a silly rhyme to remind us of the definitions as defined by the WHO: 'Never brush pink silly enormous elephants' represented neglect, bullying, physical violence, sexual violence, emotional violence and economic violence. Later, 'or comb' was added to represent cyberbullying.

Despite the hilarity, it seemed to do the trick and assisted the team as they worked through examples of unacceptable behaviour within their own communities. Having to speak the words 'out loud' became a vital part of helping them to express themselves in a culturally taboo context.

Child rights

We posed the questions, 'Do children have rights?', 'Should all children have the same rights?' and, if so, 'What are their rights?' and used the UNCRC to formulate answers. As previously stated, Uganda had signed up to this treaty, writing its own Children's Statute. The detail didn't seem to have filtered down to local level, so through an interactive matching game we were able to demonstrate the similarities between the two documents. It was interesting to see that on paper cultural differences made little impact with regard to child protection. It was clear that it was 'attitude' that needed to change, and lack of knowledge played a big part in this. There was a wealth of good feeling in our group about trying to change things for the better, so we tried to help them to do just that.

Figure 8.3 Some of the project team

Biblical prompts

As previously mentioned, approaching safeguarding from a faith-based perspective can be another helpful tool. Not only do religions help form the basis of worldviews, but familiar scripture readings can be used as great springboards for debate. St Paul's was a Christian school, although children of all faiths were welcome, so we used some recognisable scriptures about children from the Bible to challenge preconceived opinions within the culture. One example from Psalm 127 says, 'Children are God's best gift,' suggesting that children should be valued and may even be considered to be special. Discussing this became intrinsic in changing attitudes to children and the group became more inspired to want to change things.

Writing a policy

In the workplace in the UK, it is commonplace to be given policy documents that we readily read, absorb and apply. At St Paul's, there were no policy documents as such, so we had the opportunity of supporting the team through the process of writing them from scratch.

Although this was time consuming, the benefits were enormous because the team had to think in detail about what makes a good school. Subsequently, they bought in to the process and completely took ownership of implementing the policies. Of course, one of those was about safeguarding children.

It took a three-day workshop to create the child protection policy. By the time it was finished, it marked a change in worldview and a determination to draw a line in the sand. It was an opportunity to model a different way, attempting to change attitudes of those working in the school and living in the local community and providing a generation of children with a 'safe place' to learn. It was hoped that with teaching and debate, this new generation would have good role models who, in turn, would carry forward a new approach as adults. It was amazing and wonderful to watch.

Figure 8.4 The new school (with early years)

Writing a safeguarding policy from scratch is not as daunting as it might seem. You can use trigger sentences to get people started. For instance, we split the policy up into three parts: a statement of intent; a statement of protection; and a statement of confirmation. St Paul's statement read:

> St Paul's School believes that all children should be protected, respected, cared for, encouraged to reach their full potential…and grow into responsible adults that are self supporting etc.
>
> St Paul's aims to make sure that the Board, the director, head teacher and staff, neighbours, visitors etc. do not act in ways that are abusive, can be misinterpreted as abuse or put a child in a position of danger.
>
> We at St Paul's agree that as individuals and a corporate body we will take every step possible to uphold our child protection policy.

The final version contained an extended list of hopes and dreams for the children at the school, followed by an equally long list of staff or visitors who potentially might have contact with their pupils. I love the way it clearly states their intentions and is displayed proudly for all to see. Because of their ownership, the team still ensure that all staff are regularly retrained, along with any new teachers. The head teacher told me that since this policy was put in place, the whole atmosphere of the school has changed and the school is proud to provide their children with a safe space in which to learn.

Indicators

Having established an end goal, it was now much easier to explore the subject in more depth and plan a method and strategy to keep children safe. As a group, we workshopped 'key indicators' of abuse, ways children disclose, appropriate and inappropriate behaviour and barriers to reporting abuse.

For some families in Uganda, poverty is so extreme that simply feeding their children on a daily basis becomes an overwhelming challenge. At St Paul's there were some children like this, whose families had never been given a chance, finding themselves prisoners to life's circumstances. It was an interesting challenge to draw a dividing line between 'deprivation' and intentional 'neglect'. Either way, children were suffering and needed some support and help if possible.

We looked at the following areas of abuse: neglect; bullying and cyberbullying; and physical, sexual, emotional and economic violence; and we came up with a list of indicators. Most were common signs, but there were a few shockers that came out of the African setting such as burns, scalding with hot water, fear of being locked in the dark and not coming to school. We concluded that a change in a child's behaviour is not necessarily proof of abuse, but it can alert us to the possibility and help us to decide what to do next.

Appropriate and inappropriate behaviour

People, and cultures for that matter, have very different opinions about what constitutes acceptable behaviour towards children and what constitutes child abuse. In the next session, we debated at length until we could agree on appropriate and inappropriate behaviour towards children, ensuring that in the future staff actions would not only be appropriate but also would never be misunderstood as abusive and would always be beyond reproach. A little role play kept the mood light but also served to break down barriers as we tackled tricky subjects such as: not using language that will mentally or emotionally scar a child; not encouraging any crushes from a child; not acting in ways that would embarrass, shame or humiliate a child especially in public; not promising to keep a secret if a child discloses to you.

The most interesting debate centred on the use of corporal punishment. Although this had been prohibited in 1997, it was commonplace in most schools (in 2016 it became illegal). However, for teachers who knew nothing else, and who were struggling to keep control of classes of over a hundred, it was very difficult to adapt to a new way of teaching.

Again, we were faced with the challenge of trying to foster a change in perspective and a different way of doing things. As we began to tell stories of schools where teachers used such things as 'positive praise', 'time out', 'golden time', stickers for rewards and much more, their eyes nearly popped out of their heads. They resolved to give it a try, but I could tell that they were very unsure about it all. The head teacher said, 'At first we thought it wouldn't be possible, but later it started working. It's like somebody saying you should wear gumboots to dig a hole when you normally don't; when you try new things you realise they are possible.'

How wonderful it was when we returned a year later to find that they had surprised themselves, and the whole school had been transformed. There were stickers for everything: best piece of work, most helpful child, head teacher's award and many more. The change in approach had suddenly given teachers and pupils something positive to work towards and there was to be no going back to the restrictive, controlling methods of corporal punishment. Who would have thought that a child protection workshop would have made such a difference to children's learning? But it did.

Barriers

On our second visit, it became obvious that there were inbuilt barriers that made reporting cases of abuse difficult and in some cases almost impossible, particularly within the African culture.

As I was also learning on the job, even I had to think about what I would do in a situation where a child had confided in me about someone who I respected and thought to be a good teacher. I wondered how I would be able to tell if the child was telling the truth without a witness. It was hard to accept that people who abused could appear to be nice. There was a lot of deception and the truth was difficult to find; abuses were surrounded by a culture of stigma, secrecy and silence. Having no framework or support system from the outside was making it difficult for teachers to report disclosures, in case children had merely made up a story for attention and teachers' reputations were damaged for life. Having said that, patriarchal society in Uganda often renders children at the bottom of the pile, with men seeing abusive behaviour as their cultural right. This makes it easier for abusive teachers to cover their tracks without challenge.

Either way, something needed to be done to help both children and teachers, so we set about 'unpacking' the reasons why children don't report and the reasons why teachers don't report.

Making the topic very visible: the Barriers game was invented

Initially, we tackled 'why children don't tell'. In the Barriers game, you sit a doll (to represent a child) on a chair at one end of the room and sit the group facing the 'child'. You then ask the group to shout out the reasons why children don't tell about abuse and then write the reasons on sticky notes. Using boxes, if they are available (we used chairs), you stick the notes to the boxes and begin to build a barrier between the child and the group. Eventually, there will be so many reasons that the child won't be able to see the teachers and the teachers won't be able to see the child any longer. You then discuss how you can take down the barriers, and physically dismantle the barricade as you come up with solutions.

Some of the reasons for children not telling were: not knowing whom to tell; fear that nobody would believe them; being worried that it's their fault; thinking they will make matters worse; being concerned that they would be hurt or killed; and being worried about being thrown out of school or home. This made for interesting, thought-provoking discussion and actually began to form the bare bones of a school policy.

Then you repeat the game, looking at 'why adults don't report'. This time, you can sit a senior member of staff, like the head teacher, on the chair. It is a great way of breaking down barriers between staff and management, as you are practising real-life reporting to the appropriate people. Playing the game together opens up new channels of communication, so that when you have a real case of abuse, it is already easier to 'talk'.

Some reasons for staff not talking were: not knowing whom to tell; not believing a child; thinking 'It happened to me and I just had to get on with life'; fear of being wrong; fear of the consequences; too much paperwork; thinking 'He's a "man", he should take it on the chin'; thinking 'He/she's a trouble maker'; and fear of losing their job. Again, some very interesting outcomes emerged and there was a lot to consider about how to make the school a safe place for both children and adults.

Reporting

One of the recurring themes was that both children and adults did not know whom to tell. I guess it's no good being in possession of a fire extinguisher if you don't know how to use it when there is a fire.

Over the next few hours, we explored 'who' should report, 'when' to report and 'how' to report. The challenge was that we were starting from scratch, because as far as we knew there was nothing in place anywhere in the country. The advantage was that the team could design procedures that were fit for purpose within their own setting and, having created them, would own them.

It was soon established that 'everyone' should report, but 'when?' was a more interesting question. The fear of making a mistake or making things worse overshadowed the discussions. In Uganda there is a 'no-shame' culture and being proactive or reporting someone doesn't come naturally; exposing the truth is seen as provocative and authority and respect are hierarchical. Eventually, it was decided that what was required for most was to 'report not sort'.

By introducing strict confidentiality procedures, staff gained the confidence to report incidents, and this process continues today.

We discussed the benefits of a system where anyone could be confident in reporting the slightest thing, even if it didn't seem all that important. Sometimes when this happens it enables the safeguarding officer to observe a pattern of behaviour, especially if there are three or more independent reports of 'nothing much' – we called it 'Three stones make a wall'. This concept seemed to be key in helping to build confidence in the group. It was decided that it was better to report ten false alarms than miss the one time when a child was harmed.

The group was able to design a flowchart as a procedure for reporting by answering the following questions: What should happen immediately? What should happen over time? Who should be involved? Should the police or other outside organisations be involved? Should the school board be involved?

With little or no help from outside, including the police who are not adequately trained or resourced, the group agonised over how to help a schoolgirl who had recently been raped. Their dilemma was that the man would probably bribe the police to drop the case. Meanwhile, it wouldn't be long before the whole village would know, as the local police were not known for their discretion. The girl could then become an outcast, making it difficult for her to marry. Their discussion went along the lines of, 'If we are trying to protect the girl and we know justice is unlikely, for the girl's sake and to keep her safe, is it better to keep quiet as a means of protecting her? Or, on the other hand, is it better to be honest, as the truth will often find you out?' Tough! These kinds of dilemmas must always be worked out 'in country', as imposed rules simply don't achieve best outcomes.

Two safeguarding officers were appointed – one for the boys and one for the girls – and they were easily accessible to the children.

A suggestions box was used, and all suggestions were regularly reviewed by the safeguarding officers with any that were not related to safeguarding issues being reviewed by the school management team. A red card was provided in every classroom, which teachers could ask another child to take to the head teacher if they needed instant back up. He would come immediately, meaning a teacher would not have to leave a child or their class.

On the basis that prevention is better than cure and implementation is everything, we spent a lot of time on the purpose of recording and how to record something well. This was built around role play and scenarios and involved themes such as: being clear and specific; separating fact from opinion; recording evidence; decisions that are made; and writing neatly.

Finally, all teachers were given the St Paul's reporting procedure on a small card to keep in their pocket that said: 'Make child safe; Use Red card; Record facts; Report to DSO (Designated Safeguarding Officer); Keep child safe.'

The teachers told me:

> The sequence works and brings order which simplifies the challenges. Complaints against teachers are put in the suggestions box, children are free to report to the DSOs and the worst cases are taken to the head teacher. But these days we don't experience so many cases.

Policies and rolling out

This was the beginning of safeguarding for St Paul's, and it was a huge amount to take on board. I cannot praise this group of teachers enough for their enthusiasm, tenacity in trying to grasp new ways of thinking and determination to improve things for the benefit of the children in their school and community. Once they had started this work, it became obvious that they wanted to further develop their newfound knowledge. Within the school setting they began to formulate new guidelines (policies) that could be used throughout the school and that would help all staff and children to improve safety.

On one occasion, we spent three days exploring what makes a good school. This involved imagining and questioning how teaching methods, care and safety, environment, and relationship with the community could be improved. On one day we walked around the school grounds with a map, marking on it all the spots where we thought children could be vulnerable, even during lesson times. From here, staff formed policies that covered: bullying; neglect and economic abuse; and physical, sexual and emotional abuse. Teachers said: 'We owned a behaviour change in school where absenteeism, escapism and dropouts reduced. Now children enjoy being at school.'

Several years later, faced with the juxtaposition of families who had no clean water or electricity in their homes but had access to mobile phones, they formulated their social media policy. As the internet slowly crept into the far reaches of Uganda, they realised that they were in possession of something that had the potential to change their lives, both positively and negatively. Initially, they could not believe that if they were on Facebook with no privacy settings, I could see what they were doing. I surprised them once by asking, 'How was your trip to see your relatives in Kampala?' Reading in the newspaper about a girl who had been groomed online and arranged to meet her 'friend' at a hotel in Kampala and was then murdered brought the dangers very close to home. It made the team determined to train their children in how to stay safe on the internet on a mobile phone. They even wrote a whole IT curriculum to be rolled out throughout the year.

Safeguarding training for the boarding staff was also considered. Traditionally in Uganda, most children board for their senior years. Dorms can sleep 50 children or more on double- or triple-decker bunks, with supervision often scant and staff untrained. St Paul's, which had made boarding provision for children who lived a long way from school (several miles) or came from an impoverished home, quickly reduced the number of beds in dorms and incorporated small rooms within the blocks to sleep staff. Staff were trained, good supervision was provided and children felt safer, happier and more prepared to learn.

The ripple effect

The ripple effect of safeguarding continued to roll out into the community and surrounding area. Social workers were appointed to be the link between the school and the community, regularly visiting homes to encourage families and support children. Their findings inspired the school to empower families to help themselves and their children. They decided to provide very poor families with small starter kits, such as seeds, a chicken or a goat, giving them the opportunity to improve their lives and helping them to feed and support their children. Women grouped together and began small saving schemes to enable them to pay for medical fees for their children if needed. During this time the school was becoming a respected voice in the community and it spread the message about how to keep children safe. The school was invited to share knowledge with other schools in the area and social workers even began to talk to local leaders about protecting vulnerable adults in the community. A change in worldview was beginning to transform a whole community, and it had all begun with a small group of teachers who had grasped hold of something and wanted to change things for the better. One teacher said, 'I as a teacher learned how to handle children and make them love school as their home.'

A shared journey

This story is about a shared journey with a school team and a rural community in western Uganda over a period of ten years. In the beginning we didn't know how to start, and we had to learn as we went along. We discovered that anyone with a passion can inspire change for the good; you just have to take the first step, and before you know it people will have picked up the ball and be running full speed ahead with it. I particularly love the way St Paul's has made safeguarding central to its ethos and made it work within its culture and community. Should you ever visit the school, you would find a vibrant, happy community where teachers care about their pupils and children feel safe and want to learn.

Today, CPA is still working with St Paul's. We were excited to hear that in 2015 the children came top in the district in their Primary Leavers Exams, with the highest results going to one of the scholarship children. St Paul's continues to forge ahead as a beacon school, setting a great example for other schools in the area and providing a safe environment for children with animated and imaginative learning.

I conclude that it is possible to respect other cultures but challenge things that oppose human rights; you can't always prevent everything bad from happening but you can try to change attitudes, which in turn can empower children and adults alike to do their best in all situations.

I would encourage you to give it a try and you may be surprised at the results.

As a post script, the old tin shack, originally the nursery classroom, is now being used as a tuck shop and I recently heard that the head teacher had started giving 'Head Teacher awards for good parents' – that really made me smile.

Many thanks go to Polly Coombes and Joseph Hardwick, the UK team who shared the journey with me.

References

Raising Voices (2005a) *The Good School Toolkit.* Kampala: Raising Voices. Accessed on 11/6/2018 at http://raisingvoices.org/good-school

Raising Voices (2005b) *Violence Against Children: The Voices of Ugandan Children and Adults.* Kampala: Raising Voices, in partnership with Save the Children Uganda.

Save the Children UK (2006) *Keeping Children Safe: A Toolkit for Child Protection.* London: Save the Children UK.

WHO (1999) *Report of the Consultation on Child Abuse Prevention.* Geneva: World Health Organization.

CHAPTER 9

Early Years Interventions

Gina Taylor

Foundation 2 Teacher and SENCO
Holly Primary School

Chapter overview

This chapter explores a research hypothesis concerning attachment and nurture in the early years and how nurturing intervention and circle time can promote wellbeing. The attachments that a child forms from birth onwards initiate the development of schema, which are subconsciously drawn upon in everyday life. This schematic framework is the basis of a child's social and emotional understanding and learning. Personal, social and emotional development is one the three prime areas of educational learning in the Early Years Foundation Stage (EYFS). Research was undertaken to discover how the delivery of nurturing interventions and circle time could progress the social and emotional skills of all children in early years education and in particular for those who exhibited attachment issues.

A mixed methodology for research was employed and included: observations of a nurture facility and semi-structured interviews with staff, leadership, children and parents in order to ascertain their perception of worth in the nurture approach. Further to this, action research focused on one school that did not adopt the nurture room approach for pedagogy and intervention. The views of parents and guardians with children in the Foundation Stage at the focus school were gained via a questionnaire, asking how they thought their child coped socially and emotionally. Case studies of four children were examined to determine the efficacy of nurture and circle time interventions in enhancing these children's social and emotional skill-set. The case studies encompassed scoring of behavioural attitudes on a Boxall profile, their progression in the Early Years Development Matters assessment tool and observations both before and after the research period. The results indicated that there is merit in pedagogical intervention of a nurture and circle time style and showed some evidence of improved social and emotional literacy.

The phases of research can best be summarised as follows:

- an investigation into the nurture room concept through observations and semi-structured interviews with nurture room staff, leadership and children

- inquiry to ascertain the perceived importance of social and emotional literacy by parents and guardians by means of a questionnaire

- child case studies, including observations and assessment of intervention efficacy via EYFS profile scores and Boxall profiles, actioned at the commencement and culmination of research.

Nurture rooms observations, research and own practice reflection

The nurture room concept was first devised by educational psychologist Marjorie Boxall in the 1970s. She had observed that a large number of children commenced education with 'severe social, emotional and behavioural needs' (The Nurture Group, 2015, p. 2). They simply were not ready for the structure of everyday school life. The idea of a nurture room is to create a child-centred, homely environment to emulate the experiences that a child would have in their first three years of life – a period when attachments are formed and neurological pathways are created effectively – and thus allow for 're-parenting' of the child (Bishop, 2008, p. 5).

I visited a school with a nurture facility in an average-sized primary school in the Midlands. The majority of pupils where from white British backgrounds and spoke English as their first language. The number of children eligible for Pupil Premium additional funding and the number of children with Special Educational Needs (SEN) were above average.

My immediate impressions were of the genuine homeliness of the nurture area. In this case, the 'room' was a separate building, which was once the caretaker's house. As such, it was afforded the luxury of being set up in different 'zones' like a house, with a living room, kitchen and dining area. This had the effect of detaching the site from the main body of the school and added to the sense that this place was somewhere special. On talking to the children in the facility, their responses were all favourable:

> 'I meet all my friends and 'cos you can have cereal here and when I've had cereal it's good.'

> 'Your family can come here and visitors.'

> 'It feels like I'm at home because it is home.'

> 'I like it, we go on adventures.'

One could take this as evidence that the children loved being in the nurture facility, and one parent I spoke to said their child couldn't wait to join it.

The unit was run by two members of staff and overseen by the SENCO who was also the deputy head teacher. The day was very structured, and a predictable daily routine was followed; the repetition and routine strengthen connections in the brain (Dowling, 2014, p. 81). On entering the nurture rooms, all children added to a feelings tree; these were pre-printed words that the children attached to a faux tree next to their own picture. All the children were then asked why they had chosen that particular feeling. One girl said she was happy, 'Cos she was there'. The children then settled to an activity that supported their classroom learning. This draws on Vygotsky's Zone of Proximal Development (1978), as the activity is specifically tailored to the child's learning stage, is achievable and expands what the child already knows. The main emphasis from our standpoint was that the learning was in achievable, small steps, which gave learning ownership to the child, promoting pride in achievement and visible progress.

At the time of my observation, six children were in the nurture facility and varied in age. All had differing needs and levels of social and emotional skills. When asked how the staff identify a need for the facility, they said referrals mostly originated from the class teacher via the SENCO. A Boxall profile was then completed, from which a level of need was determined. The profile data is tracked on a graph and revisited on a termly basis to assess levels of need and evidence success. This later led to the use of the Boxall profile to assess the development of the case-study children.

Once all the children had arrived for that first morning session, they went into the 'Relaxed Zone', where they registered and then took it in turns to talk and share their news. This form of 'circle time' adhered to the principles of circle time as advocated by Roffey (2006, pp. 4–5): democracy, respect, community, inclusion, choice and safety. Each child had the choice to speak or not, took turns and listened to the speaker and all were included. This influenced the number of circle time activities introduced throughout the action research project.

A child's motivation, whether intrinsic or extrinsic, must be founded in the child themselves. The child has to be aware of the interaction between cause and effect. If they have low self-esteem, it could be argued that the gentle promotion of self-worth and belief would be a foundation for the exchange of causality and would therefore promote the desire for praise. Activities in the nurture room were based around building social and interaction skills. The activity witnessed promoted turn taking and memory skills. One child in particular was very eager to have a go and struggled with patience. By use of positive and peripheral praise, the child was supported in waiting for his turn.

In summary, the nurture facility was viewed as a comfortable 'home from home' by children, staff, senior management and parents. This was evident in the observations made and efficacy was displayed in the Boxall profile trackers. Some of the elements seen in the nurture facility were applicable to the action research and did influence practice in general, such as the circle time news in the Relaxed Zone and the activities based around building interaction. Circle time was used as a vehicle to build confidence and belonging to the group and gave the children a 'voice'. The breakfast routine, which encompassed individual roles for the children – laying the table, asking what each child would like, helping to prepare, serve and tidy up – would not be feasible in the research setting due to a lack of facilities. So, this 'family style' sharing of food was incorporated into a daily snack time, which promoted manners and gave individual roles to the children, such as handing out the milk or fruit. This was preferable to a snack bar, whereby the children could help themselves and in doing so miss out on the nurturing element of sitting together, giving and receiving food. The only element I felt unable to transfer into daily practice was the feelings tree. After several attempts to talk about feelings with my cohort who were aged between three and four years, I determined that the majority were too young to be able to understand or vocalise their feelings effectively. During the attempts made, the children were 'happy' and, when asked why, they mostly reiterated what was previously said by others. In this instance, then, I would be more inclined to implement a feelings tree to full-time Foundation Stage 2 children who are aged four and five after introducing visuals and learning about feelings, as I believe they would be more responsive and have a greater understanding of and ability to vocalise feelings.

Perceived importance of social and emotional literacy by parents, guardians and professionals

In order to ascertain the views of parents and guardians (referred to in this text as Primary Care Givers (PCGs)), questionnaires were distributed to them about how they viewed their child socially and emotionally. Staff at the research setting received questionnaires that aimed to give an overall picture of how they promoted social and emotional skills, as well as their views on the subject as a whole. The questionnaire was sent out to parents of Foundation 1 (nursery) and Foundation 2 (reception) children.

Parent questionnaires

The questions had a scoring system of 0 to 4. Scoring a 4 meant that the parents felt that the statement was true of their child and 0 that the statement was untrue. Additional space was provided for each statement for comments.

The views on children's confidence are shown in Table 9.1.

Table 9.1

Statement	Scores				
	4	3	2	1	0
I am confident in new situations	30%	34%	11%	15%	10%

This illustrated quite a broad spectrum of parental views on their children's confidence; although the majority saw their child as quite confident, over a quarter felt their children lacked confidence.

This, interestingly, was in contrast to another confidence-related statement, shown in Table 9.2.

Table 9.2

Statement	Scores				
	4	3	2	1	0
I can make friends and play well with other children at home.	72%	24%	4%		

This difference could be attributed to parents' perceptions of their offspring whilst in their care, as children initially explore their surroundings and return to a base for reassurance – in this case their parent. This anomaly may also derive from parents' experiences of dropping their child off at school. Personal observations indicated that children are initially upset at being separated from their main carer and in some cases exhibit a high state of anxiety. This often dissolves after five minutes when they have been reassured and distracted by a practitioner.

The comments varied: 'has always struggled with new situations' and being 'shy' was a common thread, in contrast to this, another parent stated that their child 'took everything in their stride', thus illustrating the differing perceptions of parents and children.

Encouragingly, on self-esteem statements, 88 per cent of children were thought of as feeling valued and understood and 96 per cent of parents said that the children were able to say what they were good at doing. This illustrates a very high level of perception of child self-esteem. Parental support was evident, with over 90 per cent scoring either 4 and 3 for the following statements:

- I am supported to make choices and allowed to say no.

- I am given time to speak and am listened to.

An argument could be made that the answers given may be perceived by the person completing the questionnaire as the 'right' answer; in some cases this may be true, however, my own knowledge of these parents and caregivers gives me cause to refute this and believe that the answers are genuine.

Further to this picture of good social and emotional literacy, 80 per cent of questionnaires listed a score of 4 and the remaining 20 per cent as 3 with regards to the statement, 'My child is happy at school.'

One could argue that, as a limited number of questionnaires were returned, these figures are misleading and that parent confidence in expressing concerns may be lacking, however, whilst still maintaining an unbiased view, I believe that these figures are a true reflection of parent perceptions overall. When considering the research focus on how to promote social emotional learning in conjunction with the results of the questionnaires, an additional reflective question arose: if these children were seen by their PGCs as happy, with high self-esteem and being generally confident, would an improvement in their social and emotional skillset be evident after the research and how would it present itself?

The answer to this question may lie in the development of the children's abilities to self-regulate. The PGC questionnaires gave an indication that this was an area where tailored pedagogy could enable children to control impulse and anger responses: to the statement 'I can stop myself from getting angry,' 56 per cent scored a 4 or 3, meaning just over half were able to do this, whilst the remaining 44 per cent scored 2, which could be said to indicate a lack of self-regulation and resilience. Similarly, 20 per cent would find it difficult to sort out a problem without becoming aggressive. For the focus children to be at Age Related Expectations (ARE), the age band they scored at should mirror their actual age in months, for example Child A at initial assessment was 40 months so should be somewhere between mid 30–50 months and low 40–60 months and therefore score 5, 6 or 7. Where in fact they were within the 22–36 months age range and below ARE.

In summary, the PCG questionnaires gave an interesting qualitative insight into the views of parents and guardians on their children's social and emotional wellbeing. The overall picture presented as one of a 'good' level of confidence, self-esteem and support from home with issues of self-regulation and control being highlighted. The implications taken from this for further aspects of this research were that levels of social and emotional skills could be enhanced, as could the children's abilities to understand turn taking and develop patience and calming techniques to avoid states of high anxiety and stress when needs were not immediately met.

Case studies

In order to ascertain the efficacy of interventions to promote social and emotional wellbeing in the early years, case studies were carried out focusing on four children in my class who I had determined as having an additional need in this area. This need was evident through behaviour, interactions and assessments carried out as part of a pedagogical role. In order to counter any question of gender bias or anomalies, two girls and two boys were chosen, all the children were in F1, aged three to four and from homes where both parents were present and they all had siblings. Child A was withdrawn and found it difficult to interact with peers. Child B had difficulties with boundaries and exhibited defiant behaviours and hyperactivity. Child C had pronounced attachment issues due to previous experiences. Child D had speech and toileting difficulties and exhibited defiant behaviours. Each child had a Boxall profile completed at the commencement of research and again at the end of the research term as an indicator of progress and efficacy of the interventions. In addition to this, a chronology of behaviours was also actioned by the key workers of these children. In most incidences, either I as their class teacher or the teaching assistant completed the above, and objectivity remained throughout.

The Boxall profile

The Boxall profile was created by education psychologist Marjorie Boxall to be used in conjunction with nurture rooms. The profile is a two-part checklist to be completed by staff and provides a framework for assessment of children with social and emotional behavioural difficulties and aids the planning of focused intervention.

The profile itself consists of two elements:

- The first concerns developmental strands, encompassing organisation of experience and internalisation of controls.

- The second offers a diagnostic profile that describes self-limiting features, undeveloped behaviour and unsupported behaviour.

The scores to several questions are plotted on a graph, which displays an average score for 'competently functioning children' in these same areas (see Figure 9.1).

All of the case study children were operating considerably outside the expected parameters of competently functioning children, indicated in the bottom line on Figure 9.1. This indicates that all of the case-study children had areas of need and should benefit from interventions. The only strands where a child was within expected levels was child A in the area 'is biddable and accepts constraints'. I felt that this was misleading, because, although at face value this child was indeed 'biddable', as her teacher I had the benefit of a greater understanding of her and as such knew that she severely lacked the confidence to do anything other than 'sit still without talking or causing a disturbance'.

Three of the case study children scored highly across diagnostic profile, indicating that they had attachment issues and, as such, interventions were designed to simulate nurturing experiences and games were chosen that would develop turn taking. Circle time experiences were used to build self-esteem and were actioned in small groups of half the class and a larger group with the class as a whole. It was noted that children C and D benefitted more during smaller groups, as the adult's attention could be more focused on them. The interventions and observations were built into planning, so that all children would benefit from them, and took place over two terms in the academic year. The interventions were with smaller groups still and the language of pedagogy was also modified with reference to this research in terms of how praise was used and the setting of clear boundaries. As a practitioner, I learned very quickly that the words 'No' and 'Stop' could be catalysts for acceleration of anxious behaviour.

After the two terms, another Boxall profile was completed for each case study child to determine the efficacy of the interventions and adjustments in pedagogical style. Across all areas the scores altered favourably, bringing the children closer to the competently functioning parameters. However, none of the children were within these parameters, demonstrating that, although improvements were shown, these children cannot be fixed overnight and their learning and increase in self-worth is an ongoing process. One could argue that the changes may have occurred within the children regardless of any intervention, as their understanding of boundaries and social capabilities would have increased naturally as they grew and became older. Yet, it is still fair to assume that the interventions did have some worth, as was witnessed personally.

Development matters: Personal Social and Emotional Development (PSED) assessments

Part of the role of the early years practitioner is to assess on an ongoing basis the development of the children in early years education. This is facilitated through the Early Education/Department for Education document, *Development Matters in the Early Years Foundation Stage* (2012). Though not statutory, this guidance is widely adopted throughout education as a framework for assessment and is used in the setting where the research took place. By concentrating on the prime area of learning and development, PSED and its aspects of making relationships, self-confidence and self-awareness and managing feelings and behaviour for the purpose of this research, I was able to monitor progression of learning and ability. The categories to assess progression are age related in months and statements of achievement fall into each age category.

As the focus children's teacher, I was responsible for the assessment of children in my class. The assessments are normally carried out in the half term that they first attend school and subsequently at the end of each term. The graphs in Figures 9.1 and 9.2 illustrate the initial research period assessments and the final assessments after interventions had taken place (this also coincided with the end of the school year).

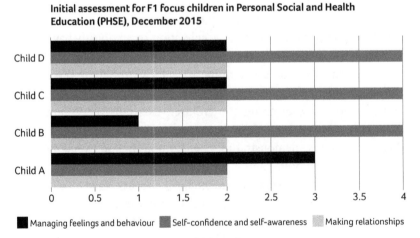

Figure 9.1 Initial EYFS assessment

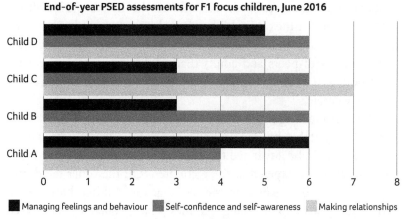

Figure 9.2 End-of-research EYFS assessment

When viewing Figures 9.1 and 9.2, is it useful to note that the lower axis in Figure 9.2 has a higher range.

Table 9.3 explains the lower axis; a number has been attributed to the age band in the EYFS assessments.

Table 9.3 EYFS age bands and scores in relation to Figures 9.1 and 9.2

Score	1	3	4	5	6	7	8
Age band	Mid 22–36 months	High 22–36 months	Low 30–50 months	Mid 30–50 months	High 30–50 months	Low 40–60 months	Mid 40–60 months

For the focus children to be at Age Related Expectations (ARE), the age band they scored at should mirror their actual age in months, for example Child A at initial assessment was 40 months so should be somewhere between Mid 30–50 months and Low 40–60 months and therefore score 5, 6 or 7.

All the focus children were aged between 39 and 42 months at initial assessment and, as such, should have scored 5, 6 or 7.

In the second and final assessment, all the children were aged between 46 and 48 months. If they were at ARE, a score between 6 and 8 would have been recorded in Figure 9.2 .

It is evident from the initial assessment that all of the focus children were below ARE for PSED. Three out of four children had good self-confidence and self-awareness. Child A (as mentioned) had low confidence, as discussed with reference to the Boxall profile above. Child C was above the other children in making relationships, however, this child has attachment issues and, as such, demonstrates 'friendly behaviours' with peers and adults (Early Education/Department for Education, 2012, p. 9); this could therefore be argued as not being entirely accurate.

When comparing the two sets of data seen in Figures 9.1 and 9.2, it is evident that the children have all made significant progress in these areas. This could be attributed to the efficacy of the circle time groups and interventions targeted at these children. On the other hand, this could arguably be credited to the fact that the children have grown and, as such, matured, meaning that these changes may have occurred naturally. Despite this, the evidence given does hold, as these children did progress and I personally believe that the additional interventions played a part in this.

Discussion of findings

When reflecting back to the original research hypothesis of whether nurturing interventions and circle time can promote social and emotional wellbeing in the early years, several sub questions and areas for investigation arose:

- What are parental views on their children's self-esteem?

- What interventions have been successful in previous studies and in other settings and how has their efficacy been measured?

- Are the findings applicable to the existing setting and influential in ongoing implementation and if so will interventions improve social and emotional skills?

The scope for this research was huge, so in order to discuss the findings of the sub-questions, each question will be considered in turn.

What are parental views on their children's self-esteem?

The parental questionnaire yielded some interesting results. As discussed, most parents thought of their children as being confident, and approximately half found the children to have anger and self-regulation issues. This in turn fed into the type of interventions and pedagogical techniques employed within the classroom and led to extended reading around the subject of mindfulness and circle time. Another indication of behaviour was evident in the question regarding behaviour and boundaries at home and at school: more adults thought that their children behaved better at school than at home. This could be due to perceptions and information given to parents regarding their children. In personal observations and my discussions with parents in an everyday teacher/parent context and apart from this research, many parents have observed that their children are better behaved at school. This may derive from the 'routine' of school life and the clear and obvious boundaries that are in place to enable children to begin to self-regulate, which is a component of being socially and emotionally literate (Dowling, 2014; Roffey, 2006). It is possible that the difference in behaviours could be a consequence of a lack of social interactions prior to school entry and may refer to Radesky's suggested 'behavioural regulation tool' in the form of electronic devices replacing human conversation (Radesky, Schumacher and Zuckerman, 2015, p. 7). This juxtaposition of behaviours was described by Tony Attwood as being like Jekyll and Hyde; this was, however, in relation to Asperger syndrome but may be equally applicable to other children, whereby the effort to conform and and behave in a particular way may result in a pressure0cooker effect once the child is at home (Attwood, 1998, p. 39). Therefore, the difference or perceived difference between school and home behaviours may be an area for further exploration and enquiry through further research.

Overall, the questionnaires gave an impression that the emotional wellbeing of their children was of concern to parents, as one would have expected. The poor rate of return of the questionnaires could be explained as an indicator that the parents saw the research or research area as unimportant; however, personal knowledge of the parents and the answers given in the questionnaires leads me to believe otherwise.

What interventions have been successful in previous studies and in other settings and how has their efficacy been measured?

The nurture facility observed at another school was evidently successful and was viewed as such by the parents, practitioner and management. The children also liked being in the nurture facility. One could argue that this may have been due to the fact that they were out of the classroom and therefore away from the 'learning' environment and their nurture time could have been seen by them as a treat. The promise of breakfast may also be viewed as an encouragement for better interaction and behaviour, as, in my own, experience children remember and react positively to situations involving food. Yet, the very act of giving and receiving food is a nurturing concept.

The interventions used by the nurture facility that were based on those suggested in the Boxall profile materials were of worth and, as such, influenced those implemented in my own setting. This is corroborated by Ofsted in 2011 and Education Scotland in 2008 which stated: 'Nurture groups are very effective in developing children's confidence. All of the activities are designed to enhance children's self-respect, sense of worth and self-esteem' (p. 12). The observations made during the visit to the other setting have been influential in the pedagogy in my current setting and the feelings tree that was not applicable to nursery-aged children due to their undeveloped understanding of their feelings has now been implemented in Foundation Stage 2 where the children are a year older.

This observation of understanding through play has implications for pedagogical practice, as one is able to understand a child more by observing them at their most relaxed and engaged when in a state of play. Much has been written about play as therapy and may be an area for further personal research (Malchiodi and Crenshaw, 2014; Wilson and Ryan, 2005).

THE EFFICACY OF THE NURTURE ROOM CONCEPT IS SEEN IN
THE CHILDREN BEING ABLE TO RETURN TO NORMAL CLASSES

There is evidence to suggest that intervention should be actioned at the earliest possible stage (Allen, 2011; Sylva *et al.*, 2003). In this research, improvement was seen in the children's progression made on the Foundation Stage Profile and the difference in the pre and post Boxall profile. Again, these results could be due to the maturation of the children and their greater awareness of themselves and school behaviour expectations. I would argue that the interventions that were employed had a positive effect on all of the children's self-esteem, and in particular helped with the self-regulation and self-esteem of the focus children and aided in preparing them for full-time school in Foundation Stage 2.

Are the findings applicable to the existing setting and influential in ongoing implementation and if so will interventions improve social and emotional skills?

The findings in the review of literature and the investigation into nurture rooms were applicable to the existing setting; the research was actioned in situ and progression and improvement of the personal social and emotional worth of the children in question was evident. The research could have gone further in pursuing this area of the curriculum but needed to be realistic in that the pedagogical requirements for the other areas of development also had to be delivered and monitored in order to teach these children effectively and prepare them for full-time school.

My own practice has been greatly influenced by the research, and circle times to develop social and emotional skills are now planned into teaching schedules for all children. I am also aware of interventions that may help children with a need in this area and am able to share this knowledge with colleagues. The endorsement of progressive educational theorists of child-centred learning have influenced how I teach, in that rather than plan every stage of the day, a rough working outline is now prepared that is adaptable to the children's interests, circle time discussions or events during the day. Through personal observation, I can see that the children are more engaged and excited by this incidental learning than a more prescriptive sit-down-and-do approach. If a child has missed out on the stages of learning that allow their brains to develop and realise their self-worth, then it is essential that what they say and think are seen as important.

The research did show improvement and progression in the social skills of the focus children. This was demonstrated in the progression in the Early Years Foundation Stage Profile (see Figures 9.1 and 9.2) and the pre- and post-intervention Boxall profiles. It was apparent that although the focus children did see progression, they were still exhibiting social and emotional behaviours that were below ARE, demonstrating that there is no quick fix for these children and that the repair and development of social and emotional skills is a long, ongoing process; each child is as complex as the experiences they are exposed to. Despite the limited timeframe of the research, some positive results were evident and illustrated that interventions and circle time of a nurturing nature could begin to build self-esteem and help to further the social and emotional development of children in early years education.

References

Allen, G. (2011) *Early Intervention: The Next Steps*. London. The Cabinet Office.

Attwood, T. (1998) *Asperger's Syndrome: A Guide for Parents and Professionals*. London: Jessica Kingsley Publishers.

Bishop, S. (2008) *Running a Nurture Group*. London: Sage.

Dowling, M. (2014) *Young Children's Personal, Social and Emotional Development* (4th ed.). Sage: London.

Early Education/Department for Education (2012) *Development Matters in the Early Years Foundation Stage (EYFS)*. London. Accessed on 11/6/2018 at: www.foundationyears.org.uk/files/2012/03/Development-Matters-FINAL-PRINT-AMENDED.pdf

Education Scotland (2008) *Developing Successful Learners in Nurturing Schools: The Impact of Nurture Groups in Primary Schools*. Accessed on 12/7/18 at: http://dera.ioe.ac.uk/218/7/ingps_Redacted.pdf

Malchiodi, C.A. and Crenshaw, D.A. (eds) (2014) *Creative Arts and Play Therapy for Attachment Problems*. London: Guildford Press.

Ofsted (2011) *Supporting Children with Challenging Behaviour through a Nurture Group Approach*. Manchester: Ofsted. Accessed on 12/7/18 at: www.ofsted.gov.uk/publications/100230

Radesky, J.S., Schumacher, S. and Zuckerman, B. (2015) 'Mobile and Interactive Media Use by Young Children: The Good, the Bad, and the Unknown.' *Paediatrics 135*, 1.

Roffey, S. (2006) *Circle Time for Emotional Literacy*. London: Paul Chapman Publishing.

Sylva, K., Melhuish, E., Sammons, P., Siraj-Blatchford, I., Taggart, B. and Elliot, K. (2003) *The Effective Provision of Pre-School Education (EPPE) Project: Findings from the Pre-school*. London: University of London.

The Nurture Group (2015) *Nurture Groups: What Are They? What Are Their Outcomes? Why Are They Needed? How Do They Work?* London: The Nurture Group Network. Accessed on 11/6/2018 at www.nurturegroups.org/sites/default/files/ngn_-_nurture_groups-2015.pdf

Vygotsky, L. (1978) *Mind in Society: The Development of Higher Physiological Processes*. Cambridge, MA: Harvard University Press.

Wilson, K. and Ryan, V. (2005) *Play Therapy: A Non-Directive Approach for Children and Adolescents*. Oxford: Elsevier.

CHAPTER 10

The Quest to Determine a Child's Understanding Through the Written Feedback Process

WITH EMPHASIS ON THOSE CHILDREN ASSESSED AS VULNERABLE

Sarah Howe and Helen Thornalley

*Senior Lecturer in Primary Education,
Bishop Grosseteste University;
Course Lead Physical Education and Dance,
Bishop Grosseteste University*

Chapter overview

This chapter is devoted to written feedback and considers its purpose and value as a means to support and improve children's learning. Throughout this narrative, 'feedback' and 'marking' are interchangeable terms. The term 'practitioner' denotes a range of professionals within the learning environment. This includes teachers, trainee teachers, teacher assistants and leadership teams.

We define 'marking' as 'the act of responding to, checking, correcting and providing a grade/mark for a child's written work'. Ultimately, this activity should determine progress made against intended learning objectives and positively impact on learning. We untangle current debate and research surrounding written feedback as a formative tool for both children and teachers. If practitioners provide feedback without strong pedagogic values and principles, this process can cause harm to the child's learning development and confidence, and potential waste of the practitioner's valuable resource of time. Crucially, this will hinder children's progress and induce confusion and anxiety, and, for learners with low self-esteem, present barriers to learning. Thus, marking becomes counter-intuitive to the desired learning outcomes. Consequently, these children become 'vulnerable' or 'disadvantaged', especially if processes mismatch skills and levels of cognitive development.

This chapter intends to induce reflection, justification and debate, particularly around children who can become more vulnerable and disadvantaged through the process of assessment. Following key discussion points, 'Pauses for Reflection' encourage discussion and examination in settings. In order to best experience this dialogue, we suggest you reflect on the 'Form' and 'Function' of feedback in your settings, through the positionality of both learner and teacher. Inevitably, these reflective discourses should take into account the value and efficiency of marking and feedback policy and procedures.

Who really carries the weight?

In this chapter, we define vulnerable children as those easily at risk of being emotionally, or mentally, hurt or influenced by written feedback processes.

By the end of this chapter, you should be able to: discuss some of the issues that are debated and concerns surrounding written feedback (marking); reflect upon aspects of your teaching practice (this includes whether you consider your feedback strategies to be 'manageable', 'meaningful' and 'motivational'); understand ways in which written feedback systems can be detrimental to learners and learning; and appreciate why this subject needs to be debated further in your settings.

The elephant in the room: some perspectives on written feedback

The term 'marking' is emotive for many, depending on the lens through which they view this activity and their particular stance on 'how', 'why' and 'if' written feedback can empower learners. As per the metaphorical idiom 'the elephant in the room', there is currently concern about how marking is undertaken in some settings. Everyone is aware of the risk associated with this topic, yet many choose to ignore current debate due to the challenges associated with complex narratives and uncertainties surrounding feedback.

The continuum of truths surrounding feedback for both learners and teachers, as well as researchers, who all seek to ascertain its value and position in learning and teaching appears to be growing. The current debate and divergences of opinion surrounding the notion of marking as a valuable form of formative feedback is recognised by many as unclear (Elliott *et al.*, 2016; Gardner, 2012). Hence, these discourses of debate and challenge sit not only within policy and literature divisions, but also, and possibly more poignantly, within school communities. Our narratives and reflections from our own working environments, which include learners, teachers and teacher educators, have led to the formulation of the following three working discourses.

- Key stakeholders tell us marking and learning must be interchangeable and synonymous with pedagogic quality.

- Teacher assessment (marking) is an essential professional skill tantamount to a requirement.

- Marking is a fundamental tool for all teachers. Comments or marks against a learning objective inform progress and act as a barometer for reporting on learning and teaching.

Putting these perspectives into context

Interest in this subject had surged following the publication of findings in *A Marked Improvement? A Review of the Evidence on Written Marking* (Elliott *et al.*, 2016). The key purpose of this review was to 'find evidence that would inform teachers' decision-making about marking' (p. 4). This then fuelled the debate on the quality of marking and provided many practitioners with a platform to internalise the rationale for processes used. Our recent school experience suggests that policy making and pedagogical and strategic activity in many settings are showing impact from this review's findings. In the government's attempt to improve educational learning outcomes, studies on feedback tend to demonstrate high impact on learning (Education Endowment Foundation (EEF), 2017), and somewhat justify the recognition of the elephant in the room as being a positive figure.

Consequently, the rationale behind marking feedback has substance, when accelerating progress, and continues to hold a large space within the cabinets of education (Department for Education (DfE), 2015; EEF, 2017; James, 2011; Ofsted, 2017a). Nevertheless, there is arguably still limited robust evidence and research on how formative assessment, including *written* feedback, can have measurable impact on learning (Elliott *et al.*, 2016; Florez and Sammons, 2013). This void in knowledge and understanding has led to a continuing examination around teacher behaviour and workload and the call to challenge emerging marking fads (Independent Teacher Workload Review Group, 2016). This includes some high-intensity and burdensome fads such as 'three stars and a wish' and 'purple polish'. A list of written feedback strategies and approaches used in primary schools is located in the Appendix.

A crucial question is whether teachers, teacher educators, teaching assistants and leaders are pausing for long enough to consider the value of marking from a child's perspective. What is the children's view on marking and its value on their learning? Are responses positive? What do children get from 'three Fs', these being the 'Form', 'Function' and 'Fun' in marking?

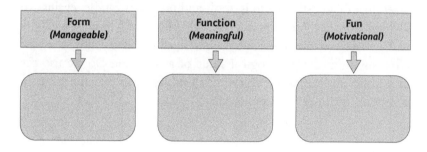

There appears to be the constant challenge of divorcing what the individual learner requires in terms of positive, constructive feedback, from both internal and external accountabilities (Florez and Sammons, 2013). This is when adherence to personal values and beliefs is paramount. This includes a child-centred approach to learning. Consequently, there would seem to be emerging tensions and power struggles when the notion of assessment is challenged. This is influenced by 'prevailing beliefs and theories in education' (Berry and Adamson, 2011, p. 3). Paradoxically, this could be construed as an 'intrinsically unethical activity' if assessment practice is dictated by external demands such as testing and Ofsted criteria and recommendation (Dubiel, 2016, p. 79). This poses several additional moral dilemmas. By conforming to the perceived boundaries found within assessment criteria, are we exposing children's vulnerability, and, unconsciously and unethically, forgetting the true needs of each child? Crucially, the core purpose and methodology of written feedback (form, function and fun), especially the impact on the child, are central to classroom practice.

Formative assessment: how does written feedback (marking) inform the learner and teacher?

Assessment is no longer viewed as a separate entity to teaching and is considered a key feature of a well-structured learning environment. Practitioners need to understand not just assessment processes, but also core purposes. The need to use formative assessment to secure progress and provide regular feedback, including accurate marking, is an expectation of the Teachers' Standards, crucially Teacher Standard 6 (DfE, 2011). Assessment draws parallels with research given that diagnostic methods, tools and processes can be 'evaluative, investigative, interpretative and critical' (Berry and Adamson, 2011, p. 4). Therefore, the multi-dimensional qualities Berry and Adamson offer highlight the pedagogical value of assessment. Do we use this diagnostic tool kit when assessing? This leads to two fundamental questions for the learner and teacher:

Increasingly, authors and researchers acknowledge that formative assessment is an essential feature of effective teaching and learning pedagogy, and its implementation can drive learning forwards (Coe *et al.*, 2014). If used well, written feedback becomes the connective fluid within learning and teaching and can become a purposeful bond as practitioners complete a six-phase reflective process to 'stop', 'pause', 'assess', 'reflect', 'intervene' and 'check' at different points in the lesson.

Assessment is an ongoing activity that should naturally happen throughout the school day. It becomes the lubrication between learning events, providing movement and progression in learning.

Research implications

In order to comprehend formative principles, activity and functions of assessment, the significance of innovative research that has informed contemporary provision is pivotal, particularly that of Black and Wiliam – *Inside the Black Box* – (1998), Hattie and Timperley (2007) and the EEF.[1] Data on the positive effect sizes of 0.4–0.7 (Black and Wiliam, 1998) represents the 'typically developing pupil', as well as those with Special Educational Needs. All of these indicators have become a catalyst for further inquiry by researchers and policy makers. Interestingly, effect sizes are slightly higher for children with Special Educational Needs and Disabilities (Fuchs and Fuchs, 1986). In the 'Visible Learning' discourse acknowledged by Hattie and Yates (2014), together with what is known about learning, formative assessment/ feedback is a top strategy in raising achievement. Although Hattie and Yates also caution that this can be misleading, as the 'variability of the effectiveness of feedback is huge' (p. 66). Alongside this, the evidence synthesis produced by the Sutton Trust EEF *Teaching and Learning Toolkit* (Education Endowment Foundation, 2017) suggests that high-quality feedback can lead to eight months' improvement in one year. Thus, the debate brings forward the saliency of truth that, when assessment is effective, it promotes progress in all learners.

Practitioners need to remind themselves, and recognise, that marking is one of many forms of feedback and these encouraging effect sizes embrace all forms of feedback. Caution is needed, depending on the age and stage of the children, especially in the early years – a key stage where marking could be considered futile. As Wiliam (2011) suggests, 'much of the feedback that students get has little or no effect on their learning and some kinds of feedback are actually counterproductive' (p. 107). Clarke (2014) further supports this claim, suggesting that 'most marking has little impact on pupil progress' (p. 145). Some educationalists express concern that, nearly 20 years after the publishing of *Inside the Black Box* (Black and Wiliam, 1998), assessment is still misunderstood, possibly due to an overemphasis on summative assessment and some perceived demands for expedient data (Berry, 2011; Dubiel, 2016; Faragher, 2014; Harlen, 2012). This suggests that knowing where the children are and *not* how they got there could be the motivation of some governments, including that of

---

1   www.educationendowmentfoundation.org.uk

the UK. In addition to this, some practitioners may simply not have the time, energy or inclination to question their practice due to other workload challenges.

Formative assessment should not be seen as the 'sugar the pill' in evidence-driven and testing cultures (Stobart, 2012, p. 239). This is not a replacement for the key principles but, instead, complements the tools and knowledge that practitioners have at their disposal. If undertaken with a level of mastery that is underpinned by the social notion of learning together, formative assessment is the construction, not reproduction, of knowledge and should not be solely used for testing against adult-defined tasks, for example, the end-of-key-stage Statutory Assessment Tests (SATs).

Perhaps this misconception by some of the role of formative assessment has resulted in this type of assessment not being part of pedagogy but, instead, becoming mini-summative assessments. A controversial view, reinforced by additional international research findings, indicates that some teachers can understand the benefits of formative assessment yet do not fully implement such pedagogy, resulting in assessment being 'outcome-orientated' (Antoniou and James, 2014, p. 154). Hence, in reality, based on our current experience, it appears that some practitioners consider SATs, coupled with the Ofsted inspection framework, to impact upon accountability and assessment methodology. During school visits and observations, including dialogue with head teachers, there appears to some truth in our understanding.

Therefore, the 'Form', 'Function' and 'Fun' that is created within formative written assessment is disturbingly misunderstood. Hattie and Yates (2014) suggest feedback has the potential to empower learning, with the caveat that it enables the learner to 'move forwards, to plot, plan, adjust, re-think, and thus exercise self-regulation in realistic and balanced ways' (p. 66). So, in order to address, with any credibility, 'how', 'why' and 'if' written feedback is purposeful, it is crucial that a clear definition of formative assessment is articulated.

The key characteristics of formative assessment
Formative assessment should:

- be developmental
- be responsive

- stimulate further learning and teaching

- appraise, deepen and sustain knowledge and understanding, and should inevitably empower and affect subsequent behaviours and thinking.

If not, the process is futile. Ideally, assessment strategies involve the holistic development of the learner and teacher together in engaging activities, during real time, as a means of determining understanding, thinking and progress. If these directions of travel lead us towards both holistic and collaborative moments of learning, this will result in cementing together clear 'Form', 'Function' and even 'Fun' within formative marking activity.

REFLECTIONS

- Consider which characteristics of formative assessment reflect your setting's philosophy, pedagogy and practice.

- Is your pedagogy and understanding replicated accurately in policies, practice and procedures?

- How do you know this?

- Work as a team to produce your own working definition of formative assessment.

Additionally, some consider formative assessment to be a 'gap minder' metaphor (Roskos and Neuman, 2012, p. 535). Its role is to identify and address the gap between where learners are and where they could be, which, in turn, can influence the structure of a lesson, anticipating misunderstandings and any associated feedback. The skills used by practitioners, once the gap has been identified, are crucial, especially for the most vulnerable learners who may be harmed by unfit processes. Weed et al. (2015) in their work on why individuals avoid taking up the challenge of activities, identify that some see, feel and become uncomfortable with their own abilities. If the learners see the attainment gap as too big, too hard or too unattainable, progress is limited and motivation diminished.

Our observations, supported by research, indicate that the most effective teachers anticipate barriers and misconceptions and check for learner understanding (Coe *et al.*, 2014). This practitioner's knowledge and understanding of 'great' teaching may soften any perceived challenges and hook the children back into learning. This is particularly so for those who feel vulnerable when assessment is being used as an indicator of their knowledge and understanding. In addition, engineering a learning environment that facilitates active and energetic learning is crucial. Learners are challenged by but may not feel confident in the supportive assessment process. Feedback should provide logical connections and prompt active information processing. If this is not the case, gaps in learning remain. This could be viewed as particularly important for the subjects of English and mathematics within the primary curriculum (DfE, 2013). Unless feedback is motivational and meaningful, this can switch off the learner.

The term 'formative' can be misused unless its content is instructional, reactive and modifies learning (the same conviction applies to marking). Hence, the term 'responsive' formative assessment, adorned by Dubiel (2016, p. 96) to describe ongoing pedagogical behaviour, has substantial relevance. This is assessment at its best. It has 'Form' and 'Function' and the 'elephant in the room' is embraced.

To conclude, feedback varies in form, dependent upon the overarching learning objective and learning methodologies. These could include questioning, probing designated reflective periods, mini-plenaries and oral, coded and written comments. Our recent observations reveal that these strategies can occur at different stages in the learning and teaching journey, including the beginning, to facilitate teaching and learning. Sometimes, practitioners cannot plan for these and must, instead, rely on real-time observations, comments and judgements.

What is effective written feedback and how do we know this?

Hargreaves (2011) astutely drew upon a teacher's comment that feedback is the 'breakfast of champions' (p. 125); marking can motivate and empower the learner, promoting 'assessment literacy' (Clarke, 2014). This then creates the 'Fun' within the learning process. If practitioners value and understand the value of formative assessment processes, then comprehending the core educational value of marking and the degrees of measurable impact and teacher behaviour is a key to this enquiry. Prominent research (Elliott *et al.*, 2016), alongside disentangling Ofsted myths, such as those linked to written feedback frequency, type and volume (Ofsted, 2017b) suggests that marking should not be a laborious routine that creates some temporary noise, congratulating learners with isolated magnanimous statements such as 'good' (Stern and Backhouse, 2011). Instead, it should be a personal dialogue, which both the learner and teacher 'hear', 'understand' and 'use' to inform next steps and reach a goal. The power of assessment should be reflected through the lens of target setting, where measurability and reporting are agreed during this learning partnership.

The following eight considerations are now explored. Combined, these can impact positively on the written feedback process, especially for those assessed as vulnerable.

Consideration 1: a 'meaningful' and 'manageable' mantra

As previously discussed, since the publication in 2016 of *A Marked Improvement? A Review of the Evidence on Written Marking* (Elliott *et al.*), there appears to be a surge in the quest for marking to be 'meaningful' and 'manageable' in many school policies and procedures. This is fuelled through our previous discourses and the need to chip into the real value of marking, particularly if the process, when absorbed by the learner, hinders motivation. Furthermore, some of our recent observations of practice reaffirm that effective, timely oral feedback helps to embed and swiftly accelerate learning, making this 'meaningful'. Our observations reveal dialogic teaching techniques, such as oral feedback, to be the most popular strategy used. Although, where appropriate, written feedback comments and marks can strengthen the impact. Although this strategy supports the notion of 'manageability', it also coincides with some of the recommendations in *The Teacher Workload Challenge: Analysis of Teacher Consultation Responses* (DfE, 2015) and the need to find strategies to reflect on time-consuming marking, especially if this has little educational impact and is considered 'unnecessary' and 'unproductive' (p. 15). It should be about getting a balance between 'quality and speed' (Elliott *et al.*, 2016, p. 22) and eliminating unnecessary workload around marking (Independent Teacher Workload Review Group, 2016).

Consideration 2: real-time oral feedback

As far as possible, teachers should provide real-time oral feedback to support an individual child's learning within this early years age group. This philosophy is particularly applicable for vulnerable children. Assessment should be spontaneous and quick and mechanistically operate in the moment (Schön, 1987). This requires higher-order questioning, scaffolding and probing questions. Thus, through the effective addressing of misconceptions and prompting deeper thinking, written comments have a range of purposes. Caution as to the timing and choice of wording/terms is needed.

Recent dialogue with several teachers indicates that fewer teachers are taking marking home, instead providing more live oral and written feedback at whole-class, group and individual level. This strategy does require critical and analytical skills in questioning, which relates to the way that taxonomies, such as Bloom's (1994), can be used to the full.

REFLECTIONS

- Reflect upon your skills to question children.

- How do you engineer meaningful discussions with the children?

- Have you formed the question in a way that is understood by the learner?

- For example, is this dichotomous (seeking a two-part answer such as yes/no), multi-dimensional or open?

- Which questioning method supports each learner best?

- When is the question worth asking? Could it confuse or interrupt learning?

- Do you model giving and receiving feedback?

Consideration 3: a high-quality time to reflect upon learning

It is fundamental that practitioners provide a dedicated, improvement reflection time for children, during which they are able to consider and address any written feedback (Elliott *et al.*, 2016).

This may include replying to comments and questions, addressing targets and marking symbols/codes or correcting errors and elaborating on ideas. If children are not learning from their errors, progress is limited – this is particularly important to the vulnerable learner who needs to understand and draw meaning from comments.

Learners need time to complete the previously stated six-phase reflective process. They need to 'stop', 'pause', 'assess', 'reflect', 'intervene' and 'check' at different points in their learning. The reshaping and learning from feedback is a powerful aspect of any feedback loop, which Lewin (1951), Schön (1987), McNiff (2013) and McNiff and Whitehead (2010) have been coining for several years. The practice of highlighting generic successful features and any misconceptions at the beginning of subsequent lessons appears to be a successful strategy. Some teachers make notes when marking, and, where relevant, examples of marked work are showcased to aid or reinforce deeper understanding.

According to Elliott *et al.* (2016), just over 20 per cent of primary school teachers provide few or no opportunities for children to respond to their marking comments (p. 15). Crucially, practitioners need to understand and teach children how to learn through assessment activity. In summary, we learn more from children's actions and conversations than we do by studying these learning and assessment theories in isolation.

Consideration 4: secure subject and curriculum knowledge

When marking against objectives, the quality of teacher assessment requires accuracy, consistency and trustworthiness. Our personal observations reveal that standards set for judging the same work may vary. It is fundamental that teachers formalise and moderate judgements to avoid ambiguity. Marking is only effective if the practitioner has a secure subject and curriculum knowledge and understands the learning objectives (LO) and success criteria (SC), together with that year group's age-related expectations. Practitioners need to make the learning explicit, and our observations suggest teachers appear to provide the best feedback in subject/curriculum areas in which they are most confident. Again, this highlights the importance of developing a secure, and scholarly, approach to subject/curriculum knowledge in order to decipher any misunderstanding as outlined in Teacher Standard 3 (DfE, 2011). This, in turn, establishes a growth mind-set mentality in both the learner and teacher (Dweck, 2017).

This point is further strengthened by Crichton and McDaid's (2016) associated small-scale exploratory study. They found 'almost all teachers, apart from those qualifying in the last 5 years said they were not very confident in writing LIs (learning intentions) and SC' (p. 198). Additionally, our observations suggest that without good subject/curriculum knowledge, marking could result in a list of personal likes and dislikes. These might disengage the learner and teacher, causing vulnerability to all. We must be mindful that in our quest for marking to link to the LOs, marking is also multi-dimensional in purpose and process. It can link to observed learning characteristics as promoted within the Early Years Foundation Stage (DfE, 2017), for example, perseverance and self-belief and, additionally, 'learning power' (Claxton, 2002; Claxton, Chambers and Powell, 2011). By this we mean how we help learners become better at, and more confident with, the process of learning, thus, ultimately, promoting lifelong learning techniques.

REFLECTIONS

- Do you have secure subject/curriculum knowledge?

- Are quality learning outcomes rooted by secure knowledge of relevant subject/curriculum understanding?

- Within written feedback methods, how are learning objectives acknowledged?

- Where relevant, is there consistency in marking, particularly within classes and across year groups?

- Do you highlight examples of learning that reflect the intended learning outcomes, for example, within a designated learning wall, which may encompass exemplary learning (and any misconceptions)?

Consideration 5: the nature of comments

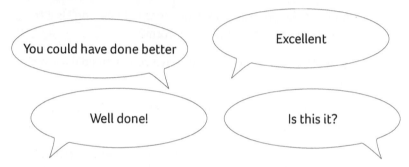

Do evaluative comments, such as these illustrated above, have a positive impact on learning? Do they inform the learner and provide useful feedback?

It appears that written formative comments are the most common marking process as well as the most varied 'in terms of quality and impact' (Butt, 2010, p. 75). Practitioners need to consider whether their comments are constructive and ask – what does this comment offer the learner? Our experience indicates that these comments vary; they can:

- evaluate or rate against the learning objective

- praise or criticise the learning and learner

- motivate learning

- challenge the learner's knowledge, skills and understanding.

Language used during feedback might unwittingly lower self-esteem and muddle the learner, especially if it is about how they have done in relation to the expected learning objective. This can cause harm and stress by being too personal, extensive and meaningless. Practitioners must ensure that they take into account learning barriers and learner effort in order to ensure progress. As suggested by Frederickson and Cline (2015), it is essential that those practitioners providing the feedback also accept part responsibility for some failures, and, through our own observations, this is possibly why the 'elephant in the room' is present in many classrooms.

REFLECTIONS

- What is the purpose of your comment?

- How does the process help to deconstruct learning? Is it to evaluate, investigate, praise or inform?

- If you use the comment 'good', have you justified why this is so?

- Do the learners understand your comments? Is the learner able to read the comments?

- Are these comments overloading learners with too much information?

- Could it be more useful to focus on just one achievable improvement at a time?

Consideration 6: mini goals for learning

Written formative comments that comprise future targets and goals directly related to LO/SC are considered effective practice (Clarke, 2014; Wiliam, 2011). Our recent observations reveal that a large proportion of practitioners write targets, wishes or goals in some manner for most, or all, of the work marked. This is advocated in Teacher Standard 2, where practitioners are asked to guide children to reflect on their own progress and next steps in learning (DfE, 2011). This is perceived as high-quality professional practice.

Recent research suggests that learners' perception and use of targets are varied, often having greater success when they are involved in the setting or writing of these (Clarke, 2014; Elliott et al., 2016). Surprisingly, Crichton and McDaid's research findings (2016) suggest

LO/SC to be 'rarely discussed' thoroughly in class. Our observations pinpoint two potential pedagogic constraints, these being teacher competency and teacher workload. Ideally, if these two features are improved, learning would be at its optimum level for both the learner and teacher.

Some schools are starting to use rubrics. These can increase self-regulation, especially where children have been involved in the writing of success criteria and marking against this (Wiliam, 2011). However, a degree of caution is needed. Rubrics have been thought, by some, to cause stress and high-performance avoidance (Panadero and Romero, 2014). Dweck (2017) suggests that some children can avoid challenge and develop a fixed mind-set. Additionally, feedback from teachers, supported by research, suggests that higher achievers tend to underestimate, and lower achievers to overestimate, their achievement when marking against these success criteria (Panadero and Romero, 2014).

Consequently, in the practitioner's effort to follow a meandering pathway of learning and formative assessment, next steps are often navigated by the learners' unique learning pathways, which may not naturally mirror each other. The power of the teacher is to understand attainment and how close this is to the perceived learning outcomes. We recognise that some learning is not formulaic, and the skill of the teacher is to understand each child's learning potential and challenge them accordingly. This is particularly so for the vulnerable and talented learners, for which objectives/next steps are limitative. This, in turn, could cap future learning.

REFLECTIONS

- Does your written marking provide valuable next steps for the learners and practitioners?

- Do you provide opportunities for the learners to set personal targets?

- Is there actionable information to support the learner to meet this goal/target?

- Is there ever a need to caution the writing of targets to avoid the capping of learning?

Research by Hattie and Yates (2014) suggests that children want to know how to improve their work, however much depends on their growth mind-set and how they interpret targets. Our dialogue with children reveals that most could readily relay targets, especially in Key Stage 2. For marking to be meaningful, particularly for the vulnerable child, it has to be centred on a few clear and concise future learning objectives, especially short-term ones. Thus, the power of learning has to be through mini goal setting.

Consideration 7: valuing and promoting metacognition

Metacognitive strategies, together with evidence of a growth mind-set culture, form the foundation of formative assessment (Clarke, 2014; Dweck, 2017). Interesting, and pertinent to this discourse, are concerns that teachers need to be mindful of generating learner dependency upon teachers. Formative assessment gives considerable emphasis on the learner taking control of their learning through constructivist teaching, which facilitates 'self-analysing, self-referencing, self-evaluating and self-correcting' (Berry and Adamson, 2011, p. 8). These could be considered as learned lifelong skills and attributes. Practitioners should strive for learners to be our partners in the learning process. The greater the involvement of the learner in the marking process, the more awareness the learner has of their individual competencies and capabilities, and, inevitably, this will impact positively on learning. To do this, there needs to be appropriate challenge and a level of analytical discourse. Acquisition is dependent upon the learner acquiring the skills and knowledge to make this a purposeful activity. We recognise that this requires modelling by the adult and peers, together with effective lesson structure and time.

Self-assessment and self-regulation appear to have growing prominence in schools. Practice includes self-marking, traffic lighting and other self-evaluation strategies. Capable children appear to find self-assessment easier (Butt, 2010). Effects can be variable for several reasons, including the learner's competency to judge their work and be able to critically make correlations with the teacher and/or peers (Brown and Harris, 2014). Equally, in reality, we need to be mindful that some learners may not want to appear egotistical, especially in Key Stage 2.

Peer feedback, if undertaken correctly, can impact positively on learning outcomes. Central to this process is the need for an established culture for giving and receiving honest and concise feedback. If undertaken in an atmosphere of challenge and awareness, it can be a strategy for 'learning to learn' (Smith, Lovett and Turner, 2009). This reflects a socio-constructivist view of education, following Vygotsky's (1978) Zone of Proximal Development, in which one learner is guided by a more skilled and knowledgeable learner. Additionally, Wiliam (2011, pp. 133–134) has identified four possible factors that signify success. These are:

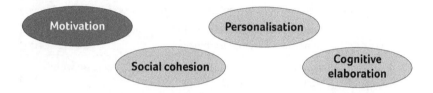

REFLECTIONS

– Are you valuing, and planning for, self- and peer-marking learning events that teach children how to learn? Have you modelled this process to your children?

– Have you and your colleagues created a culture that embraces honesty and supportive criticism?

Consideration 8: questions to consider when reflecting on assessment/marking and feedback policy and practice

These reflective questions are intended to ignite reflection, justification and debate, and should be considered in conjunction with the school's marking and feedback policy.

Policy and procedures	Does the policy reflect the core purpose of written formative feedback to improve learning? (Marking should impact positively on learning and behaviours and bridge gaps between current attainment and ultimate goals)
	Whom is the marking for?
	Is the learner at the heart of this policy making?
	When was the marking (and feedback) policy last reviewed by all stakeholders in order to ensure it reflected practice and the values of the school?
	Are policy and procedures steered by outcomes, not processes?
Pedagogy and methodology	Does the policy incorporate key research and policy recommendations and accurately reflect working practice?
	How can we show and explain that policy and practice are impacting on future learning?
Intended learning	How do teachers' views of feedback policy compare with those of the learners?
	Is the marking linked to the intended learning objective?
	Does written feedback inform the learner, clearly, of their performance against this?
	Do learning intentions demonstrate good teacher subject knowledge and understanding of age-related expectations?
Targets	How is the marking informing the learner of future targets and goals in order to drive learning forwards?
	Are these sufficiently challenging, demonstrating high expectations from the teacher?
	Are targets clear, concise and easy to interpret?
Written comments	Are written comments purposeful and related to the learning?
	Do comments take into account the learning needs and development stage of the learner?
	Are comments succinct and relevant to learner behaviour?
	Do comments bridge the gap between current performance and the ultimate goal?
	Are written comments used for learners lacking the reading and comprehension skills required to interpret them?
	Is oral feedback given, where it is deemed more appropriate?
Motivation and self-regulation	Is the written marking motivating the learner to improve? How are staff creating an ethos that embraces mistakes as a vital form of learning?
	Is there evidence of self-regulation and a growth mind-set?

Approach	Are the approaches used appropriate in meeting specific marking aims?
	Which forms of marking do teachers and learners find useful and why?
	Does the marking method applied take account of the stages of child development and the way children learn?
	Is careful consideration given to the needs of vulnerable children and any ethical considerations?
Planning for marking	How is marking feedback built into planning systems?
	Is this carefully considered as part of the lesson and learning process?
	Is it central to classroom practice?
Collaborative marking	Do we recognise the value of collaborative and shared marking? Are there opportunities for peer marking?
	Are the learners taught to peer-assess and is marking assessed alongside that of the teachers?
	Is marking modelled by both the teacher and learner?
Checks and balances	Could we sometimes be diverting learners from their own responsibly to check and self-assess? For example, through providing such immediate and thorough marking, could there be an over-reliance on feedback?
Consistency	Are all stakeholders committed to our marking feedback policy, pedagogy and methodology?
	Where appropriate, is a consistent approach evident in working practice and across the school?
Learner understanding	Do learners understand the purpose of the marking and how the quality of their achievement is judged?
	Do learners critique examples of marked work in order to promote and support the marking process?
Planning and timing	How immediate is the written feedback?
	Is marking planned for and, where appropriate, completed during real time within the lesson and alongside the learner?
	Is adequate time provided for learners to respond to their marking?
Teacher workload	Is our policy manageable and mindful of teacher workload?
	Are aspects of the policy making unreasonable demands on staff, and learners, and taking them away from other tasks, which may have a greater impact on educational outcomes?
	Are we encouraging professional autonomy and allowing staff to decide if, and in what form, written marking is appropriate?

Conclusion: who really carries the weight?

This chapter acknowledges that children who are highly motivated by the learning are *usually* learning. Marking must help to motivate the learner, as well as promote curiosity and move learning forwards. Highly motivated teachers possess high learning expectations for all – constantly striving, through research and enquiry, to improve written feedback impact. They engender this behaviour through meaningful methodologies that have a combination of 'Form', 'Function' and 'Fun' when assessing. Written feedback relies on an individual teacher's interpretation of some complex principles of formative assessment, alongside a strong understanding of each child's unique needs and learning goals. Again, manageability and workload are put under the spotlight. However, with the continued practitioner expectations to embrace learning preferences, motivations and barriers to learning, practitioners should consider the philosophical educational practices, especially those deemed child-centred.

When this feedback is thoughtfully considered, it can positively influence learning and classroom behaviour, thus raising attainment and lifelong learning skills for all learners. When it goes wrong, primarily due to a mismatch in procedures to a child, it can result in panic, anxiety and confusion, often resulting in disengagement. This is especially so for those children who deviate considerably from age-related expectations. For some children, written feedback is not appropriate and, instead, timely and sensitive oral feedback is highly effective. This activity depends on the school's ability to provide quality thinking time for these interactions. Misinterpretations of formative assessment can seemingly be the root of ineffective written feedback and any misconceptions, weighing down and exposing vulnerability and disadvantage.

Masses of feedback does not automatically denote learning, especially with vulnerable children. This brings us back to the debate on 'quality, not quantity'. The pressures put on schools, perceived to be a result of the current Ofsted regime, together with some high-stake testing and unrealistic marking policies, calls for practitioners to 'stop', reflect on their understanding of the Teachers' Standards and apply intelligent checks and balances. If practice is having little impact on learning and results in children having poor motivation (no 'Fun'), low self-esteem and the experience of failure, it is time to reflect again on teaching, feedback systems and practitioner values. The ultimate purpose of any feedback must be to improve outcomes and bridge gaps in learning, not widen these.

There is no single ingredient or recipe for successful practice. However, if written feedback is considered a formative process, there is every chance progress will be evident, especially if practitioners establish an environment of trust, self-belief and growth mind-set. Hence, the need to construe the concept of formative assessment, and some confusion as policies are refined and rewritten, has been one of the most challenging and significant features of this chapter.

Without categorically understanding the function of marking, practitioners can be demotivated, especially if they are unable to articulate the similarities and differences between marking procedures and practices. Mantra for marking as 'meaningful (Function), manageable (Form) and motivating (Fun)' activity is central to ensuring that written feedback is effective and purposeful. We propose that stakeholders are also 'mindful' of how children learn. For some, timely oral feedback – a reflective discussion – will be more valuable. As we critique feedback systems, especially written, what is the impact on mental health and wellbeing? Where is the weight distributed?

It would appear that the best teachers do not mark *more*, they mark *better*. Marking should not overwhelm the child or be an isolated event – it is a regular activity with the practitioner strategically overtly and covertly eavesdropping on the learner's learning. Marking can be timed to coincide with the beginning, middle and end of learning cycles to have maximum impact. The learners should understand that marking and feedback are learning – these go hand in hand. Yet, how do they get to this point? Our school experience tells us that this is through understanding and embracing practice and mistakes as part of the learning process and not just mundanely following practices.

Finally, we should not sacrifice teaching pedagogy during the marking process, especially when adhering to some seemingly ineffective and dysfunctional marking policies, which can generate vulnerability. To conclude, if written feedback is recognised as a formative assessment tool, we would maintain that, in nearly all cases, by the time children's work is loaded into the boot of a teacher's car for marking, it is too late...depersonalised. The moment to feed back and 'drive learning forwards' has gone. This, in turn, can result in a cycle of failure for some of our most vulnerable children in schools. Unfit strategies will desensitise the learner through meaningless, demotivating and unmanageable processes. The cost of this is profound with regard to time, energy and the moment.

The 'elephant in the room' again becomes a metaphorical idiom for the significance and risk that some written feedback policies and procedures have on children's learning and wellbeing. The concern is present (as obvious as an elephant in a room) but can be avoided as a topic for vigorous debate and challenge in some settings. Consequently, the elephant will fix itself in the corner, laughing at our ignorance as we pursue futile systems that are both tiring and purposeless.

So, who carries the weight? The learner or the practitioner? We believe that the answer is wholly dependent on the individual's learning and teaching pedagogy.

Strengthening marking practice and pedagogy for all learners: key future considerations for written feedback and formative assessment in primary schools

In the writing of this chapter, there appears to be a call to reclaim and justify marking as a valuable part of formative assessment. We have identified the following future considerations with regard to vulnerable learners. These thoughts should alleviate some tensions highlighted in this chapter and ensure that marking is meaningful, thus impacting positively on learning and teaching behaviour and educational outcomes, whilst being mindful of our responsibility to effectively justify and manage teacher workload.

- To design a formative marking tool kit for practitioners that impacts positively on learning, particularly for our most vulnerable learners. This should be founded on robust research that is evidenced in working practice. This guide should: inspire; avoid contradiction and misconceptions; comprise some solutions and case studies; and address key questions posed by relevant stakeholders.

- To ensure that relevant policies are regularly reviewed with staff and understood by all stakeholders. Crucially, this should be mirrored in practice and take into consideration the voice of the learner in order to bridge any gaps between markers' and receivers' perception of marking and prevent vulnerability.

- To ensure that marking feedback intrinsically links to LO/SC targets and has a higher prominence during the planning stage. Where relevant, planning should signify the markers for identified cohorts, account for opportunities for oral/written feedback at different points in the lesson and include designated response periods. The ultimate aim is that most formative marking would occur within the lesson period. Consequently, practitioners should embrace actions from written comments, visual learning experiences and oral articulation of thought. Feedback must take place in lesson time, as this is when all the parties in learning are present (learner, peers, teaching assistant, teacher). For it is within this collective moment that feedback has greatest impact.

- With reference to credible research, to address a misconception by some, including parents/carers, that 'more marking equates to better marking' and good teaching. To consider alternative strategies, other than written feedback, that may be more appropriate to some learners' developmental needs and learning styles. This may include making full use of digital technologies within a safe and supportive learning environment.

References

Antoniou, P. and James, M. (2014) 'Exploring formative assessment in primary school classrooms: Developing a framework of actions and strategies.' *Educational Assessment Evaluation and Accountability 26*, 153–176.

Berry, R. (2011) 'Assessment Reforms Around the World.' In R. Berry and B. Adamson (eds) *Assessment Reform in Education: Policy and Practice.* London: Springer.

Berry. R. and Adamson, B. (eds) (2011) *Assessment Reform in Education: Policy and Practice.* London: Springer.

Black, P. and Wiliam, D. (1998) *Inside the Black Box: Raising Standards through Classroom Assessment.* London: School of Education.

Bloom, B.S. (1994) 'Reflections on the Development and Use of the Taxonomy'. In K.J. Rehage, L.W. Anderson and L.A Sosniak *Bloom's Taxonomy: A Forty-Year Retrospective. Yearbook of the National Society for the Study of Education 93.* Chicago: National Society for the Study of Education.

Brown, G. and Harris, L. (2014) 'The future of self-assessment in classroom practice: Reframing self-assessment as a core competency.' *Frontline Learning Research 2*, 1.

Butt, G. (2010) *Making Assessment Matter.* London: Continuum International Publishing Group.

Clarke, S. (2014) *Outstanding Formative Assessment: Culture and Practice.* London: Hodder Education.

Claxton, G. (2002) *Building Learning Power: Helping Young People Become Better Learners.* Bristol: TLO Limited.

Claxton, G., Chambers, M. and Powell. G. (2011) *The Learning Powered School: Pioneering 21st Century Education.* Bristol: TLO Limited.

Coe, R., Aloisi, C., Higgins, S. and Elliot Major, L. (2014) 'What Makes Great Teaching? Review of the Underpinning Research.' Accessed on 13/6/2018 at www.suttontrust.com/wp-content/uploads/2014/10/What-makes-great-teaching-FINAL-4.11.14.pdf

Crichton, H. and McDaid, A. (2016) 'Learning intentions and success criteria: Learners' and teachers' views.' *The Curriculum Journal 27*, 2, 190–203.

Department for Education (2011) *Teachers' Standards: Guidance for school leaders, school staff and governing bodies.* Accessed on 13/6/2018 at www.gov.uk/government/publications/teachers-standards

Department for Education (2013) *The National Curriculum in England. Key Stages 1 and 2 Framework Document.* Accessed on 13/6/2018 at www.gov.uk/government/uploads/system/uploads/attachment_data/file/425601/PRIMARY_national_curriculum.pdf

Department for Education (2015) *Workload Challenge: Analysis of Teacher Consultation Responses. Research Report.* Selby: CooperGibson Research.

Department for Education (2017) *Statutory Framework for the Early Years Foundation Stage: Setting the Standards for Learning, Development and Care for Children from Birth to Five.* Accessed on 13/6/2018 at www.gov.uk/government/uploads/system/uploads/attachment_data/file/596629/EYFS_STATUTORY_FRAMEWORK_2017.pdf

Dubiel, J. (2016) *Effective Assessment in the Early Years Foundation Stage* (2nd ed.). London: Sage.

Dweck, C. (2017) *Mindset: Changing the Way You Think to Fulfil Your Potential.* London: Robinson.

Education Endowment Foundation (2017) *Feedback.* Accessed on 13/6/2018 at https://educationendowmentfoundation.org.uk/resources/teaching-learning-toolkit

Elliott, V., Baird, J., Hopfenbeck, T., Ingram, J. *et al.* (2016) *A Marked Improvement? A Review of the Evidence on Written Marking.* London: EEF and University of Oxford. Accessed on 13/6/2018 at https://educationendowmentfoundation.org.uk/public/files/Publications/EEF_Marking_Review_April_2016.pdf

Faragher, S. (2014) *Understanding Assessment in Primary Education.* London: Sage.

Florez, M. and Sammons, P. (2013) *Assessment for Learning: Effects and Impact.* Reading: CfBT.

Frederickson, N. and Cline, T. (2015) *Special Educational Needs, Inclusion and Diversity.* Maidenhead: Open University Press/McGraw-Hill Education.

Fuchs, L. and Fuchs, D. (1986) 'Effects of systematic formative evaluation: A meta-analysis.' *Exceptional Children 53*, 199–208.

Gardner, J. (2012) 'Quality Assessment Practice.' In J. Gardner (ed.) *Assessment for Learning.* London: Sage.

Hargreaves, E. (2011) 'Teachers' Feedback to Pupils: "Like So Many Bottles Thrown Out to Sea"?' In R. Berry and B. Adamson (eds) *Assessment Reform in Education: Policy and Practice.* London: Springer.

Harlen, W. (2012) 'The Role of Assessment in Developing Motivation for Learning.' In J. Gardner (ed.) *Assessment for Learning.* London: Sage.

Hattie, J. and Timperley, H. (2007) 'The power of feedback.' *Review of Educational Research 77*, 1, 81–112.

Hattie, J. and Yates, G. (2014) *Visible Learning and the Science of How We Learn.* Abingdon: Routledge.

Independent Teacher Workload Review Group (2016) *Eliminating Unnecessary Workload Around Marking.* Accessed on 7/6/2018 at www.gov.uk/government/uploads/system/uploads/attachment_data/file/511256/Eliminating-unnecessary-workload-around-marking.pdf

James, M. (2011) 'Assessment for Learning: Research and Policy in the (Dis) United Kingdom.' In R. Berry and B. Adamson (eds) *Assessment Reform in Education: Policy and Practice.* London: Springer.

Lewin, K. (1951) *Field Theory in Social Science; Selected Theoretical Papers.* New York: Harper and Row.

McNiff, J. (2013) *Action Research. Principles and Practices* (3rd ed.). London: Routledge.

McNiff, J. and Whitehead, J. (2010) *You and Your Research Project.* London: Routledge.

Ofsted (2017a) *School Inspection Handbook: Handbook for Inspecting Schools in England Under Section 5 of the Education Act 2005/October 2015.* Accessed on 13/6/2018 at www.gov.uk/government/uploads/system/uploads/attachment_data/file/654625/School_inspection_handbook_section_5.pdf

Ofsted (2017b) *Guidance: Ofsted Inspections: Myths.* Accessed on 13/6/2018 at www.gov.uk/government/publications/school-inspection-handbook-from-september-2015/ofsted-inspections-mythbusting

Panadero, E. and Romero, M. (2014) 'To rubric or not to rubric? The effects of self-assessment on self-regulation, performance and self-efficacy.' *Assessment in Education: Principles, Policy and Practice 21*, 2, 133–148.

Roskos, K. and Neuman, S. (2012) 'Formative assessment – simply, no additives.' *The Reading Teacher 65*, 8, 534–538.

Schön, D.A. (1987) *Educating the Reflective Practitioner: Toward a New Design for Teaching and Learning in the Professions.* San Francisco, CA: Jossey-Bass.

Smith, A., Lovett, M. and Turner, J. (2009) *Learning to Learn in Practice. The L2 Approach.* Carmarthen: Crown House Publishing Ltd.

Stern, J. and Backhouse, A. (2011) 'Dialogic Feedback for Children and Teachers: Evaluating the "spirit of assessment".' *International Journal of Children's Spirituality, 16*, 4, 331–346.

Stobart, G. (2012) 'Validity in Formative Assessment.' In J. Gardner (ed.) *Assessment for Learning.* London: Sage.

Vygotsky, L. (1978) *Mind in Society: Development of Higher Psychological Processes.* Cambridge, MA: Harvard University Press.

Weed, M., Coren, E., Fiore, J., Welland, I. *et al.* (2015) 'The Olympic Games and raising sport participation: A systematic review of evidence and an interrogation of policy for a demonstration effect.' *European Sport Management Quarterly 15*, 2, 195–226.

Wiliam, D. (2011) *Embedded Formative Assessment.* Bloomington, IN: Solution Tree Press.

| CHAPTER 11 |

Exploring Approaches to Learning Outdoors

Beverley Keen

*Course Leader, BA (Hons) Early Childhood Education
leading to QTS (two-year route)
Leeds Beckett University*

Chapter overview

This chapter considers the potential of the outdoor environment to support vulnerable children both within the context of the outdoor learning environment attached to an Early Years Foundation Stage (EYFS) and through approaches such as Forest Schools. As discussed in Chapter 1, the Children's Commissioner for England (Cordis Bright, 2017, p. 5) has identified 32 groups of vulnerable children and nine domains of the different types of vulnerability. The report identifies the importance of developing the children's self-esteem, self-efficacy and sense of belonging through maximising their sense of agency and control within a positive and supportive environment. The outdoor learning environment attached to early years classrooms and approaches to using the outdoors such as Forest Schools have the potential to provide effective, positive experiences to develop these attributes within young children.

Using the outdoor learning area attached to an EYFS-setting classroom to empower vulnerable children

CASE STUDY 1: NOAH
Using the outdoor learning environment
to empower a vulnerable child

Using the Children's Commissioner's (Cordis Bright, 2017) definition, Noah is a vulnerable child due to having a range of Special Educational Needs. He is dyslexic, has a developmental coordination delay (dyspraxia) and a speech delay of about 18 months. Noah had seen the outdoors as something he interacts with since he was a small child, exploring the garden and nearby field and woodland with his parents enthusiastically.

The ethos of using the outdoor EYFS unit he attended as a reception child enabled him to build on and develop his strengths and interests, empowering him as a learner. The outdoor area was a large space, including a tarmac area, grass, woodland, a huge sandpit with water pump, a fire pit and a slope and contained a large selection of loose-part resources. The school provided the children with waterproofs and the area was accessed throughout the year, whatever the weather. The setting's approach was Reggio Emilia inspired, with the learning being child initiated and project based (with the projects led by the children), which was reflected both indoors and outside.

As a creative child, Noah's imagination was fired by the outdoor area. With his speech delay, he often had difficulties in expressing his ideas; however, the adults took time to listen and talk to him, allowed him to persevere and at times articulated his ideas to the other children. Because Noah was so imaginative, his ideas were then often the ones that the group decided to follow and the ones that the other children found exciting. One project inspired by Noah's ideas led to the children creating a large-scale pirate boat, complete with a plank to walk off. Playing on a large scale and using loose parts to create his designs were particularly important to Noah, as he found fine motor skill activities difficult. Noah enjoyed exploring the space at different heights, particularly climbing trees and hanging off branches. Although the setting did have rules, these were designed for the children to navigate themselves, such as markers on the trees to delineate how high they could climb, which enabled him to take some responsibility for his own safety, rather than having an adult continually enforcing the limits.

When interviewed for this case study, his mum commented, 'It took a great weight off my mind, knowing he wasn't being forced into a way of being that was against his developmental needs at that point.'

For children within the EYFS in England, there is a clear statement within the Statutory Framework about the requirement for the children to have an opportunity for outdoor play every day.

> Providers must provide access to an outdoor play area or, if that is not possible, ensure that outdoor activities are planned and taken on a daily basis (unless circumstances make this inappropriate, for example unsafe weather conditions). Providers must follow their legal responsibilities under the Equality Act 2010 (for example, the provisions on reasonable adjustments). (DfE, 2017, p. 30)

As Case Study 1 shows, for many vulnerable children the outdoors creates an environment where their strengths and interests are valued and developed. Bilton (2010, p. 1) discusses how the outdoors is a 'complete learning environment which caters for all children's needs – cognitive, linguistic, emotional and physical'. However, it is important to recognise that just physically being outside doesn't automatically provide an empowering experience for children or create positive outcomes in all areas of learning (Merewether, 2015; Waite and Pratt 2017; Waters and Maynard, 2010). It is important to carefully consider the nature of the physical space, how the space is resourced, how the children interact with each other and the adults, and how these variables interact together to create the most effective, stimulating and positive learning experience for all children.

Wherever possible, the physical outdoor environment should include a range of different surfaces, including hard surfaces (such as tarmac), grassy areas, muddy areas, bushes, shrubs and woodland to encourage different types of play and incorporating opportunities for different types of movement. The outdoor learning environment should provide children with the space to move on a larger scale, at different speeds and in different ways. For some children within EYFS settings and classrooms, this daily access to the outdoors might be their only opportunity to play outside. This may be due to living in housing without access to a garden such as flats or terraced housing, living in areas where there isn't access to community outside play areas within walking distance, financial constraints making it difficult to afford travel to areas to play outside and parental concerns about the risks of playing outdoors. Moving on a larger scale enables the children to develop gross motor skills such as running, jumping, changing direction and speed, balancing and their awareness of their body within space, whilst having the opportunity to use wheeled toys develops skills such as coordination. For children like Noah, this area provides them with the space to experiment with their movements in an informal play context, rather than in a structured PE session where there is the pressure to produce a prescribed movement at a specific time. The outdoor environment should ideally also enable the children to investigate moving at height, for example having trees identified as suitable for climbing. In many outdoor areas, a fixed climbing frame has been provided to encourage the children to climb. However, as Herrington *et al.* (n.d.) found in their research, for the majority of the time this type of fixed equipment is unoccupied by the children because they are unable to adapt and shape it to fit their play. It is important therefore to consider how you can provide flexible climbing opportunities, which can be adapted and developed by the children, such as the use of planks, crates and low-level moveable frames.

The outdoors can offer the children a different way of being (White, 2011) and opportunities for playing, investigating, creating and engaging in imaginative ways. For a child such as Noah, this enables them to explore their creativity in a range of different ways without the restrictions that the indoor space can impose. Haywood-Bird (2017, p. 1023) suggests that the outdoor space can provide children with a 'wide open canvas of creation' where children have the agency to choose who to play with, where to play, what to play and choose or create their own props. Whilst Whitehurst (2009, cited in Bilton, 2010) suggests pretend play is the most dominant form of play outside, Merewether (2015, p. 105) recognises that being outside alone is not enough; the area needs to be resourced with a wide range of loose-part natural materials, which stimulate the children's imagination to create 'whatever they want it to be' (Broadhead and

Burt, 2012, p. 48). If the outdoor environment includes a woodland area, there may already be a wide range of natural loose-part materials available, such as sticks and branches, stones, leaves, trees and shrubs to provide possible starting points for structures. If the location of this area doesn't naturally provide this environment, it is important to bring in and provide a range of natural resources within the setting, as well as providing a wide range of manmade loose-part resources, such as materials, pipes, tubes and crates. The inclusion of loose-part resources is important because of the flexibility and opportunities it provides the children to use their imaginations to follow their own interests, to explore prior experiences and to have the agency to create their own play worlds. This provides some vulnerable children with a safe space to explore emotions and prior experiences through their dramatic play. Broadhead and Burt (2012, p. 48) suggests these types of opportunities are important in enabling the children to develop their personal identities and their resilience.

The outdoor learning environment can be a valuable resource for developing children's language and communication skills. ICAN (2017) suggests that 10 per cent of children have a speech, language and communication need, and up to 50 per cent of children in some areas of deprivation have delayed language. King and Saxton (2010) identity the importance of practitioners creating shared contexts for talk with children. This context for this talk outside might be: the ever-changing nature of the outdoor environment, due to the weather or seasonal changes; an episode of child-initiated play in the mud kitchen; the mini-beasts the child has found underneath a stone. King and Saxton (2010) discuss the importance of allowing children to introduce their own topics of discussion, which might then be taken up by the adult on behalf of the child to share with the wider group. This was important for Noah, whose expressive language was delayed, because it enabled his imaginative ideas to be shared and become the focus for outdoor child-initiated projects for a wider group of children, which in turn developed his self-esteem. However, it is important to consider what kind of language is being stimulated in different outdoor environments. Research by Waters and Maynard (2010, p. 482) found that the shared context of visits to a country park where the children were able to participate in a period of child-initiated play stimulated rich language interactions and episodes of shared sustained thinking. These interactions were often focused on the children's expressions of wonder, awe and excitement about aspects of the environment they were playing within. Richardson and Murray (2017) compared the impact on children's utterances between the indoor setting, outdoor attached to the setting and a Forest School setting in the natural environment. They found that there was richer lexical diversity, with higher levels of verb, exclamation and adjective usage, for the majority of the children in the natural environment. However, within this small-scale study, there was no significant difference between the language use in the indoor or outdoor areas at the school, which they felt was due to, 'Schools providing outdoor classrooms which practitioners plan children's learning creating a safe but sterile environment' (p. 457). Perhaps, then, a key role for the teacher is to consider how they can ensure that their outdoor environments are exciting, stimulating and 'non-sterile' spaces of communication.

Using the Forest-School approach to support vulnerable children

The next part of this chapter explores the Forest-School approach to using the outdoors and the potential this approach has to support the needs of vulnerable children. The Forest-School approach is focused on providing children with the opportunity for independent learning, based on following their own interests in a woodland environment. The role of the practitioner is to scaffold, facilitate, support, encourage and develop these interests, rather than to lead learning based on specific learning outcomes. This approach has been adopted by many early years settings and schools working with children aged three to eight years, although the approach and the potential benefits are relevant to children of all ages.

The Forest-School approach to learning is a cultural construct; although it originated in Denmark and the overall ethos will be very similar, the way that the approach is interpreted and implemented in different countries will vary. Within England, the Forest School National Governing Body (NGB) created a definition of the ethos for Forest Schools in February 2012, which was based on the definition in Murray and O'Brien's 2005 evaluation. This states, 'Forest School is an inspirational process, that offers ALL learners regular opportunities to achieve, develop confidence and self-esteem, through hands on learning experiences in a local woodland or natural environment with trees'

(Forest School Association, 2017). To achieve this holistic ethos, the NGB has created a series of key principles that underpin the English approach. Within these principles, the emphasis on Forest School as a process, a sequence of regular visits to a woodland area, rather than a one-off event, is an important aspect of the approach.

The positive impact of Forest School on the participant's self-esteem is often highlighted as a key benefit of Forest School. For vulnerable children, developing and maintaining their self-esteem is a key factor in their successful progress. Archimedes (2013, p. 52) identified that self-esteem is related to a number of factors including security (ease and trust), selfhood (ease and trust), affiliation (belonging and connectedness), mission (purpose and responsibility) and competence (feeling of success). The Forest-School approach provides opportunities to develop these feelings due to the relationship between the environment, the nature of the activities and the nature of the interactions with the participants. Baumeister *et al.* (2003, cited in Maynard, 2007, p. 324) suggest that, 'high self-esteem is likely to be the result of experiencing success'. The Forest-School approach encourages success for the participants because of the open-ended nature of the resources and because they can set themselves problems to solve (such as making a rope swing or a den) independently, with a group of peers or with the support of an adult if they choose to ask for it, but, importantly, they are able to take responsibility for making their own decisions. Swarbrick, Eastwood and Tutton (2004, p. 143) suggest, 'this type of practical activity with real relevance to children and adults generates high quality interactions, genuine open questioning, leading to a rich and diverse curriculum'. It is important for children to feel real success during the sessions, which might be when they have challenged themselves to take an 'acceptable risk' such as climbing a tree for the first time or using a knot they have learnt to fasten part of their den together. Knight (2013, p. 45) suggests, 'Confidence and self-esteem are improved as skills develop and no one fails. This has a snowball type effect, because as confidence grows so the child finds more exciting things to do, which they will succeed at, thus improving their sense of self-esteem even more.' This is important for the role of the Forest-School practitioners because they have to provide enough potential structure and encouragement to build in the gradual development of challenging activities, whilst providing the children with enough freedom to follow their own interests.

Forest-School practitioners can support this process by developing a very good understanding of their children through extended observations of their play and through having time to have one-to-one in-depth conversations based on what is currently capturing the child's imagination and attention. This enables them to build on the child's interests and fascinations, and to provide opportunities for the children to 'be who they want to be', building on their strengths. In order to facilitate this, Forest-School practitioners must give the children extended time and space to follow their interests. Also, there must be open-ended outcomes, which are decided by the child rather than judged against pre-set outcomes. The Forest-School ethos supports this approach, where the process, not the product, is the most important. This is very important for vulnerable children because it empowers them with a sense of agency within the process and control over their own learning. A study by Haywood-Bird (2017, p. 1022), which focused on children aged two-and-half through to five years within a forest setting in the US, found, 'these children feel completely empowered by the environment to facilitate their own choices of where to be in the forest, how to play in the forest, and who to play with in the forest'.

As the Children's Commissioner report (Cordis Bright, 2017, p. 8) identified, developing vulnerable children's resilience is seen as an important factor in supporting their needs. Resilience is defined as, 'positive adaptation despite the presence of risk, which may include poverty, parental bereavement, parental mental illness, and/or abuse' (Gotman and Schoon, cited in Natural England, 2016, p. 89). The aim of Forest School is not to create these types of experiences, but to provide the conditions that foster the mind-set that enables people to deal with these experiences positively. In Forest-School sessions, the children often demonstrate resilience when carrying out activities, for example a child may have several attempts to climb a tree before they work out the most effective route to get to the height they are aiming for, or they may have several attempts at building parts of a den before succeeding.

Forest School provides children with an open-ended, natural environment, where they are able to engage in adventurous and, at times, 'risky' play. Tovey (2010, p. 82) suggests that, 'Risk taking allows children to vary the familiar, to try out new ideas or ways of doing things and to be innovative in their thinking.' This might be trying out different ways of moving down the muddy bank, experimenting with different ways of reaching a particular branch on a tree or experimenting with how to balance a particularly large piece of dead wood to create a den. The structure of Forest-School sessions, the repeated visits to the same area of woodland and the opportunity to explore and become familiar with this environment all develop this sense of security for the children. Knight (2013) believes this sense of security will then promote the confidence for the children to risk take within their play, whilst Sandsette (2007) and Stephenson (2003) (cited in Tovey, 2010, p. 80) both found that, 'children typically increase the challenge or level of risk as they repeat their play,' which repeated visits to the Forest-School setting promotes.

The view of the child within Forest School promotes appropriate risk taking, because the children are viewed as competent learners in their own right, who are encouraged to set and solve their own challenges creatively. This is important for many vulnerable children, who might be viewed as needing additional support or interventions within other learning contexts. Little and Wyver (2010, cited in Broadhead and Burt, 2012, p. 108) found in their research that children aged four and five were capable of making risk judgements during their play and demonstrated a, 'good level of understanding of the relationship between their capabilities, their behaviour and potential injury outcomes'. Similarly, Dowling (2005) felt that young children can understand the need to be safe, providing the example of a child checking that a plank is secure to walk across, and suggests that, 'most children will take the responsibility very seriously and grow in self-confidence as they make decisions' (p. 155) and suggests that they take responsibility for each other's safety. I observed an example of this in a Forest-School session, where a group of children had made a rope swing off a raised platform, including propping a crate against the front: when the smallest child was about to go, she put her foot on the crate to test if it was stable to stand on, turned around and discussed it with two other children and they decided it wasn't, so, as a group, they then tied the crate on so that it wouldn't slip – all without adult guidance. In Forest School it is not that the practitioner allows children to take 'unsafe risk', which would have a strong chance of causing significant harm; rather it is the Forest-School practitioner's role to develop the children's confidence and understanding in taking 'acceptable risk'.

The woodland environment proves an exciting context for these experiences. Broadhead and Burt (2012, pp. 99–100) suggest that children take 'calculated risk' in 'settings where adults are seeking to create optimum opportunities for independent action and interaction; settings where adult leadership of play is minimised and where children's capacities to make choices that correspond with their interests and experiences are maximised'. This statement seems to closely match the ethos of Forest School. For a vulnerable child such as Noah, this ethos provides him with the opportunity to develop his strengths in an empowering environment, which provides him with a sense of agency and control over his own learning. Taking risk is an important aspect of child development and a life skill. Dweck (2000, cited in Tovey, 2010) believed that characteristics of effective learners include having a willingness to try new things, take risks and have an 'I can do' attitude. Tovey (2010, p. 83) also suggests that risk taking in play 'appears to be positively associated with emotional wellbeing, resilience and mental health'.

Whilst the Forest-School approach provides children with extended periods for child-initiated play and opportunities to develop resilience through risk taking, it also contains rhythms and routines. McArdle, Harrison and Harrison's (2013) research considered the impact on promoting resilience of a ten-week Forest-School type experience, where children from challenging backgrounds aged four and five years attended a nature/nurture programme one afternoon each week. Many of these vulnerable children had attachment issues or a lack of nurturing relationships within their home backgrounds. Such children often find change and transitions difficult and stressful. Their research identified that routines, such as songs to welcome the children by name into the woodland and to signpost transitions such as snack time and home time, were important elements in creating, 'familiar landmarks that were consistent and reliable' (p. 247) and created a sense of security for the children. Similarly, games such as '1, 2, 3 where are you?' and routines such as having a time for reflection at the end of each session and returning to a familiar area of the woods each week enable the children to develop a sense of ease and confidence about attending Forest-School sessions.

The opportunity to engage in 'appropriate risk taking' also promotes positive behaviour. A central aspect of this is the development of the child's self-perception – if the child has a low self-perception, which often occurs within vulnerable children, this will often affect their behaviour negatively, which in turn reinforces their low self-image. Gill (2007) and Lindon (2003) (cited in Knight, 2013, p. 39) suggest that, 'where children feel their environment offers insufficient challenge, they will seek challenges etc. elsewhere', often demonstrating unsocial behaviour.

CASE STUDY 2: TOM
The impact of attending Forest-School sessions with a vulnerable Key Stage 1 (KS1) child

Tom is a six-year-old child who attended a series of afternoon Forest-School sessions as part of a group of children from a Year 2 class. He could be categorised as a child with family-related vulnerabilities, due to his parents using substances problematically, which had a negative impact on his behaviour in school. In discussion with him, he said that he was always in trouble and sent to stand outside the head teacher's door at school. Initially, he found having the freedom to choose his own activities and the different role of the adults challenging and showed a range of anti-social behaviour, upsetting other children in the group to gain attention from the adults. He seemed to want adult attention and was happy if this was gained through poor behaviour. Rather than 'being in trouble' and being removed from the session, the strategies of encouraging him to find a different group of children to play with or to becoming involved in a different type of play were used. This had the initial result of him flitting from group to group until he became interested in joining a game where he needed a bow. His initial response was to demand someone made one for him, however, with some sensitive interactions, he was supported in using the tools to make one for himself, which he was very proud of. This prompted an interest in tying knots, which he quickly picked up. As the sessions progressed, he became more settled at Forest School and frequently returned to knot tying because he was successful, and it was something he started to teach other children when they wanted a bow/sword.

The Forest-School ethos places the emphasis on the child being able to test their own boundaries and challenge themselves positively, rather than challenging 'authority'. The relationship between the Forest-School practitioner and the participant is important, because the practitioner sets the boundaries that this risk taking can take place within, for example, playing '1, 2 3 where are you?' at the start of a session to set the physical boundaries of play and setting other limits such as the height of trees (or which trees) the children can climb. Within these boundaries, the child should then feel that they can experiment with their activities, with encouragement when necessary from the adult, rather than feel the adult is constantly restricting their interests. This requires the practitioner to stand back and observe, rather than constantly intervene in, the activities. However, the role of the adult as an observer and facilitator, rather than constant rule setter and teacher, can also be challenging for some children (see Case Study 2). Within Forest School, the practitioner needs to respond sensitively to this child, so that they are able to break this negative cycle. Forest School provides a unique environment for a child to develop their strengths. Through careful observation of the child, the Forest-School practitioner can identify the child's interests and their dominant schemas and interject at the point before a child's behaviour is becoming unacceptable, steering them towards an activity that will actively engage their attention positively and at which they will potentially be successful, developing their self-esteem. A sensitive interaction at an early point can defuse the situation and enables the child to re-engage positively in the session.

The transition to KS1 and beyond

CASE STUDY 3: NOAH
The impact of the transition to more formal learning in KS1 on a vulnerable child

As a Year 1 child, Noah's experiences of using the outdoor environment were reduced to the playground at break and lunchtimes or as a reward in golden time. The emphasis became focused on indoor, sitting-at-a-table learning where fine motor skills, phonics, mathematics and literacy were prioritised. All the things that had been his strengths and were visible in reception because of the opportunities for working creatively in the outdoors on a bigger scale – where he could demonstrate mastery and which he felt were visible to his teachers and his friends – disappeared. This resulted in Noah's self-confidence and self-belief reducing, and by Christmas he no longer wanted to go to school, a place he had enthusiastically attended six months before.

In many ways, the nature of the transition from the EYFS to KS1 has the potential to empower or disempower vulnerable children. In the EYFS, the statutory requirement for access to the outdoor environment on a daily basis (DfE, 2017), and the strong emphasis within the characteristics of learning on child-led learning, problem-solving, creativity and resilience, can provide these children with effective, supportive learning environments for their specific needs. However, within the space of the six-week summer holidays, for many children there is a transition into KS1 where the emphasis is often on adult-planned, objective-led lessons, where the ability to sit still and represent your understanding on paper is foregrounded. As Case Study 3 identifies, for a vulnerable child such as Noah, there is a danger that, although their strengths are still present, the learning environment means they are no longer visible to and valued by the teacher or their peers, which impacts on the child's self-belief and sense of self-worth.

The implementation of the Forest-School sessions into KS1 and KS2 can provide the continuation of outdoor learning experiences for these children. However, as this is often only for one half day each week, it is important that the outdoor learning environment is incorporated more widely into the KS1 and KS2 curriculum. Many KS1 settings have access to an outdoor area from the classroom. It is important that children still have the opportunity to be involved in child-initiated play as well as adult-focused lessons in this environment and that it is seen as an integral part of the learning process, rather than a reward for good work. The National Connections Demonstration Project 2012–16 (Natural England, 2016) worked with 125 schools in the south-west of England to develop the use of the outdoor learning environment, either in the school grounds or local area, across the curriculum. The research findings showed that over 90 per cent of the 40,434 children involved felt the experiences of learning outdoors in subjects such as

English and mathematics had a positive impact on their enjoyment of lessons, connection to nature, social skills, engagement with learning and health and wellbeing, and 85 per cent felt the experiences positively impacted on their behaviour. As the school participating was in areas of multiple deprivation, these positive findings suggest that we can still potentially create very positive learning environments for vulnerable children using the outdoors in KS1 upwards.

REFLECTIONS

- How could you create an enabling outdoor learning environment attached to your EYFS classroom that supports and empowers the vulnerable children within your setting?

- If you do not have access to Forest-School sessions, how could you recreate similar opportunities for loose-part and risky play within your own school grounds?

- How can you ensure that the importance of using the outdoor learning environment is maintained effectively once the child has made the transition into KS1?

References

Archimedes (2013) *Forest School Handouts*. Sheffield: Archimedes Trading.

Bilton, H. (2010) *Outdoor Learning in the Early Years: Management and Innovation*. London: David Fulton Publishers.

Broadhead, P. and Burt, A. (2012) *Understanding Young Children's Learning through Play: Building Playful Pedagogies*. London: Routledge.

Cordis Bright (2017) *Defining Child Vulnerability: Definitions, Frameworks and Groups*. London: Children's Commissioner for England.

Department for Education (2017) *Statutory Framework for the Early Years Foundation Stage: Setting the Standards for Learning, Development and Care for Children from Birth to Five*. London: Department for Education.

Dowling, M. (2005) *Young Children's Personal, Social and Emotional Development* (2nd ed.). London: Paul Chapman Publishing.

Forest School Association (2017) *Principles and Criteria for Good Practice*. Accessed on 18/6/2018 at www.forestschoolassociation.org/full-principles-and-criteria-for-good-practice

Haywood-Bird, E. (2017) 'Playing with power: An outdoor classroom exploration.' *Early Child Development and Care 187*, 5–6, 1015–1027.

Herrington, S., Lesmeister, C., Nicholls, J. and Stefiuk, K. (n.d.) *7Cs: An Informational Guide to Young Children's Outdoor Play Spaces.* Accessed on 18/6/2018 www.wstcoast.org/playspaces/outsidecriteria/7Cs.pdf

ICAN (2017) *ICAN.* Accessed on 18/6/2018 www.ican.org.uk

King, S. and Saxton, M. (2010) 'Opportunities for language development: Small group conversations in the nursery class.' *Educational and Child Psychology 27*, 4, 31–44.

Knight, S. (2013) *Forest School and Outdoor Learning in the Early Years* (2nd ed.). London: Sage.

Maynard, T. (2007) 'Forest Schools in Great Britain: An initial exploration.' *Contemporary Issues in Early Childhood 8*, 4, 320–331.

McArdle, K., Harrison, T. and Harrison, D. (2013) 'Does a nurturing approach that uses an outdoor play environment build resilience in children from a challenging background?' *Journal of Adventure Education and Outdoor Learning 13*, 3, 238–254.

Merewether, J. (2015) 'Young children's perspectives of outdoor learning spaces: What matters?' *Australasian Journal of Early Childhood 40*, 1, 99.

Murray, R. and O'Brien, L. (2005) *'Such enthusiasm – a joy to see': An evaluation of Forest School in England.* Forestry Commission and nef.

Natural England (2016) *Natural Connections Demonstration Project, 2012–2016: Final Report.* Worcester: Natural England.

Richardson, T. and Murray, J. (2017) 'Are young children's utterances affected by characteristics of their learning environments? A multiple case study.' *Early Child Development and Care 187*, 3–4, 457–468.

Swarbrick, N., Eastwood, G. and Tutton, K. (2004) 'Self-esteem and successful interaction as part of the forest school project.' *Support for Learning 19*, 3, 142–146.

Tovey, H. (2010) 'Playing on the Edge: Perceptions of Risk and Danger in Outdoor Play.' In P. Broadhead, J. Howard and E. Wood (eds) *Play and Learning in the Early Years.* London: Sage.

Waite, S. and Pratt, N. (2017) 'Theoretical Perspectives on Learning Outside the Classroom.' In S. Waite (ed.) *Children Learning Outside the Classroom from Birth to Eleven.* London: Sage

Waters, J. and Maynard, T. (2010) 'What's so interesting outside? A study of child-initiated interaction with teachers in the natural outdoor environment.' *European Early Childhood Education Research Journal 18*, 4, 473–483.

White, J. (2011) *Outdoor Provision in the Early Years.* London: Sage.

PART 4

A Positive Process

CHAPTER 12

Health and Wellbeing

Pat Beckley

Senior Lecturer for Research
Bishop Grosseteste University

Chapter overview

This chapter considers the prerequisites needed to secure children's health and wellbeing while they are in the early years and the implications this may have on their future outlook, educational progress and life chances. Specific aspects of development are noted, we well as their importance for inclusion in an early years framework of learning. Examples of difficulties arising from a lack of early inclusion of key factors that have a significant impact on wellbeing in later life will be described.

The UK Early Years Foundation Stage (EYFS) framework (DfE, 2017) seeks to provide children with quality and consistency, a secure foundation, partnership working and equality of opportunity. It states that it must ensure that, 'every child is included and supported'. It also states that:

> Personal, social and emotional development involves helping children to develop a positive sense of themselves, and others; to form positive relationships and develop respect for others; to develop social skills and learn how to manage feelings; to understand appropriate behaviour in groups; and to have confidence in their own abilities. (p.8)

Personal, social and emotional aspects and physical development are two of the three prime areas according to the EYFS framework (DfE, 2017). Language development (see Chapter 5) is the third prime area for children from birth to aged eight. This area can also significantly impact on a child's sense of wellbeing. The emphasis on these areas highlights their importance for children's development concerning health and wellbeing; they have major implications for a child's future outlook and possible life chances as they grow older.

REFLECTIONS

- What factors do you consider to be vital to promote health and wellbeing for young children?

- What strategies would you use for an individual child?

- What strategies could be used for larger numbers of young children in groups, settings or schools?

Health and wellbeing within the early years key themes

The prime and specific areas in the EYFS framework are underpinned through themes covering a unique child, positive relationships and enabling environment, which together enable learning and development to take place. They echo Bronfenbrenner's (1979) view of the child understanding the world around them through a widening awareness of it. According to *Development Matters in the Early Years Foundation Stage* (Early Education/DfE, 2012, p. 1):

> Children have a right, spelled out in the United Nations Convention on the Rights of the Child, to provision which enables them to develop their personalities, talents and abilities irrespective of ethnicity, culture or religion, home language, family background, learning difficulties, disabilities or gender.

Children need sufficient confidence to be able to initiate an activity in play and take a risk in their learning, engaging in new experiences. Resilience is required to maintain interest in a task and focus on a problem they have devised. A belief in their own ability is needed to enable them to regain focus after a disappointment of a challenge they have faced in their activities. A sense of wellbeing can be developed through a belief and self-understanding of the value of their work and how it is achieved.

Whatever a person's personality, whether they enjoy their own company or feel happiest surrounded by others, relationships play a vital role in securing wellbeing. This can follow Bronfenbrenner's outline (1979) demonstrating the need for secure attachments with those closest to them and developing into a wider network of relationships and social interactions (see Chapter 9). Young children may demonstrate different social relationships as they develop their knowledge and awareness of how to engage and react in different social circumstances. Initially, this may take the form of observing the world around them, which leads to parallel play, where they access activities alongside another child without actually interacting with them. Further development can lead to complex interactions involving small or larger groups, involving problem-solving tasks and assuming a range of roles within the group, depending on the child's preferred approach, such as a leadership role or organiser. Secure relationships with significant adults are essential to provide the foundations for young children to access available opportunities. They provide a model to demonstrate how the child can navigate complex situations around them, for example personal difficulties or social interactions, and either everyday occurrences such as shopping procedures or more challenging circumstances such as an illness.

The environment provided can influence the level of security felt by the child and how they can respond to opportunities and experiences within it.

REFLECTIONS

- What aspects would you consider should be included in discussions about young children's health and wellbeing?

- What factors in the environment do you consider essential for a child's health and wellbeing?

- How can a child's sense of wellbeing be enhanced in the environment?

It is essential that a young child is safe and secure in the environment (see Chapter 8). It must comply with the requirements for health and safety legislation and be suitable for the age and number of children. Procedures for emergencies or fire need to be considered and there must be appropriate fire detection and control equipment, such as fire blankets, and readily accessible exits. Once this safe environment is established, there are other factors that impact on the child. A welcoming atmosphere will encourage a child to enjoy the experience and take those first steps to independence. Adults preparing the environment influence the welcome given to each child, for example, through routines at the start of the session and the approach demonstrated towards the child and the adult with them. Other factors also matter, including the building the setting is in and whether it appears welcoming or, perhaps, austere. The room may seem very formal and alien to a child who has spent a large amount of their life so far in a living room at home. Furnishings and resources can add to the atmosphere and support a child's decision as to whether the environment is a suitable place or one to be feared. Even the adults' clothing in a setting can suggest what type of environment the setting is going to be, for example, formal or casual wear or a corporate brand of uniform.

Health and wellbeing within the prime areas of the EYFS

The EYFS framework provides key aspects of development that suggest ways to ensure health and wellbeing. These cover:

- personal, social and emotional development: making relationships, self-confidence and self-awareness and managing behaviour

- physical development: moving and handling, health and self-care

- communication and language: listening and attention, understanding and speaking.

Within the personal, social and emotional area, aspects of personal health and wellbeing need to address the child's developing ability to become independent and be confident to leave the attachment of significant others and happy with other known carers.

Personal factors

Bowlby (1951) claims that children need to form attachments with others, as this will help them to survive. A fear of strangers is also an important mechanism to help young children survive. However, this has implications for other adults who will need to gain the trust of young children in order for the child to feel safe. Bowlby argues that failure to secure a relationship with a significant parent at a very early stage in a child's life could result in difficulties in later life. The child exhibits behaviour, for example crying, to gain the attention of the parent or carer and seek reassurance. If this bond is broken, significantly for the first five years of the child's life, particularly in the first two-and-a-half years, then the child could exhibit 'maternal deprivation' with a failure to develop an attachment. This could have implications in later life. Mcleod (2007, p. 3) states that 'the long-term consequences of maternal deprivation could include: delinquency, reduced intelligence, increased aggression, depression and affectionless psychopathy.' McLeod explains that 'affectionless psychopathy is an inability to show affection or concern for others. Such individuals act on impulse with little regard for the consequences of their actions. For example, showing no guilt for anti-social behaviour' (2007, p. 3).

Robertson and Bowlby (1952) found three progressive stages of distress in short-term separation from a parent/carer. This comprised protest, despair and detachment. Protest included such aspects as the child crying, shouting or screaming as the parent leaves; in despair the child appears quiet but does not participate although coaxed; detachment happens when the child begins to participate in activities with others but rejects the parent or carer when they return.

Children respond to early signals from the parent or carer about their worth, such as whether they are loved, rejected or responded to angrily. This gives them a pattern of their estimation of their worth and adults' responses to it from an early age, which can be established as a lifelong pattern of internal cognition of self-worth and others' responses in interactions with them.

Rutter (1981) suggested that there were different levels of parent bonding, with a loss or deprivation to privation, where the quality of the interactions between parent and child were flawed. This could range from such aspects as lack of interaction, lack of stimulation or negative, aggressive communication.

When a child is secure in the knowledge and understanding that the environment is positive towards them, they will be able to take advantage of opportunities and develop their skills and abilities with the confidence to do so.

Social competence

Children learn, internalising their thoughts and ideas while building new concepts, through talking with other peers and adults. Those who are lacking the skills and ability to interact with their peers and adults are at a significant disadvantage concerning both their educational development and their social and emotional health and wellbeing. If a child is lonely or isolated at an early age, it can set a pattern of lack of interaction, which could be challenging to change in later life. There are many reasons why a child may be isolated, such as a home situation where there is little contact with others including children, undiagnosed hearing difficulties, limited contact outside the home or lack of interactions between family members. Children may not have experienced social ways of having discussions with others or routine greetings.

Emotional considerations

Bowlby's discussion of maternal deprivation and the effect that difficulties in security and bonding between a child and a significant parent or carer might have has been considered earlier in this section. Parental or carer impact can have a profound influence on a child's emotional security and ability to develop. Positive perspectives encourage brain stimulation and promote the best possible outcomes for children. Conversely, negative perspectives can determine outcomes, giving a child a lack of belief in the ability to succeed and dampening motivation. This can result in a failure to attempt an activity, with the child believing the outcome to be already determined. Emotional confidence can give children excitement in learning new experiences, exploring new resources and surroundings and knowing they will gain a positive, supportive response to their endeavours whether they achieve what was anticipated or not. They can become aware of their own feelings and emotions and know how to deal appropriately with them. Young children can also be empathetic to others, supporting those around them, as they are emotionally secure.

Physical development

The ability to access resources, communicate through writing and lead a healthy life through a well-balanced diet and appropriate movement and exercise all help children to become independent and enable them to participate in the wider community. The importance of literacy skills is identified in the specific area concerning literacy but, to be able to access writing, children will need to develop the ability to use tools, including those for writing, to acquire the necessary skills to produce written forms or other products using manipulative skills, for example with woodwork tools. Having the ability to explore surroundings also requires the skills needed to manipulate resources, such as the use of a mouse on a computer.

Healthy eating has become an issue for national discussion due to findings of the effects of a poor diet and access to frequent sugary drinks and the effect on teeth and general health. Health problems, such as diabetes and obesity, have been discussed in terms of poor diet and its impact on the workings of the human body and its healthy development. Young children can gain a knowledge of healthy eating and know about what they are eating. Physical exercise can promote healthy bodies, which in turn transmits signals through the system that improve the sense of emotional wellbeing.

Communication and language

The ability to communicate, along with the use and understanding of language, links, in health and wellbeing terms for young children, to the importance of being able to voice personal feelings, ideas and emotions and to understand others around them. It supports the ability to follow instructions and routines, respond to other children and adults, interact and become members of peer groups and share their experiences. A lack of skills in this area of the EYFS can have profound implications for later development, as discussed in greater detail in Chapter 5.

Specific areas of the EYFS and health and wellbeing

The specific areas of the EYFS – that is literacy, mathematics, understanding the world and expressive arts and design – also feature in the identification of ways to support vulnerable children. The specific areas, on a par in importance with the prime areas, form a basis to further develop a child's knowledge and understanding of the society they live in. It is evident that the areas enable children to access further literary understanding, become proficient in managing mathematical experiences such as shopping and provide insights into the wider world through learning about other cultures and communities, while enhancing creativity and the ability to give expression to emotions and ideas through expressive art and design. While individual young children may need further support to grasp aspects of an area of study, others may be empowered by an ability or specific skill in an area, which can impact on their self-esteem and confidence and all other areas of the EYFS framework.

CASE STUDY

Andrew was reluctant to come to an early years setting and, when he did arrive, he lacked confidence in participating in the activities available. His mother mentioned at the beginning of a session that she too had been very reluctant to go to school and had not enjoyed the experience. She demonstrated some reluctance to enter the early years indoor provision. The key worker noticed Andrew did enjoy using the woodwork table. This also gave him a subject to discuss with his peers and he seemed to forget his shyness when talking about his favourite subject. Andrew accessed the woodwork table whenever he could and showed a flair for the work, producing products that were praised by his peers. The adults discussed his progress. Some felt he was making such good progress he should continue with his love of woodwork, while others noted he was missing other activities and should be given equal access to all resources. It was decided to encourage his woodwork skills while providing experiences in other areas that drew on them, for example drawing or painting his designs and finished products or recording what was needed to make them. He grew in confidence and his holistic development flourished.

He continued his love of working with wood and later became a successful joiner.

Vulnerable children

There are a wide range of factors in a young child's early years that may cause them to be considered vulnerable. There may have been identification prior to the child entering a setting or some event may occur during the child's formative years, for example the death of a parent or economic pressures affecting a family. 'Vulnerable' does not simply cover those with Special Educational Needs and/or Disability but could include economic, social and health risks. A child born in the UK is fortunate to be able to access facilities that enable assessment at birth to determine at the earliest stage possible if there are underlying difficulties. It may not be possible for such an early diagnosis to identify all health issues but other health officials, such as health visitors, track babies' welfare to identify concerns that may arise in their development. The Two-Year check also provides a further tracking point to gain further support for a toddler's development if needed. It is useful in a setting to identify any possible challenges a child may face as they progress. According to the Department for Education and Department of Health guidance, *Special Educational Needs and Disability Code of Practice: 0 to 25 years* (2015, p. 79):

> Providers must have arrangements in place to support children with SEN or disabilities. These arrangements should include a clear approach to identifying and responding to SEN. The benefits of early identification are widely recognised – identifying need at the earliest point, and then making effective provision, improves long-term outcomes for children.

Special needs requirements may already have been identified but it is useful to informally keep track of children who may be assessed as borderline for extra support. Children develop at different rates, sometimes developing rapidly while at other times having a period of consolidation of new skills learned. The informal tracking therefore may not always appear to be necessary, but it could pick up a difficulty that could be significant.

Partnerships

The importance of key, significant adults on young children's health and wellbeing has already been highlighted in the chapter. It remains crucial to work in partnership with parents or carers as the child develops. It is important to liaise with parents or carers when children access an early years setting, to provide security and enable collaboration and support for the child. This can include initial assessments of a child's achievements and possible areas where they may need more focused support. The EYFS framework (Department for Education, 2017, p. 31) states, 'Maintained schools and maintained nursery schools must identify a member of staff to act as Special Needs Coordinator (SENCO) and other providers (in group provision) are expected to identify a SENCO.' Childminders are also encouraged to identify a person to act as SENCO, including those in a childminding agency network.

Identification of children with Special Educational Needs

The process of identification of a special need or disability may have begun, and parents, carers and practitioners can work together to support the child, devising an appropriate routine to ensure the child is accessing suitable personalised care and help. Early identification from those closest to the child is crucial. Home-based groups, such as Portage, can support development and care at home. Specialised support for parents and settings may also be available to provide care for the child and help adults to continue to deliver necessary procedures in the interim between their visits. There may have been access to the Education, Health and Care (EHC) plan process for more complex needs, which includes multiagency working to support the welfare of the child. These plans were disseminated in the Children and Families Act (2014) and include assessments and review processes of all children and young people from birth to 25 years. The EYFS framework can provide guidelines for activities and support the identification of attainment through the developmental process, while acknowledging that children develop at differing rates through swift progress and consolidation periods. The Two-Year progress check can give further information about progress and whether additional support or focused input due to a developmental delay are required.

The check can provide information for planning a child's next steps and the appropriate support and resources required for this to promote children's health and wellbeing.

Health

A holistic view of the child could include healthy eating and accessing sufficient exercise to remain healthy and grow healthily. These factors promote a sense of wellbeing, cognitive engagement and energy and stimulate the child to attempt new experiences. Liaison between parents, carers and providers will help to promote the good health of the children. This should include any health issues the child may have, the most appropriate ways to support the child and how these can be routinely addressed. Procedures should be in place to follow should a child become ill. The EYFS framework (DfE 2017, p. 27) clearly states, 'Prescription medicines must not be administered unless they have been prescribed for a child by a doctor, dentist, nurse or pharmacist (medicines containing aspirin should only be given if prescribed by a doctor).' It continues, 'Medicine (both prescription and non-prescription) must only be administered to a child where written permission for that particular medicine has been obtained from the child's parent and/or carer.' If it is agreed that a medicine is administered at a setting, it must be logged in case later reference is required. Many settings or schools have a specific book for this occurrence. If food is available, a healthy choice should be considered, with the utmost regard for cleanliness. Parents or carers must be liaised with to find out if the child has any dietary requirements, such as a nut allergy, and for information about how critical the requirement is and the consequences that may arise should the dietary request not be followed. This information could be vital, and it is appropriate to have an adult who has attended a first aid course to address any incident swiftly, should the need arise. Any accident or emergency should be logged and the parent or carer informed as appropriate.

CASE STUDY

Louise, a nursery child, had been identified by staff as not responding to them during the play sessions. Louise's interactions were tracked, and it was noted that she did not respond if the room was particularly busy and rather noisy or if the speaking was some distance away from her. Louise's key worker organised physical activities with her group and gave some instructions for actions for the group when they were not directly facing her. While Louise happily participated following the instructions, when the adult turned so that she could not see her face, Louise failed to respond. The key worker mentioned a possible hearing loss to the parents when they came to collect Louise. When she was taken for a hearing check, it was found she had glue ear and at times had limited hearing. The parents had not realised they had been compensating for Louise's hearing loss, for example by turning the television to a higher volume setting, and it was not until the key worker mentioned it that it became apparent.

Strategies to promote the health and wellbeing of vulnerable young children

Children with Special Educational Needs are generally thought to have one or more of the following broad bands of need: communication and language; cognition and learning; social, emotional and mental health; sensory and/or physical needs (DfE and DoH, 2015, p. 85). Careful tracking can ensure those children identified can make progress with further inputs. Interventions can be planned and organised for an individual child or specific groups (see Chapter 9). Children may have already been identified prior to entering a care group or setting but, at times, a practitioner may have a sense of something being 'not quite right' and track the situation to observe and gain evidence that further support is needed, such as in the case study concerning Louise above.

Summative assessments at two and five years old provide a check for children's development – looking at whether they are on track, emerging or beyond what is expected. This can include a cycle of observations and assessments to inform planning, implementing the plans, reviewing the outcomes and reflecting on them, and then taking actions to further develop the support for the child. This process is frequently termed a 'Plan, Do, Review' cycle.

There are numerous strategies that can be put in place but possibly the most crucial aspect is to have a personalised plan for the child to meet the specific needs. For example, a child may be anxious about meeting a new foster carer, visiting a children's home or during a transition period when they are entering a new school and meeting other children – and possibly unable to understand English when it is used as a first language in schools. Strategies put in place in the early years of a child's life can have a crucial influence on future life chances as the child forms patterns of thinking and self-awareness. Positive experiences and support to overcome challenges and demonstrate resilience can do much to help, although the child may need further help in later life if negative memories of previous experiences return.

Partnerships between those involved, strong teamwork and key workers in a welcoming environment can all help to give a positive experience and calm any anxiety that may have been felt by the child. Planning activities such as circle time to gain insights into children's ideas and thoughts and promote children's interactions can help a child feel welcome and understood. Routines during the day provide security and before- and after-session clubs can give food to ensure children are not hungry.

CASE STUDY

Karl had been abused as a toddler and was suicidal when he was four years old. He feared most things in his early years setting but enjoyed watching the children through the window into the outdoors area. He was afraid to play outdoors, and other children were afraid to play with the rather grey, old-looking young boy. The team decided to be welcoming but gave him space to observe. After many weeks, he relaxed and eventually went outdoors and joined the group of children playing who were, by this time, eager to play with him and help him be happy.

As discussed throughout the chapter, health and wellbeing for vulnerable children can take many forms, therefore there are myriads of ways young children can be supported to access experiences and resources with other children and adults to take full advantage of their surroundings, while exploring opportunities for them to progress and develop as valued individuals and members of communities.

References

Bowlby, J. (1951) *Maternal Care and Mental Health: A report prepared on behalf of the World Health Organisation as a contribution to the United Nations programme for the welfare of homeless children.* Geneva: World Health Organization.

Bronfenbrenner, U. (1979) *The Ecology of Human Development.* London: Harvard University Press.

Department for Education (2017) *Statutory Framework for the Early Years Foundation Stage: Setting the Standards for Learning, Development and Care for Children from Birth to Five.* Accessed on 13/6/2018 at www.gov.uk/government/uploads/system/uploads/attachment_data/file/596629/EYFS_STATUTORY_FRAMEWORK_2017.pdf

Department for Education and Department of Health (2015) *Special Educational Needs and Disability Code of Practice: 0 to 25 years.* Accessed on 5/11/2018 at https://assets.publishing.service.gov.uk/government/uploads/system/uploads/attachment_data/file/398815/SEND_Code_of_Practice_January_2015.pdf.

Early Education/Department for Education (2012) *Development Matters in the Early Years Foundation Stage (EYFS).* London. Accessed on 11/6/2018 at: www.foundationyears.org.uk/files/2012/03/Development-Matters-FINAL-PRINT-AMENDED.pdf

McLeod, S. (2007) *Bowlby's Attachment Theory.* Accessed on 31/10/2018 at http://www.simplypsychology.org/bowlby.html

Robertson, J. and Bowlby, J. (1952) 'A two-year-old goes to hospital.' *Proceedings of the Royal Society of Medicine 46,* 425–427.

Rutter, M. (1981) 'Stress, coping and development: Some issues and some questions.' *Journal of Child Psychology and Psychiatry 22,* 4, 323–356.

Bibliography

Bowlby, J. (1969) *Attachment: Attachment and Loss* (Vol. 1). New York: Basic Books.

Bowlby, J. (1988) A *Secure Base: Parent-Child Attachment and Healthy Human Development.* New York: Basic Books.

Griggs, J. and Bussard, L. (2017) *Study of Early Education and Development (SEED): Meeting the Needs of Children with Special Educational Needs and Disabilities in the Early Years.* London: NatCen Social Research, DfE.

Longfield, A. (2017) *On Measuring the Number of Vulnerable Children in England.* London: Children's Commissioner for England.

CHAPTER 13

Interminable Transition in the Early Years

Dr Margaret C. Simms

Early Years Consultant
Newark

Chapter overview

The chapter seeks to unravel the numerous issues, for young children and the adults supporting them, associated with transitions. It highlights a child's right to be happy during these changes and how adults can overcome any challenges transitions may present to formulate positive change management.

When viewed *en bloc*, a child's first five years, from suckling to school days, evoke multifarious adult perspectives – all of which shape in some way the approach to and type of support given to the transitioning child. Early childhood transitions commonly bridge chasms between one life and another – home, childminder, nursery and school. Smudging through Bronfenbrenner's ecological circles, these *rites of passage* require – no, expect – adjustment, compliance and achievement on the part of the child. As if that is not enough to cope with, consider the notion of a child in constant change, the contemporary lived experience of interminable transition.

In a paradigm of transition, the onus of support for each child lies within a collective of significant people – early childhood professional, parent, carer, older sibling, close friend, teacher...with the probability of a unified approach being open to discussion. Still, all are responsible for the child's happiness and wellbeing, each person's mindful understanding contributing to a universal perspective of how change may be accomplished. This chapter is therefore germane to all involved in early childhood transition, none more so than the professional focused on effecting exemplary transition practice, that is: smooth and reassuring transference and reception of the child from one stage to another.

Happenstance aside, emotionally successful transition (Bryce-Clegg, 2017) of child and adult requires meticulous planning, preparation and proaction (MPPP – pronounced MPs) on the part of the practitioner; the performance of such being staged against a backdrop of reflective practice, without which empathetic love cannot be shared. Readers are therefore persuaded to utilise the following reflective process to explore personal and professional understandings of their transition paradigm.

TEACH Process of Reflection (TPR)

- Thoughts (what transition or transitions come to mind?)

- Emotions (how did you feel at the time and how do you feel about it now?)

- Actions (who did what, how and why?)

- Consequences (what impact did the actions have on individuals in the particular transition collective?)

- How has this experience affected your perspective on transition?

REFLECTIONS ACTIVITY

PERSPECTIVES, PROJECTIONS, POSITIONS

- Discuss personal and professional *perspectives* of the first five years of childhood transitions.

- Critically evaluate potential effects of *projecting* your experiencing onto the transitioning child.

- Question the need to be mindful of all parties' *positions* in the transition process.

- How unified *was* the approach in your particular collective?

Scratching at the surface of one's own perspectives in this way underpins the professional's current transition support potential and invites deeper analysis of contribution to a process that, in common transitions at least, occurs at the behest of the collective's members. The approach itself hinges on the individual's awareness of ways in which professional and personal life experiences project themselves in practice. It is by revisiting enabling *and* impeding emotions (Good and Pereira, 2010) that professionals in the making learn to focus attention on the innermost needs of the transitioning child. Expending so much emotional energy, and relinquishing it to the child, reaps rewards for one whose child-centred heart, unhampered by 'health and safety gone mad!' dines with wellie-clad toddlers at muddy picnics. To give is to gain what is lost through denial. The personally and professionally responsive professional balances the child's right to happiness on a tightrope of fear and fulfilment, knowingly giving up control to fuel the child's self-control throughout interminable transition.

Successful transition is no coincidence. It happens on purpose, being birthed from a secure base and immersed in love through every stage and situation of the child's early years. It is motivational, inspirational and attainable. Whether or not successful transition in the early years was the professional's own experience, they are part of the very fabric of practice that exudes love in the Early Years Foundation Stage. Therefore, it is the professional who determines the child's emotional and mental state of transition momentarily and continuously.

A child's right to be happy

Compounding the *United Nations Convention of the Rights of the Child* (UNCRC) (United Nations Convention on the Rights of the Child, 2017) in the right to be happy, the mindful professional is sensitive to the child's spiritual needs, thus avoiding the trap of a single-minded, superficial transition of convenience where 'everything looks okay'. To understand the power that makes or breaks a child's spirit is to believe in the Froebelian (1782–1852) ability to, 'give or deny opportunities for self-expression' (Lilley, 1967, p. 6). In transition, the spirit of a child soars or sinks at the caprice of every actor. It is worth remembering that first impressions are lasting impressions – on all sides of the collective. A look, a word, a posture – welcoming, authoritative, authoritarian or even disengaged – a child's receptive heart and brain absorb and store it all. Be it attraction or repulsion, the mood of the moment highlights the professional's capacity to effectively facilitate transition. Proaction in securing a trusted colleague's frank evaluation of it is therefore welcome (Roffey-Barentsen and Malthouse, 2013) in forward-thinking professional learning communities (Mertler, 2017).

REFLECTIONS ACTIVITY
FACILITATING FRANK EVALUATION

- Contemplate your deepest fears at being 'observed' when facilitating three-year-old Mateusz's transition from childminder to nursery on a day when his new baby sister has just been born. Bear in mind that Mateusz has transitioned from being the youngest of two brothers to the middle child in his family.

- As the observer in the above scenario, how would you ensure that you did not disturb the natural behaviour (Walsh, 2001, p. 68) of actors in the transition process?

- Critically read 'Seven Steps for Success' (pp. 72–73) in Hayes et al. (2017) Developing as a Reflective Early Years Professional: A Thematic Approach (2nd edn). How would you ensure that the giving and receiving of feedback either enhances or changes transition practice?

Change management

Many adults baulk at change yet expect little children to manage it with ease, even when, in a transition from nursery to home, a carefully modelled and highly prized box sculpture is 'forgotten' or crossly crushed into the bin by an irritated parent. A casualty of its own creativity, the child's shoulder-straightening pride descends into a pit of powerlessness. The enduring effect of such rituals on personal perspectives of supporting transition for the next generation are deserving of critical reflection. The implications of Erikson's (1902–1994) supposition that ritual is as much a skill to be developed in children as intellect (Friedman, 1999) are that now is the time to reimagine the ritual of early years transitions. As the transitioning child's 'ritual teacher[s]' (Grimes, 2000, p. 74), approximately 450,000 early years staff in England (Department for Education, 2017) are subliminally or intentionally affecting the lives of three million children by their 'relived rite of passage experiences' (Van Gennep, 2004, p. 19). Disregarding for one moment that by three years of age the intensity of attachment response subsides just enough to release a child from its attachment figure for a few hours (Bowlby, 2015), the potential for confusing loyalties in today's care-hopping children is enormous. Early childhood professionals must work alongside parents and other professionals to get it right from the start (Right from the Start, 2017). 'Strong partnerships between parents and carers can only prove advantageous for the children concerned' (Beckley, 2012, p. 38) if they have the child's happy wellbeing at heart. Then, when children are supported to positively manage change, they are also afforded fundamental opportunity for sustained empowerment and permanency anchored in self.

A mother's relived rite of passage experience

Leaving Me – Harper's mummy's story

I remember well my first day at nursery,
The gated garden and windy path to porched door,
Picture pegs and plimsoll bags.
The tall teacher's white-knuckle grasp on my hand and
Opposite shoulder, as she prised me from Mummy's skirt
Screaming a hundred decibels of tears down my hot cheeks.
Oddly, I don't remember mum fetching me back.

REFLECTIONS

- Whose rites of passage are relived in the poem? Use TPR to reflect on similar transitions.

- Where is 'power' positioned? Critically evaluate power relationships and their impact on all involved.

- Consider potential effects on Harper's spirit if she hears this story on her first day at nursery.

- Use Gibbs' Reflective Cycle to analytically process your thinking in relation to 'new starters'.

- Explore what is meant by superficial transition.

Harper's need for love, and the satisfying of it, is crucial in the above transition. Maslow did not convey to us how many times a basic need may be thwarted before the seed of 'maladjustment' is sown (Maslow, 1943, p. 381) but in the nurturing of love we cannot risk but once. Consequently, the professional's expression of love must resonate in Harper's little heart. Furthermore, any reliving of 'teacher' rituals must be love-based and timely as the inextricably linked brain wires (Lewis, Amani and Lannon, 2001) of cared-for-child and carer-adult connect.

Harper grew up and became a mummy herself. Affected by the relived experiences of her mother and mother-figure nursery teacher, Harper chose to influence her children differently.

'Bye-bye Darling. See you soon.'

Firm, warm and loving hold.
Soothing voice – yet strong.
Kindness beaming into smiles,
'Mummy won't be long.'

CREATIVE ACTIVITY

- Create a personal, early-childhood, transition story.

- Consider whether to stash, share or shred your piece, and do so.

Recapitulation

Spiritual awareness and empathetic love are central elements of smooth and reassuring early years transitioning. Personal and professional understandings of the transition paradigm and relived rites of passage are also crucial, and single-minded superficial transition is to be avoided.

- Knowing as we do that transitions commonly refer to care and education rites of passage, yet today's norm leans more towards interminable transition, the burden of transitional provision rests firmly on the shoulders of adults.

- Academic knowledge and understanding of the paradigm of early childhood transition go hand in hand with reflective exploration and practical implementation.

- Children's happiness is not a whimsical fancy but a necessity for successful transition and the growth of love. It is a child's right; the target upon which watchful professionals set their sights.

- The early childhood professional is just one member of a collective; working together, each member can affect successful transitions for young children in their care.

- Expending emotional energy is a prerequisite for professionalism in the early years.

- Successful transition should be a product of meticulous planning. It should not be left to chance.

- Proper use of power empowers the young child.

Having safely transitioned from domestic to institutionalised settings, and settled in the readiness-to-learn domain (Whitebread and Bingham, 2011), young children are again uprooted and transplanted in a preparatory class for compulsory schooling. The move may be new but the challenges it presents are familiar to the collective: relived rites of passage, separation, power struggles and the MPs – meticulous planning, preparation and proaction on the part of the practitioner. Whilst some members of the broadened collective may be blissfully unaware and others decidedly over-aware of the child's spiritual feelings, it is, again, the professional's capacity to effectively facilitate transition that is on display.

DISCUSSION

- Why might the transitions highlighted thus far be categorised as 'calendared transitions'? What other calendared transitions can you think of?

- Discuss the notion of 'curriculum-based transition'. How many curriculum-based transitions might a child have undergone by their 12th birthday?

- Judge the effects of a range of calendared and curriculum-based transition on a four-year-old child. For example, what happens to children's developmental progress when they transition from playing all day to sitting on the carpet for extended periods of time?

− Develop an argument for and against one dominant point in the following passage.

− There has never been a better time to release our youngsters from calendared and curriculum-based transitions, white-line boundaries of educational systems and one-way streets to institutionalisation; to free ourselves from legalistic notions of transition and let our hearts run, skip and play the journey of continuous transition.

When considered through the lens of interminable transition, the success of the Children Act 2006 in meeting its specific aim of establishing the Early Years Foundation Stage (EYFS) and the government's (2006) aim to, 'promote the wellbeing of young children in early years provision' (pp. 2–3) is debatable; one side arguing that transitioning children risk, challenge, lead, follow, seek and find themselves playing the EYFS; the other that coexisting EYFS assessments are restrictive and unclear (TACTYC, 2011, p. 30), causing confusion for early childhood practitioners and premature 'labelling' of young children. Whatever the professional stance, knowledge scaffolding knowledge, experience surpassing experience, the young child in transit reaches out for adult hands – safe hands, strong hands – and instinctive old hands that believe, 'This time, like all times, is a very good one, if we but know what to do with it' (Emerson, 2009, p. 57).

EXPLORATION ACTIVITY

CHILDREN'S HAPPINESS LAW

You are part of a government think-tank tasked with proposing plans for a white paper that will eventually lead to legislation aimed at ensuring the happiness of young children during times of transition. You must cover every conceivable aspect of transition. Plan, prepare and present your proposal.

Becoming a powerful overcomer

No matter how expert the professional, most children will experience times of discombobulation – on entering a new environment, being approached by an unfamiliar adult or observing from afar a completely new group of children. The early days of a young child are dappled with disorientating transition-induced anxiety. The role of the early childhood professional is to help alleviate such tension, sometimes by distraction, but more meaningfully by equipping the child to become a powerful overcomer.

If overcoming requires tools, to become powerful overcomers young children need power tools. Redefining power tools in an environment where loving reciprocal attachments not only help children cope with transitions (Wright, 2010) but also contribute to the formation of relationships in later life (Schaffer, 2003) is tantamount to success. Furthermore, personal and professional awareness of the effects of power in relationships is a prerequisite to reducing the over-dominance of authoritarian practice in favour of child-centred, appropriate, child-led enjoyment. In all simplicity, bin 'Be careful' – and just be there, trusting in the child's capacity to influence to the good their own transitions.

Having traversed the first five years of life, Year 1 is coming – ready or not. Behaviour expectations change as a new reality dawns that this is 'big school'. Here, in a mesosystem that literally and figuratively fences children in, uniformity would swallow individuality were it not for the meticulous planning, preparation and proaction that has already occurred, thereby raising the child to a place where individual challenge, creativity and compliance are able to coexist. There, behaviour management moves towards extinction as, 'deeply involved children are too busy learning to cause problems' (Ephgrave, 2017, p. 16).

In conclusion, early childhood professionals hold the keys to transitions in which happiness and the child's ability to make relationships are paramount. For the sake of the sector and their own reputation, they are duty bound to reflect, observe, contemplate and develop practice and policy to ensure the process works for every transitioning young child.

References

Beckley, P. (ed.) (2012) *Learning in Early Childhood*. London: Sage Publications.

Bowlby, R. (2015) 'Relationships.' In J. Colwell and A. Pollard (eds) *Reading for Reflective Teaching in Early Education*. London: Bloomsbury.

Bryce-Clegg, A. (2017) *Effective Transition into Year One*. London: Featherstone.

Childcare Act 2006. Accessed on 19/6/2018 at www.legislation.gov.uk/ukpga/2006/21/pdfs/ukpgaen_20060021_en.pdf

Department for Education (2017) *National Statistics Childcare and Early Years Providers Survey: 2016*. Accessed on 19/6/2018 at www.gov.uk/government/uploads/system/uploads/attachment_data/file/593646/SFR09_2017_Main_Text.pdf

Emerson, R.W. (2009) *The Essential Writings of Ralph Waldo Emerson*. Accessed on 19/6/2018 at https://books.google.co.uk/books?id=n73fdFhQxxUC&printsec=frontcover&dq=ralph+waldo+emerson&hl=en&sa=X&sqi=2&redir_esc=y#v=snippet&q=contents&f=false

Ephgrave, A. (2017) *Year One in Action*. Abingdon: Routledge.

Friedman, L. (1999) *Identity's Architect: A Biography of Erik H. Erikson*. London: Free Association Books.

Good, A. and Pereira, P. (2010) 'Using our Subjective Experience: Teaching Curriculum.' In D. Tidwell and L. Fitzgerald (eds) *Self-study and Diversity*. Rotterdam: Sense Publishers.

Grimes, R. (2000) *Deeply Into the Bone: Re-inventing Rites of Passage*. London: University of California Press.

Hayes, C., Daly, J., Duncan, M., Gill, R. and Whitehouse, A. (2017) *Developing as a Reflective Early Years Professional: A Thematic Approach* (2nd ed.). St. Albans: Critical Publishing.

Lewis, T., Amani, F. and Lannon, R. (2001) *A General Theory of Love*. New York: Random House USA Inc.

Lilley, I. (1967) *Cambridge Texts and Studies in the History of Education*. Cambridge: Cambridge University Press.

Maslow, A. (1943) 'A theory of human motivation.' *Psychological Review 50*, 4, 370–396.

Mertler, C. (2017) *Action Research in Education*. Oxford: Routledge.

Roffey-Barentsen, J. and Malthouse, R. (2013) *Reflective Practice in Education and Training*. London: Sage Publications.

Right from the Start (2017) *How we can help*. Accessed on 19/6/2018 at www.right-from-the-start.org

Schaffer, H.R. (2003) *Introducing Child Psychology*. Somerset: Wiley-Blackwell.

TACTYC (2011) *The Early Years Foundation Stage (EYFS) Review Report on Evidence*. Accessed on 19/6/2018 at http://tactyc.org.uk/pdfs/Report-EYFSreview.pdf

United Nations Committee on the Rights of the Child (2017) *Convention on the Rights of the Child*. London: UNICEF.

Van Gennep, A. (2004) *The Rites of Passage*. London and Henley: Routledge and Keegan Paul.

Walsh, M. (2001) *Research Made Real: A Guide for Students*. Oxford: Nelson Thornes.

Whitebread, D. and Bingham, S. (2011) *School Readiness: A critical review of perspectives and evidence*. Accessed on 19/6/2018 at http://imx07wlgmj301rre1jepv8h0-wpengine.netdna-ssl.com/wp-content/uploads/2018/04/Occ-Paper-2.docx

Wright, J. (2010) 'Supporting Children's Learning and Development in Practice: Developing Your Specialist Knowledge.' In P. Farrelly (ed.) *Early Years Work-Based Learning: A Guide for Students of Early Years and Early Childhood Studies.* Exeter: Learning Matters.

Bibliography

Brenner, A. (2007) *Women's Rites of Passage: How to Embrace Change and Celebrate Life.* Lanham: Roman and Littlefield.

Erikson, E.H. and Erikson, J.M. (1997) *The Life Cycle Completed.* New York: W.W. Norton and company.

| CHAPTER 14 |

Child, Family and Community

WORKING WITH EMPOWERING DISCOURSES

Julie Percival, Anne Renwick and Emmy Sealey

Senior Lecturer, University of Cumbria; Senior Lecturer, Early Years, University of Cumbria; Nursery Owner, Carlisle

Chapter overview

This chapter considers how everyday experiences and practice choices shape our understanding of vulnerability. Reviewing our thinking and our practice should lead us to consider the ways in which children, families and communities are strong and capable on their own terms. Respectful practice starts with an acknowledgement of the multifaceted lives children lead – that being vulnerable to disadvantage and adversity does not preclude being strong and capable in other facets of life. The following working definition underpins the content of this chapter:

> Discourse: A way of talking and thinking about a subject that is united by common assumptions and serves to shape people's understanding of and actions towards that subject. (Giddens and Sutton, 2014, p. 4)

Introduction

This chapter is being written as the media is preoccupied with the plight of Charlie Gard, a child not yet one year old, born with a particular life-limiting illness. His parents are fighting medical professionals through the courts and campaigning through social media to secure the treatment they believe is most appropriate for their son. A campaign website documents the 'army' of support with 109,000 followers on Instagram, more than a hundred thousand 'likes' on Facebook and thousands of 'likes' through Twitter. The Prime Minister for the UK government, the Pope and the President of the US, along with celebrity commentators, have contributed to the collective discussion. Direct donations can be made to the cause and specially designed campaign badges, mugs, wrist bands, framed prints and key rings can be purchased through the campaign website shop. Very many words have been written and spoken both for and against the stance taken by parents and professionals, covering a wide range of emotive, passionate, informed and not-so-informed opinions. A range of discourses, competing for our attention, confirming and challenging our beliefs can be detected. Maybe you have contributed to the campaign through social media, discussions with colleagues, friends and family.

TASK 1: INVESTIGATE USING A RANGE OF ONLINE SOURCES

Think about definitions of vulnerability and disadvantage mentioned in other chapters of this book. Review the online coverage of this child's circumstances using a simple internet search using Charlie's name. Look particularly at the judicial summary available at: www.judiciary.gov.uk/wp-content/uploads/2017/07/gosh-v-gard-24072017.pdf. Charlie's family have established the Charlie Gard Foundation and you can find out how they see Charlie's life journey and how they have taken their campaign forward.[1]

- How do you feel about the child, the parents and the medics?

- What is the nature of this child's vulnerability? Can you support your reasoning?

- Is it easy to identify what the best response to adversity and risk should be?

Every day in early years settings, we discuss children and families – children's progress, families' responses to our provision, small moments of wonder, fun and security along with niggles, challenges and uncertainties. Conversations, both formal and informal, become the frame of reference for our understanding of who the child is and their 'fit' with the provision and practice on offer.

---

1   www.thecharliegardfoundation.org

Our conversations help us to review our 'habits of conduct' (Edwards and Thomas, 2010, p. 411, after Oakeshott, 1962), establishing and confirming the nature of the child, what the child's needs are most likely to be and, significantly, how we might act as competent, early years professionals.

TASK 2: REFLECTION – STUDENTS' EXPERIENCES OF STAFFROOM CONVERSATIONS

Students discuss their recent experiences of being on placement in different nursery schools, particularly the arrangements for using the staffroom over lunchtime. In one school staffroom, on several occasions, staff were overheard discussing the appearance of some of the adults dropping their children off, their relationships with partners and the levels of cleanliness of the children and their homes. Another student was not allowed in the staffroom at lunchtime because confidential matters were likely to be discussed. This led to a debate about the nature of informal discussions in staffrooms. Most students felt that the staffroom was a vital place to meet up, share information and seek advice. Collective knowledge about home life helped inform their practice and once or twice stopped them from saying or doing potentially unhelpful things in the classroom. But then did it lead them to make assumptions?

Make a note of ways in which you and your colleagues talk about children and families.

- Do you notice anything about the words and phrases used about children and families?

- How do you think it might influence your practice?

Work with vulnerable children and their families starts with a recognition that the language you use to express your ideas and make sense of your experience is highly significant. Rosemary Roberts (2006) uses the power of fictional biography as an anchor for understanding children's development of self-esteem. Her character, Joanne, narrates the ups and downs of family life. The conversational style gives us a window into the family's world and Joanne's perceptions of their thoughts and feelings. Almost instantly, you are drawn into working out what is going on in the lives of the family, particularly how the children are developing socially and emotionally. Comparison and opinion are hard to suppress as we draw on personal experiences and refer to the discourses we identify with and use most regularly. Some lines of thought become powerful ways of shaping our understanding, giving us ground rules for making judgements and determining appropriate courses of action in all aspects of life. In daily practice and when dilemmas arise, we use discourses to guide our actions.

TASK 3: REFLECTION – TALK IN YOUR STAFFROOM

Consider a dilemma that has provoked discussion in your setting or school.

- What sorts of words and actions were used?

- Could you detect what the possible lines of thought, assumptions and social rules were?

- Do you think this can have an impact on the care and learning offered to the child?

Thinking back to what we know of Charlie Gard, you might notice that discourses come bundled up with powerful emotions and actions that can have quite a profound influence on people's lives.

Certain discourses embody a view of children as capable and resilient, whilst others place limitations on our expectations. Particular lines of thought might become so strongly embedded in our thinking that they are taken for granted as part of the natural order of things, not worth questioning. Subscribing to and acting in accordance with such discourses means we can share knowledge easily and stay safe as an accepted part of the group or profession. Dahlberg, Moss and Pence (2007, p. 2) make the case for actively seeking a 'multiplicity of languages' about early childhood rather than relying on dominant discourses that tell us how things are, how they should be and how we should practise. We have scope to seek out and listen to different accounts and ways of being (McNaughton, 2003/6). We can ask questions of ourselves, and of leading practitioners, researchers and policy makers, to check whether our ways of thinking about children and families are enabling or restrictive – whether they are focused on capacities to flourish or deficiencies from the norm.

We must check what we understand by words such as vulnerable, disadvantaged, troubled, at risk and in need because this shapes our practice, and this has real consequences for the children and families whose lives we label as such. Returning to Roberts (2006, p. 20):

> How we really feel and what we really think are the things with which babies are actually dealing…we need to take an honest look at what we really mind about.

Which lines of thought help us to see children, parents, families and communities as capable? Under what conditions might they flourish and how might early years professionals contribute to this?

Strong, capable children

In whatever way we choose to discuss or define vulnerable children and their families, underpinning knowledge and understanding of child development is essential. If we do not understand the way in which children develop and learn, then we cannot make informed decisions on our support for them.

As early years professionals, we must endeavour to contribute to conditions that promote children, parents, families and communities as capable individuals and groups, with responsibility for their own needs, supporting them in making decisions and helping them to flourish. A sound knowledge of child development and children's learning has to be at the heart of good practice.

We need to ensure that our knowledge of children's development is underpinned by a sound theoretical background on which to draw when we are supporting children and families. We must ensure that our understanding is based on sound, relevant theory, as well as recent medical and educational research related to good practice.

TASK 4: REFLECTION – ONE SETTING'S APPROACH TO UNDERSTANDING CHILDREN'S CAPABILITIES AND NEEDS, THEIR STRENGTHS AND CAPABILITIES

Dolly (owner-manager) reflects on her passion for her work in early years, demonstrating her deep knowledge of child development and how her life experiences have shaped her practice:

Mission statement

All children have a secure, safe and joyful experience at our nursery, where they are helped by skilled and committed practitioners to gain the knowledge, skills and emotional wellbeing they need for their future life. Inspired by Reggio Emilia, we value children's natural curiosity and inclination to explore the world around them.

My experience as a practitioner

The past 29 years have been busy and exciting as I have been the owner and manager of a well-established nursery in the North of England, thus fulfilling a lifetime ambition. Our building is purpose built and designed by my husband who is an architect and is in the grounds of our family home. It comprises a: birth to three unit; pre-school room; sensory room; conservatory that is used as an atelier exploring arts and crafts; tree house that is used as a maths area with information and communication technology (ICT) resources; covered outdoor classroom for the use of clay work and woodwork; large garden; playground. Staff and children help to look after our environment and our rabbit, two cats, five love birds, two parrots, a goldfish, a tortoise and four hens. The children take a great interest and pride in our pets and care, feed and clean them, I feel that this is a unique way of making the children feel empathy towards animals and other people, hopefully starting from a young age to care for others will have a long-lasting effect in their future lives.

We work closely with the local schools and take on students from the local university and colleges to make sure that our future young practitioners and teachers gain as much experience as possible before they venture out into the world of employment.

We have achieved 'Outstanding' twice in our Ofsted inspection, and our report has highlighted that we: 'offer highly effective teaching and learning which is excellent in meeting the needs of all children attending. An innovative learning environment which is confidently explored by all children thus making them capable learners. Robust systems for observation, planning and assessment are in place, which ensures that an excellent range of challenging, age and stage appropriate activities is available for the children, to support their rapid learning and development.'

We follow the children's interests and use 'All about me' booklets and a 'Wow or magic moments board' regularly filled in and updated by the parents to make sure that we know all our children really well. The children in the pre-school room decide on their own planning and we try and follow all the interesting suggestions they make to further increase their knowledge of their world. The children are very confident to express themselves, use good language and know that their interests will be followed, as they are always listened to by promoting children's participation in democratic decision-making. Every year when our older children leave for school, their reception class teachers and parents praise us for the children's achievements and their confidence in speaking and listening to others and their good manners.

I was brought up in Europe and have very fond memories of using the environment and exploring the outdoors with my sister and my parents. I know how valuable this experience has been to me and my sister, and I try to encourage the use of natural and everyday materials in the nursery by using Heuristic Play (Goldschmeid and Jackson, 2004) for all ages and the Reggio Emilia Approach and philosophy (Thornton and Brunton, 2005), encouraging the children to express themselves, explore and investigate, think and reflect, be involved in projects following their own interests and reinforce their identities using open small spaces. Building dens using tyres, planks, crates, stones, bricks, planting and growing, climbing trees, taking risks and using sand, mud and water are vital for a young child's sensory experiences and supporting the competent learner outdoors.

Through close observations and links with parents, we come to know the child as a whole. So how do we identify a 'vulnerable' child? This could be that a child has suddenly become withdrawn for no apparent reason; it could be something quite 'simple' like the arrival of a new sibling or the move to a new house. The loss of a family member or a pet and speech and language difficulties have been identified, as well as children who have English as an additional language or a child having physical or emotional difficulties or hearing loss. We have concerns when listening to a child in the role-play area using inappropriate language and behaviour in their play or if there are parental issues or the child is finding the transition to nursery or later on or 'school readiness' hard to cope with. Myself and my staff are all qualified between Level 3 and Level 7 in childcare and have good knowledge of health and safety, Special Educational Needs and/or Disabilities (SEND), safeguarding, speech and language and behaviour management. We have access to educational magazines and journals, we attend regular training and we always try to be abreast of any changes that have occurred in our education or health system. We have close links with our Early Years Advisors and other medical and safeguarding professionals; on the whole, we feel we have good local support, but sometimes we have to make a nuisance of ourselves by insisting on further meetings to make sure that our children and staff get the best support possible. We have regular staff meetings where we discuss positive or negative behaviour we have observed since our last meeting and make regular changes with equipment and resources in our rooms to further interest the children in their play, their involvement and wellbeing. Hopefully, through our 'open-door policy' with the parents/carers and our links with other professionals, no child in our care will be missed or left behind.

- Consider how this compares with the approaches you have in your own setting.

- How do you find out what children can do?

- How do you identify those vulnerable children who may need additional support?

- How do you support these children and their families?

- Is your knowledge of child development secure and up to date?

- How does your own personal experience enhance your practice?

Children are strong and capable learners from birth, and with supportive adults and an enabling environment, they will thrive (DfE, 2017). *Starting from the Child*, Julie Fisher's seminal text (2013), encourages practitioners to ensure that the child is at the centre of all planning, support and developments.

Understanding the importance of early relationships in the development of children's brains, attachment theory and the role of the key person (Lindon, 2013), as well as children's growing self-esteem, are all extremely important parts of any initial or continuing professional development. All those who work with children and their families, whatever their role, must ensure up to date knowledge of these fields (Gerhardt, 2014).

TASK 5: REFLECTION – ONE SETTING'S APPROACH TO ATTACHMENT AND THE ROLE OF THE KEY PERSON

Read an excerpt from a Key Person Policy, then find out what the key person remembers about Alfie.

Key person

The key person must help ensure that every child's learning and care is tailored to meet their individual needs. The key person must seek to engage and support parents and/or carers in guiding their child's development at home. They should also help families engage with more specialist support if appropriate...offer[ing] a settled relationship for the child and build[ing] a relationship with their parents. (DfE, 2017, paras 1.10 and 3.27)

Taken from one setting's Key Person Policy

- A key person plays a vital role in a child's life and must demonstrate consistency and sensitivity and be responsive to the child's needs. They must engage, interact and connect with a child and their family. They will observe, assess, record and plan and have a good understanding of up-to-date child development and theories. When children feel happy and secure in this way they are confident to explore and to try out new experiences. A close emotional relationship with a key person in the setting does not determine children's ties with their own parents and carers.

- To ensure consistent care, each child will be assigned a main key person and a second key person. The key person will be assigned to the child prior to their start date; in order for the system to be effective, they will be reviewed once the child has settled into their room at nursery. We have found that children will seek out their own special member of staff who they feel close to.

- Look at the child's 'All about me' booklet, which is updated by parents as changes occur. Parents add comments to the 'magic wow' board and hold discussions with staff at daily handovers and at parent's evenings.

- We will respect the circumstances of all families including parents who are unable to stay for a long period of time in the nursery due to work commitments and inform parents of their child's progress.

- Through purposeful relationships and getting to know the children well, individual planning will be written to follow the children's individual interests and provide opportunities to investigate these further.

- Key staff will undertake regular training in Safeguarding, Special Educational Needs, Code of Practice, Behaviour, First Aid, Manual Handling, Speech and Language, Health and Safety, Nutrition and Allergies, Food Hygiene, Multicultural and British values, English as an Additional Language, Observation and Assessment, and any other subjects that have links with their key children.

Child case study

Alfie was two when he joined nursery. He made it obvious from his first day that he hated being the centre of attention and being fussed over, but after a few weeks of attending every day, he became totally attached to his key person, who was to give him one-to-one care, and his newly found friend, Maria.

The arrival to nursery was an issue, as it was too busy for Alfie, so he would start his nursery day in the sensory room with only a few people and his friend, Maria, flicking through books that he really loved and using the Heuristic Play objects.

Alfie is deaf and wears Cochlear Implants, which he often pulls off when he gets frustrated. His physical ways of getting around are limited. He sits in a special chair to help with his posture for part of the session but gets frustrated as he has no speech, although he can sometimes use grunting sounds to make himself noticed, and has no bladder control. He likes a limited choice of food and will often throw food off his tray if he is offered something new, not even attempting to taste it. Alfie enjoys listening to certain types of music and rocks from side to side or backwards and forwards if he enjoys it. He is using a few Makaton signs; in nursery, pictures of the signs are displayed low down so that other children and staff can use them. As a result, he is fully included in all nursery activities and his emotional wellbeing is significantly enhanced through his key person's expertise.

As he attends nursery every morning, he has a lot of professionals visiting him here so that his afternoons can be spent at home with mum. The professionals are not always received in a favourable way, as Alfie only cooperates with his key person and finds their presence intrusive. We work closely with the professionals and we are given various exercises to be carried out with Alfie during the sessions. Alfie's brother, Ryan, is six and he attends a special school as he has autism. Mum is very keen for the professionals to observe Alfie, as she suspects he also has autism, and recently after a lot of observations and meetings with an educational psychologist and different medical tests, Alfie has been diagnosed with Asperger Syndrome. Alfie will be leaving nursery in August to go to the same special school as his brother Ryan.

- Consider how this compares with the approaches you have in your own setting, particularly in relation to children you may have identified as vulnerable.

- How do you support children and families through the role of the key person?

- Does your approach work well or are there changes you might make?

- How secure is your own knowledge of attachment theory and the role of the key person?

The importance of parental/carer engagement with children from pre-birth has formed the basis of much research and educational development. Sue Palmer has warned us of the toxic nature of many recent technological developments (Palmer, 2008, 2015) and Alison Gopnik's work analyses further the idea of what parenting in the 21st century might look like (Gopnik, 2009, 2016). Recent studies in brain development, using the most up-to-date scanning and brain-mapping techniques, demonstrate the effects of neglect or long-term stress on the developing brain.

TASK 6: REFLECTING ON YOUR OWN KNOWLEDGE AND PRACTICE

Read the example below of one setting's approach to understanding and supporting the needs of 'looked-after children' (DfE, 2015).

Case study

Elaine (two years, eight months) arrived at nursery with grandma and looked very unsure today, which was very unlike her! She was normally dropped off by mum and ran in, sometimes even forgetting to kiss and cuddle mum. Elaine's key person and little friends ran to greet her and led her into the den outside, which was Elaine's favourite place; she felt confident and blossomed in this area.

Elaine had been absent from nursery for a couple of months due to family issues and changes at home. Mum, a single parent, who cared for Elaine and her sister (six years old and at school), was under close supervision after her involvement with a man who was known to be a drug user, and she had now also started taking drugs, was drinking heavily and was struggling with the rehabilitation programme for drugs and alcohol abuse she had been put on to decrease her drug dependency since Elaine's birth. Unfortunately, due to these changes, Mum had started being violent towards both girls. Grandma had taken over the care of the girls in her home, as advised by the social worker, but the girls, being close to Mum, found it hard to cope with this separation and their behaviour became very unpredictable. Elaine was having screaming tantrums for no reason and throwing things across the room if she didn't get her own way. Her sister was refusing to go to bed and, once in bed, not wanting to get up for school, which she previously adored.

Grandma had contacted the social worker to stress the difficulties she was facing – she was suffering from depression herself, due to the stress she had found herself in – and the continuous arguments she was involved in with her partner, who didn't really agree with having to share her with the girls. Unfortunately, a foster parent was going to take over the care of the girls and, sadly, the family unit would be split. After unending meetings over a period of time with all the professionals, and Mum's persistence with drugs and alcohol continuing to affect her behaviour towards the girls, her suicide attempt and grandma's ill health, the girls were to be put on the adoption list, for their own safety and wellbeing.

After months of waiting for the right parents to come along, all the professionals were called to fortnightly meetings with the adoptive parents to write case studies on the girls, share information on the girls' lives, and, eventually, the transition would start taking place over the summer holidays and the girls would meet their new parents and hopefully move away with their new family to start a new life.

- How does this compare to the approaches you have in your own setting or have observed elsewhere?

- Consider other vulnerable children in your setting and your approach to supporting them.

- How successful is your current approach and are there any changes you might make?

Strong and capable parents and families

A well-chosen quote from James and Prout (1997) asserts, 'Children from birth are people in their own right and as such should be recognised as socially active participants of their families, communities and societies' (cited in Lancaster and Kirby, 2014, p. 97). Alfie and Elaine's biographies (and indeed the snippets we know of Charlie's life) are entwined with those of their parents and their family group. Many adults and young people take on parenting responsibilities and functions, bringing with them their past: they maybe biological parents or carers, have legal responsibility or have come to a significant informal arrangement for one reason or another. Close, intimate relationships form and, although this is not exclusively the case, mutually rewarding care takes place. Personal and private relationships, however, are often open to public scrutiny.

Unpublished research data gathered by one of the authors indicates that some parents judge themselves but also perceive that family, friends and indeed strangers do so too. Professionals such as teachers, health visitors and early years practitioners are believed to have opinions about their parenting, and indeed very many aspects of their life. Even before their child is born, parents may feel that their fitness to parent is in question and, as a child enters the world, these feelings can be compounded as a range of professionals play their part in the child's care, learning and development. Each unique child's capacity to thrive is influenced by the parents' wellbeing set within the socioeconomic and cultural context in which they live (Bronfenbrenner, 1979). Significantly, a child's sense of self and self-esteem is also affected by their sense of how you and your setting respond to their family and home context – both the 'positive or negative responses' (Manning-Morton and Thorp, 2015, p. 9). The discourses that we subscribe to in relation to parents and families are as important as those we hold to for children. Vulnerability and adversity are not the child's alone.

Vulnerability is challenging to identify and quantify, and professionals draw on a complex range of tools and benchmarks that vary according to current norms and expectations, which in turn are set within the political and economic climate of the day (Brotherton and Cronin, 2013). The interplay between child, parent, family, state and providers of services, all charged with how a child should be cared for and educated, can sometimes be so overwhelming that keeping a strong sense of self requires determination on the parents' behalf;

parents disengage, opt out and become 'hard to reach' (Osgood *et al.*, 2013, p. 210). And yet, policy and research seem to be intent on looking for the most effective parenting programmes and tools for assessing needs (Field, 2010, for example).

The Social Mobility Commission (SMC) (2016) provides data that indicates there are significant child development gaps in the early years. Good parenting and preparing children for school forms one of their four recommendations to government.

> Opportunities are being missed to influence parenting. There needs to be a response to this policy vacuum in order to support all parents to be good parents…by establishing an innovation fund to road test and evaluate approaches which aim to improve parenting skills. (SMC, 2016)

The underpinning discourse implies deficient parenting is at the heart of the gaps in development and learning. Strategically, we need to consider how structural features of society, along with policies and dominant practices, impact on us all. The 'stark postcode lottery of social mobility' identified by the SMC (2016) highlights who is doing well from our current ways of organising society and who is not. We need to acknowledge gaps and deficits in this context so wider structural changes can be made.

In our practice, however, we value positive personal and social wellbeing, which is recognised as a prime area of learning within the Statutory Framework for the Early Years Foundation Stage (DfE, 2017). Its importance in the early years is often argued for and seen as the 'heart' of practice (Callanan *et al.*, 2017, p. 9). This means that:

- we feed self-esteem and resilience to face life's challenges

- we look for ways to be sensitive yet assertive, not only to determine beneficial courses of action but act upon aspirations

- we nurture secure and positive identities

- we harness signs of optimism that things will work out

so that the focus is squarely on how children *flourish* (Kingdon, Gourd and Gasper, 2017, after Seligman, 2011). All parents, but particularly those who may be vulnerable, need this kind of focus: when they flourish, their child does too.

Supporting parents and families – turning the gaze from vulnerability

The child is at the heart of practice at Pen Green: the foundation for nurturing children is partnership between staff and parents (see for example the 'Pen Green Loop', Whalley, 1997). Over many years, parent–practitioner research, carefully co-constructed, has informed both practitioner and parent understandings of how children develop and learn. Provision has been investigated and revised through shared learning and respect for the unique knowledge parents and practitioners possess. The Pen Green paradigm (Fletcher, 2014) – choosing what to find out about, how to do it and how to share the findings – centres on democratic involvement in each person gaining *insight*.

The discourse that underpins this approach does not start with categorising vulnerability, labelling cultures and observed patterns of care. The insights parents have about their child and the child's world and the insight staff can offer is often pooled, and ways of expressing and using this insight are found together. If training and development are only ever led by experts, both staff and parents lose confidence in their abilities to nurture and flourish.

Supporting families to flourish depends on the 'architecture of access' (Hayward, 2014) to that support: working out how and why parents engage with your early years education and care is a vital starting point. From co-constructed research, staff and parents at Pen Green found that involvement and subsequent development of confidence, insight and capacity to nurture and organise life could be associated with organisational factors and personal dispositions.

Table 14.1 Checking the 'architecture of access' for working together (adapted from Hayward, 2014)

Organisational factors	Personal perspectives and dispositions – open to change
• Is the day structured so there is time to build relationships? • Is the environment organised so it is a parent-friendly space too? • What do you plan to do so that relationships are built not only over the induction period, but also beyond? • List the range of ways parents can get involved in learning about their child, the curriculum, their own interests and the wider community. • Do you offer these opportunities at different times and in different ways? • Do you have a designated member of staff who supports parents to access wider support services and community resources? • Do staff and parents have regular access to home-language speakers? • Do you make sure information sharing is open and accessible? • Is there any stigma attached to using the setting or support services?	• Capacity to trust that practitioners are honest and do not judge them. • Confidence to be in that environment. • Confidence to communicate. • The impact of prior use of services, schools, health, benefits and police. • Personal resilience in the face of life's challenges. • Aspirations for their child. • Concerns that the child's behaviour might be judged negatively and attributed to them. • When the time is right and I trust you… • I can tell you about my child's development – the story of their life so far in my terms. • I can talk with you about my child's play and learning if we share experiences of the actual play and learning. • I can share with you knowledge of our family and our background.

TASK 7: REFLECTION – ALFIE AND ELAINE'S FAMILY AND NURSERY PARTNERSHIPS

- Can you identify features of the practice in nursery that enabled Alfie and Elaine's carers to trust staff, share insights and make decisions for the effective care and learning of the children?

- Does your own practice start with children's and parents' capacities to flourish or their vulnerabilities?

- How do you come to understand parents' dispositions and the organisational factors that foster access and involvement in what you have to offer?

Effective, universal services for babies and young children pay attention to the ways in which the services they build are accessible *and* contextually and culturally relevant. There is no single set of practices that will hold parents and families together in times of adversity. Working on protective factors that shore up resilience and capacities to flourish helps to weaken risk through providing unique protective influences that buffer and interrupt the impact of adversity (Noltemeyer and Bush, 2013). Pen Green parent interview data illustrates how meaningful involvement in the centre provides scope for parents and families to make choices and changes through insight gained in meaningful ways. The work is not compensatory or targeted to 'narrow the gap' between disadvantaged children and their peers.

Wider social discourses

The Children's Commissioner for England has tried to:

> Work out how many vulnerable children there are in this country today…four months, 500 pages and 4 spreadsheets later and our answer is: we don't know…it isn't for the lack of trying…[and]…in one sense of course, all children are vulnerable. (2017, p. 1)

Anne Longfield's foreword to the preliminary report *On Measuring the Number of Vulnerable Children in England* asserts the need for society to rise to the challenge of identifying groups of children who are at risk so that we can better organise our services and communities making it more likely that they, 'live healthy, happy safe lives' and, 'have successful transitions to adulthood' (Children's Commissioner for England, 2017, p. 3). The study illustrates the complexity of provision, overlap of services and varying threshold of need required to access some services. Thirty-two groups of vulnerable children are identified, further grouped into four broad types of vulnerability (Children's Commissioner for England, 2017, p. 13):

- children with health-related vulnerabilities
- children with family-related vulnerabilities

- children directly supported or accommodated by the State

- children and young people whose actions put their futures at risk.

It is clearly emphasised that the purpose of the study is not to provide the basis for designing services and setting service level targets. In the ecology of the lives of children (Bronfenbrenner, 1979), the Commissioner is on the periphery of children's lives but indicative of institutions across society that lobby for attention in parliament and the media, promote the rights of the child and compete for scarce resources. Campaigning organisations raise wider political awareness and support practitioner communities of practice (Wenger-Trayner and Wenger-Trayner, 2015). The priorities evolve through communication of findings.

Action for Children (2017) are currently reviewing high re-referral rates made to children's social care for children who have not met the threshold for statutory intervention. The scrutiny of data and interviews with local authority and family services staff suggest that limitations in services are leading to increased referrals. Across the country, to varying degrees, localised Early Help services such as children's centres are in decline whilst statutory intervention is on the increase.

For the NSPCC, neglect has become a key line of enquiry and lobbying. Their vision is underpinned by the principle that preventative services (both universal and targeted, child and family focused) are best suited to meeting children's needs. Whilst the parent–child relationship is most important, the quality of surrounding relationships between parents and practitioners, between parents and their local communities and between the different practitioners in contact with the family is also highly important. A shared understanding of healthy child development across the community, parents and practitioners is seen as essential (Haynes et al., 2015).

TASK 8: REFLECTION – CONSIDER THE RANGE OF PROFESSIONALS SUPPORTING THE CARE OF ELAINE AND ALFIE

Elaine	Alfie
Nursery manager and safeguarding officer and key person	Nursery manager, SENCO and key person
School teacher	Special school teacher
Social services	Hospital professionals re Cochlear Implants (nursery communicates with them through telephone calls, emails and reports)
Police	
Health visitor	
Unity (alcohol and drug recovery services in local authority)	Speech and language therapist
	Physiotherapist
	Occupational therapist
Foster parent	Teacher for the deaf
Adoption services in local authority and away	Portage worker
	Social worker
New parents	Educational psychologist
	Dietician

- How did the nursery provide a bridge between the children, their parents and family and other professionals?

- For the children in your care, do you know which services are offering support to the child and their family?

- How would you describe your relationships with parents? Is access to them in accordance with Pen Green's 'architecture of access' (Hayward, 2014) or supportive of the concept of flourishing (Kingdon et al., 2017)?

- Do you think there is a shared understanding of child development across the professionals you work with?

Communities

Within communities, people are drawn together by choice and/ or circumstance sometimes because they live in a particular area, share common interests and develop psychological ties (Philips and Pittman, 2015). Governments might hope to harness the capacity for communities to support children and families to flourish (for example the Conservative/Coalition 'Big Society' initiative published by the Cabinet Office in 2010). The reality, however, is that a community needs to have resources that can be drawn upon – assets that members of the community can mobilise in their favour to promote their health, safety and wellbeing. Such resources are referred to as capital (Bourdieu, 1986) and, as the work of centres such as Pen Green illustrates, 'capacity building' – strengthening norms, gaining new insights and overcoming problems – adds to a community's capital. Networks of people that come together around meaningful projects add to the skills and resources of the community, supporting self-maintenance and enhancing wellbeing (Mattessich, 2015).

The starting point for community-embedded practice is an understanding of the networks and resources available to the child and their family – the cultural capital. Through this awareness, staff in a nursery, particularly the key person and manager, have the possibility of working on projects that are meaningful, collaborative and insightful. Staff take time to reflect on which community resources families use, how they form part of the child's understanding of the world and the way experiences of life outside nursery add to the child's sense of self and understanding of the world. It is possible then to weave this insight into the offered curriculum – they visit some of these places with the children, host meetings and invite members of the community into nursery for purposeful reasons, understood by all concerned. Trust is strengthened through shared understanding of the community – where to go for goods, services, help and advice. Nursery is not the 'font of all knowledge' but tries hard to be a safe space to gather *insight* and problem-solve together.

TASK 9: REFLECTION – SOCIOGRAMS OF ELAINE AND ALFIE'S REGULAR CONTACTS

- If you were to map out people and places in the lives of your key children, what might you find? Why is it important to consider the nature of these networks carefully? What discourses could be used when deciding how these might contribute to their flourishing?

Where early years services draw on established relationships from within and across the community, it is more likely that parents will participate. Where services are imposed as a form of remediation and correction (Osgood *et al.*, 2013; Skattlebol, 2016), offered to individual children and their parents so they can be educated, engagement will be low and measurable outcomes will show a relatively poor return on society's economic investment (Sammons *et al.*, 2015; Simpson *et al.*, 2017).

Whilst on a strategic level, a case can be made for governments identifying vulnerable groups and recognising the impact of adverse childhood experiences, Jackson and Needham's research (2014) leads them to question professionals' purposes in labelling children, their families and communities. Where provision is designed by professionals, based on identifying vulnerabilities and deficits, the concern is that packages of support may be bought in and delivered with limited acknowledgement of the interests, capabilities and aspirations of parents and families. The existing networks, knowledge and experiences gained from living within the community may be ignored in favour of information-sharing parents' open days and short courses on healthy eating and behaviour management. Such forms of working with parents and families offer some level of accountability but also a recognisable underpinning discourse concerned with a pre-identified, fixed understanding of vulnerability and what is needed to remove risk and adversity.

Paradoxically, despite the various mechanisms for labelling children as vulnerable, when considering practitioners' work with poverty, Simpson *et al.* (2017, pp. 183–184) found from their data a, 'normalising influence…replete with diversity and complexity reduction'. Practitioners recounted how they worked hard at treating all children the same. Despite the widely recognised discourses that contribute to child-centred pedagogy, the overriding imperative is to adopt 'normative, standardised' (*ibid.*) approaches to practice where children and, implicitly, their parents 'become passive objects' (*ibid.*), having a service delivered to them. As the work of the Children's Commissioner for England, amongst others, attests (2017), vulnerability to adversity, and adversity itself, is a complex web of interconnected factors: no one definition will capture a child and family's experiences of living within their circumstances. And sometimes, with the best will in the world, it is hard to find any indications of flourishing (Kingdon *et al.*, 2017).

Conclusion

Strong, capable and flourishing?

Vulnerable children, parents, families and their communities are understood through a variety of discourses – lines of thinking, ways of talking about and coming to understand others but also ourselves. Education cannot compensate for society (Reay, 2017, p. 11), especially when it is possible that some ways of thinking or our 'habits of conduct' (Edwards and Thomas, 2010) limit our capacity to support vulnerable children.

A child's perception of your acceptance of their family and home context (Manning-Morton and Thorp, 2015; Roberts, 2006) is connected to their wellbeing and sense of self. Placing personal, social and emotional development at the 'heart' of practice (Callanan *et al.*, 2017) is a recognised approach to supporting children's learning and development and their hopes and aspirations. Positive relationships and emotions, positive energy and opportunities for self-determination are characteristics of practice centred on flourishing (Gasper, 2017). Staff and parents flourish (Kingdon *et al.*, 2017) because practice is co-constructed, meaningful for children, staff and parents and nurturing. A variety of projects (funded and unfunded) shore up self-esteem and resilience, a sense of trust and a positive identity – not a new identity, transformed into a better parent, with a child better ready for school, but a member of a community with new insights and capacities to face adversity. Personal flourishing and organisational flourishing are closely intertwined and co-dependent (Gasper, 2017).

It is legitimate for society to marshal resources so that all can understand more about the adversities children face and pay attention to groups more vulnerable to risk. However, there are compelling reasons why effective practice starts with recognising the need to challenge assumptions and purposefully use the kind of discourse that looks for and builds upon the positive capabilities that enable children and families to flourish.

References

Action for Children (2017) *Revolving Door Part 1: Are Vulnerable Children Being Overlooked?* Watford: Action for Children.

Bourdieu, P. (1986) *Distinction: A Social Critique of the Judgement of Taste.* London: Routledge and Kegan Paul.

Bronfenbrenner, U. (1979) *The Ecology of Human Development.* London: Harvard University Press.

Brotherton, G. and Cronin, M. (2013) 'Working with Vulnerability.' In G. Brotherton and M. Cronin (eds) (2013) *Working with Vulnerable Children, Young People and Families.* Abingdon: Routledge.

Cabinet Office (2010) *Building the Big Society.* Accessed on 20/6/2018 at www.gov.uk/government/publications/building-the-big-society

Callanan, M., Anderson, M., Haywood, S., Hudson, R. and Speight, S. (2017) *Study of Early Education and Development: Good Practice in Early Education.* London: Department for Education/ NatCen Social Research. Accessed on 20/6/2018 at www.gov.uk/government/publications/good-practice-in-early-education

Children's Commissioner for England (2017) *On Measuring the Number of Vulnerable Children in England.* Accessed on 20/6/2018 at www.childrenscommissioner.gov.uk/wp-content/uploads/2017/07/CCO-On-vulnerability-Overveiw.pdf

Dahlberg, G., Moss, P. and Pence, A. (2007) *Beyond Quality in Early Childhood Education: Languages of Evaluation* (2nd ed.). Abingdon: Routledge.

Department for Education (2015) *Promoting the Health and Well-Being of Looked-After Children: Statutory Guidance for Local Authorities, Clinical Commissioning Groups and NHS England.* London: Department for Education. Accessed on 20/6/2018 at www.gov.uk/government/publications/promoting-the-health-and-wellbeing-of-looked-after-children--2

Department for Education (2017) *Statutory Framework for the Early Years Foundation Stage: Setting the Standards for Learning, Development and Care for Children from Birth to Five.* Accessed on 20/6/2018 at www.gov.uk/government/uploads/system/uploads/attachment_data/file/596629/EYFS_STATUTORY_FRAMEWORK_2017.pdf

Edwards, G. and Thomas, G. (2010) 'Can reflective practice be taught?' *Education Studies 3,* 4, 403–414.

Field, F. (2010) *The Foundation Years: Preventing Poor Children Becoming Poor Adults. The Report of the Independent Review on Child Poverty and Life Chances.* London: Cabinet Office.

Fisher, J. (2013) *Starting from the Child* (4th ed.). Maidenhead: Open University Press.

Fletcher, C. (2014) 'Preface: A Review of the Pen Green Research Paradigm.' In E. McKinnon (ed.) (2014) *Using Evidence for Advocacy and Resistance in Early Years Services.* Abingdon: Routledge.

Gasper, M. (2017) 'Parent Partnership for Flourishing in an Age of Austerity.' In Z. Kingdon, J. Gourd and M. Gasper (eds) (2017) *Flourishing in the Early Years: Contexts, Practices and Futures.* Abingdon: Routledge.

Gerhardt, S. (2014) *Why Love Matters* (2nd ed.). Abingdon: Routledge.

Giddens, A. and Sutton, P. (2014) *Essential Concepts in Sociology.* Cambridge: Polity Press.

Goldschmeid, E. and Jackson, S. (2004) *People Under Three: Young Children in Day Care* (2nd ed.). Abingdon: Routledge.

Gopnik, A. (2009) *The Philosophical Baby.* London: Bodley Head.

Gopnik, A. (2016) *The Gardener and the Carpenter.* London: Bodley Head.

Haynes, A., Cuthbert, C., Gardner, R., Telford, P. and Hodson, D. (2015) *Thriving Communities: A Framework for Preventing and Intervening Early in Child Neglect.* London: NSPCC.

Hayward, K. (2014) 'Narrative Enquiry: The Architecture of Access.' In E. McKinnon (ed.) *Using Evidence for Advocacy and Resistance in Early Years Services.* Abingdon: Routledge.

Jackson, D. and Needham, M. (2014) *Engaging with Parents in Early Years Settings.* London: Sage.

James, A. and Prout, A. (eds) (1997) *Constructing and Reconstructing Childhood: Contemporary Issues in the Sociological Study of Childhood.* London: Routledge.

Kingdon, Z., Gourd, J. and Gasper, M. (eds) (2017) *Flourishing in the Early Years: Contexts, Practices and Futures.* Abingdon: Routledge.

Lancaster, P. and Kirby, P. (2014) 'Seen and Heard: Exploring Assumptions, Beliefs and Values Underpinning Young Children's Participation.' In G. Pugh and B. Duffy (eds) (2014) *Contemporary Issues in the Early Years* (6th ed.). London: Sage.

Lindon, J. (2013) *The Key Person Approach (Positive Relationships in the Early Years).* London: Practical Pre-School Books.

Manning-Morton, J. and Thorp, M. (2015) *Two-Year-Olds in Early Years Settings: Journeys of Discovery.* Maidenhead: Open University Press.

Mattessich, P. (2015) 'Social Capital and Community Building.' In R. Philips and R.H. Pitman (eds) *Introduction to Community Development* (2nd ed.). Abingdon: Routledge.

McKinnon, E. (ed.) (2014) *Using Evidence for Advocacy and Resistance in Early Years Services: Exploring the Pen Green Research Approach.* Abingdon: Routledge.

McNaughton, G. (2003/6) *Shaping Early Childhoods: Learners, Curriculum and Contexts.* Maidenhead: Open University Press.

Noltemeyer, A.L. and Bush, K.R. (2013) 'Adversity and resilience: Synthesis of international research.' *School Psychology International 34,* 4, 474–487.

Osgood, J., Albon, D., Allen, K. and Hollingworth, S. (2013) '"Hard to Reach"' or Nomadic resistance? Families "choosing" not to participate in Early Childhood Services.' *Global Studies of Childhood 3,* 3, 208–220.

Palmer, S. (2008) *Detoxing Childhood.* London: Orion.

Palmer, S. (2015) *Toxic Childhood.* London: Orion.

Philips, R. and Pittman, R. (2015) 'A Framework for Community and Economic Development.' In R. Philips and R. Pittman (eds) *An Introduction to Community Development.* Abingdon: Routledge.

Reay, D. (2017) *Miseducation.* Bristol: Policy Press.

Roberts, R. (2006) *Self-Esteem and Early Learning.* London: Sage.

Sammons, P., Hall, J., Smees, R., Goff, J. *et al.* (2015) *The Impact of Children's Centres: Studying the Effects of Children's Centres in Promoting Better Outcomes for Young Children and their Families.* London: Department for Education/University of Oxford.

Seligman, M. (2011) *Flourishing: A New Understanding of Happiness and Well-Being and How to Achieve Them.* London: Nicholas Brearley Publishing.

Simpson, D., Loughran, S., Lumsden, E., Mazzocco, P., McDowall Clark, R. and Winterbottom, C. (2017) 'Seen but not heard: Practitioners work with poverty and the organising out of disadvantaged voices and participation in the early years.' *European Early Childhood Education Research Journal 25,* 2, 177–188.

Skattlebol, J. (2016) 'Taking advantage of early Childhood Education and Care: The priorities of low income families in their children's early years.' *Families, Relationships and Society 5*, 1, 109–125.

Social Mobility Commission (2016) *The Early Years: Building the Right Foundations Fact Sheet.* Accessed on 20/6/2018 at www.gov.uk/government/uploads/system/uploads/attachment_data/file/545818/Early_Years_factsheet.pdf

Thornton, L. and Brunton, P. (2005) *Understanding the Reggio Approach.* London: David Fulton.

Wenger-Trayner, E. and Wenger-Trayner, B. (2015) *Introduction to Communities of Practice: A Brief Overview of the Concept and Its Uses.* Accessed on 20/6/2018 at http://wenger-trayner.com/introduction-to-communities-of-practice

Whalley, M. (1997) *Working with Parents.* London: Hodder and Stoughton.

Concluding Thoughts

The introductory section queried the definition of vulnerable and who might be deemed so. The possibility of anyone fitting the category or, given certain circumstances, to become vulnerable highlights the need for care and attention to ensure all young children gain the support they need to develop as confident individuals. Winstanley states:

> there has been a shift away from seeing a difficulty as being within the person as a kind of defining characteristic. In its place we have a broader concept of trying to embrace difference and show where society should be more usefully adapted to ensure that all its members have an equal chance to participate at every level; the right not to be excluded. (cited in Bailey, 2011, p. 122)

The challenge for those involved with babies and young children is to ascertain the most appropriate ways to foster these opportunities to ensure no child is missed.

Reference

Bailey, R. (ed) (2011) *The Philosophy of Education: An Introduction*. London: Continuum.

A List of Written Feedback Strategies and Approaches Used in Primary Schools

Acknowledging goal statements (learning objectives/success criteria) The learner marks, or colours, LO/SC according to confidence level in and achievement of these.	**Comment-only marking** A written descriptive comment about the work.
Comments to work Matching work to comments. A powerful means of encouraging learners to read comments and evaluate features within the work.	**Codes – mode of feedback** The use of transparent codes such as VF (verbal feedback) and PA (peer assessed) to describe the type of feedback provided.
Codes and symbols Understood and agreed marking codes and symbols. For example, // refers to new paragraph. These are often used to reduce teacher time.	**D.I.R.T.** 'Dedicated Improvement and Reflection' framework. This can involve self-assessment, peer-assessment and teacher assessment against LO/SC.
Future learning goals/targets Identifying next steps in order to close the gap in learning.	**Grades or scores** Agreed grades or scores as assigned to work by the learner and/or marker. Scores usually refer to a number, grades or a letter. These are usually given for effort, achievement and confidence levels.

Highlighting learning Learning objectives and success criteria are visible and, if achieved, acknowledged with a mark.	**Highlighter lines** The use of different colour markers to correlate evidence against LO/SC.
Informative and constructive feedback Qualitative information about particular aspects of the work which may include performance against the intended learning or future targets for development.	**Marking rubrics** A set of expectations for assessing learning against. These usually include LO/SC. This form of rubric can help to delineate learning goals e.g. Green/Gold Criteria – 'I'm going for gold.'
'Now' and 'then' steps This comprises a positive statement about the learning together with future action that is required. (It is a similar approach to 'Stars and wishes'.)	**Polishing pens** Using some different colour markers to highlight achievements and improvements. For example, 'Brilliant Blue' denotes success and 'Think Pink' denotes the need to think again about their working.
Peer-written marking The exchanging of written comments, grades and judgements based on agreed criteria – it usually includes the initials of the marker/s.	**Prompts** Written feedback prompts can facilitate further learning. These can *remind*, *scaffold learning* and provide *examples*.
Question setting The learning is marked through a series of questions that the learner has to respond to. Questions will be differentiated appropriately – for example, higher order questioning and help to seek clarification.	**Reflective commenting** The learner is asked to reflect on their learning in a learning log or journal. The teacher will often provide questions or prompts to instigate responses.
Responsive written feedback The marker acknowledges both success and any future developmental points. For example, the 'Stars and wishes' approach.	**Spaces/margins** Providing a designated area for responses or improvements to be made so these are visible.
Secretarial marking Acknowledging spelling, punctuation or grammar mistakes, which need to be addressed, usually with codes. For example, *s* for spelling.	**Self-marking** The learner marks their own work against specified criteria.

Stars and wishes	Traffic-lighting marking
A means of providing concise written feedback. This includes statements/comments about positive aspects of the learning and suggestions for further improvement. Often referred to as 'Three stars and a wish'.	The use of colours to reflect understanding and learning. This can also be used to rate the teaching.
Triple marking This form of marking involves the teacher responding to any previous written feedback following further input from the learner – learner responses are acknowledged.	

Contributors

Dr Pat Beckley (editor) has worked in education, initially as a Key Stage 2 coordinator, followed by many years of leading an early years unit, particularly supporting children and families in challenging circumstances. As an 'outstanding teacher' with Advanced Skills Teacher status and National Professional Qualification for Headship (NPQH), she supported early years settings and schools. Her work in higher education, where she became a senior fellow of the Higher Education Academy, involved leading early years and primary Initial Teacher Education (ITE) programmes and participating in the design of national initiatives and comparative research with colleagues in Europe, especially Norway, and Africa.

Nishi Bremner was born in West London and, after gaining a BSc Joint Honours degree in Maths and Management from King's College, London, she trained as a teacher at South Bank University, London. She gained a PGCE in Primary Education, specialising in the early years, almost 20 years ago. She has successfully taught in Inner London, Surrey and Spain, teaching right through from nursery to Year 2. She moved to Lincolnshire six years ago with her husband and two children and is now deputy head teacher (and full-time reception teacher) in a small market town in Lincolnshire.

Elizabeth Farrar has taught across the primary age range, leading English, PSHE, Geography and ICT, and was a head teacher for six years. She is interested in the fields of sociolinguistics, phonetics and phonology. For her doctoral research she is exploring educational issues surrounding poverty of language in primary school age pupils.

Sarah Howe is currently a senior lecturer in Primary Education at Bishop Grosseteste University, Lincoln. Her 29-year career in education includes experience in Initial Teacher Training, as an early years consultant and as a head teacher in infant schools in the Middle East, Belgium and England. Whilst teaching at Bishop Grosseteste University, Sarah has pursued her interest in, and research on, 'Assessment for Learning'. She actively promotes formative assessment as an invaluable tool for raising learning potential and teaching efficiency.

Beverley Keen is the course leader of the BA (Hons) Early Childhood Education leading to QTS at Leeds Beckett University. She has a particular interest in the use of the outdoor learning environment. Prior to working in higher education, she taught early years and primary children and was involved in a North Yorkshire LEA research project on the use of dialogic talk within classrooms.

Dr Julia Lindley-Baker coordinates and teaches on undergraduate programmes in Special Educational Needs and Inclusion (SENI) across Bishop Grosseteste University, following ten years as vice principal of a Special Educational Needs college. Her research background is in special education. Julia has delivered training locally, nationally and internationally and is a senior fellow of the Higher Education Academy.

Antony Luby is a former senior lecturer at Bishop Grosseteste University, Lincoln, and a final year doctoral student at the University of Glasgow. He has a Master's degree in Theology, Pedagogy and Education from the Universities of Aberdeen, Oxford and Strathclyde. A highly experienced practitioner and chartered teacher, Antony has more than 60 publications in academic and professional journals and the educational press.

Yinka Olusoga began her career as a primary teacher, gaining experience working in multi-ethnic communities and with children with additional needs. She then specialised in early years. Since 2006 she has led the PGCE Primary Education (Early Years, 3–7), leading to QTS. Yinka's doctoral research examines the social construction of the working-class school child in key historical documents from the 18th and early 19th centuries. She has also been involved in research on child-initiated play and student teachers' experiences of implementing play pedagogies in schools.

Julie Percival is a senior lecturer at the University of Cumbria, teaching on Education Studies and Early Years Education and Development programmes. Previously, her role included programme leader for routes to Early Teacher Status. Julie has taught in a variety of contexts: special schools, mainstream primary and early years settings. As an advisory teacher and area SENCO, she worked in multiagency teams, supporting children and families alongside pedagogical support for practitioners working in private, voluntary and independent settings. Whilst at the University of Huddersfield, Julie developed an interest in early years practitioner identity and her current research uses material culture to inform her doctoral studies.

Anne Renwick was a senior lecturer at the University of Cumbria, teaching across the full range of early years programmes, until her recent retirement. She has worked in a number of primary schools in Cumbria and the north-east of England, teaching nursery, reception and Key Stage 1 children. Before joining the University of Cumbria, Anne was employed as a senior early years advisory teacher for Cumbria Children's Services, supporting practitioners in a range of early years schools and settings. Anne has developed her own research on the subject of professional development for the children's workforce and her Master's dissertation focused on support for teachers working in children's centres. Her recent research centres on transition into higher education and the development of teacher identity in undergraduate QTS students.

Emmy Sealey has owned and managed a purpose-built nursery for 29 years and has worked in childcare for the last 40 years, managing to achieve two 'Outstanding' outcomes in her recent Ofsted inspections. She has started three nurseries in her career in childcare in Cumbria and has been lead practitioner as part of a Children's Services team specialising in the 'outdoor environment and continuous provision'. She has been involved in helping other nurseries and student practitioners develop Heuristic Play in their settings, which was the focus of her Master's dissertation. She has recently received 'The Lifetime Achievement Award' for her contribution to childcare in Cumbria. The last three years have been focused on developing a Reggio Emilia-inspired centre used by all age groups, from babies to adults, with the focus of using recycled materials to create their own individual masterpieces and progressing into a similar style 'school' for

3- to 11-year-olds, concentrating on the child's emotional wellbeing, opened in September 2018.

Rosey Shelbourne is one of the founders of CPA (Christian Partners in Africa), and has been part of the team since the very beginning. Over the past 22 years she has been involved in a variety of projects in Ethiopia, Uganda, Mozambique and Malawi and has particularly enjoyed meeting and working with lots of lovely and interesting people. As a former primary school teacher, she is passionate about education and safeguarding children. Her main focus recently has been working with children and with writing and delivering 'safeguarding training' in an African context.

Dr Margaret C. Simms works in higher education and is the programme area coordinator at Vision West Nottinghamshire College University Centre. The privilege of teaching is learning; this Margaret enjoys to the full. She writes to encourage others on their journey – as she too was encouraged.

Gina Taylor is foundation leader of learning and has previously taught across the Foundation Stage and as special needs coordinator in schools in the Nottinghamshire area. She completed a Masters in Education in 2017 and latterly the National SENCO Award. She believes passionately in early years education and the importance of developing social and emotional skills for wellbeing.

Helen Thornalley is senior lecturer at Bishop Grosseteste University, Lincoln, teaching in Teacher Education with ITE and Master's students. Formally a secondary school teacher in physical education and head of sixth form, her educational career has allowed her to teach overseas for the British Council in Kenya, China and London, developing scholarly research projects with the educationalist Sir John Rowling, Paralympic athletes, the All England Lawn Tennis and Croquet Club and the Schools Dance Company established by Darcey Bussell. All of these projects have a specialist interest in extending the learners through appropriate feedback and questioning within the fields of health, exercise and sport with EYFS pupils to professional teachers within schools.

Index